Selling Students Short

Selling Students Short

Classroom Bargains and Academic
Reform in the American High School

Michael W. Sedlak
Christopher W. Wheeler
Diana C. Pullin
Philip A. Cusick

Teachers College, Columbia University
New York and London

Published by Teachers College Press, 1234 Amsterdam Avenue,
New York, N.Y. 10027

Library of Congress Cataloging-in-Publication Data

Selling students short.

Bibliography: p. 191
Includes index.
1. High schools—United States. 2. Teacher-student relationships—United
States. 3. School management and organization—United States. 4. School
discipline—United States. 5. Achievement motivation. I. Sedlak, Michael W.
II. Columbia University. Teachers College.
LB1607.S43 1986   373.73   86-14539
ISBN 0-8077-2818-7
ISBN 0-8077-2817-9 (pbk.)

Manufactured in the United States of America

91 90 89 88 87 86   1 2 3 4 5 6

⋕ Contents

⚏ Acknowledgements

We would like to express our appreciation to those who have supported the preparation of this book. We developed concepts and arguments and tried to unravel their implications for the current reform movement as part of a National Institute of Education contract to Michigan State University's College of Education. Our project officer, Enid Simmons, provided encouragement and the intellectual freedom that we needed to explore such a timely and politicized topic. Our colleagues at the Institute for Research on Teaching have been indispensible. We are particularly indebted to Jere Brophy, Andy Porter, and Jack Schwille for their thoughtful consideration of earlier drafts of this book. To Andy Porter we owe our collaborative existence itself. In response to the opportunity provided by the NIE, he brought together our unlikely team, composed of an historian, a political scientist, an attorney, and an organizational theorist. We continue to be grateful for his creativity in establishing and nurturing our collaboration. Other colleagues and friends have argued with, and encouraged us, in our struggle with this enterprise: Margret Buchmann, Robert Church, David Cohen, Robert Hampel, David Labaree, Linda McNeil, George Madaus, Douglas Mitchell, and Paul Peterson. Several of our doctoral students contributed in a variety of ways to the project, from tracking down elusive and fugitive source materials to responding critically to drafts of the manuscript; we would like to recognize the distinctive contributions of Jay Busch, Becky Kirschner, Gemette Reid, Jim Stanaway, and John Zeuli. Despite all of the assistance and goodwill, however, problems undoubtedly persist. For those errors of fact or interpretation that remain, one or another of the authors is responsible; actually, it is one of the other authors who is responsible.

In the olden days authors customarily thanked secretaries and typists for deciphering and transcribing their horrible penmanship. At worst, all that could go wrong in the process was the transposition of a letter or two. With word processing, however, the potential for incapacitating loss is mortifying, as when control keys are accidentally touched or the machines quietly rebel. Four authors writing and revising in different and incompatible formats multiplies the threat of catastrophe. Our thousands of pages of drafts have somehow survived revision and word processing unscathed. For this we would like to express our gratitude to Ann Marie Stevens, Jennifer Arnold, Sandy Callis, Paula Deal, Cindy Casey, Katherine Graesslin, Pamela Harrington, Rebecca Nawrocki, Judith Pavona, Jennifer Wallace, and Robin White. Kathy Crown deserves our warmest thanks for her indispensable assistance in preparing the index.

Finally, we extend our thanks and appreciation to Lois Patton, Audrey Kingstrom, Carole Saltz, Mel Berk, and Nina George, of Teachers College Press, who had the foresight to accept this study for publication and the imagination to improve its contents.

▩ Preface

Our public educational system stands accused of subverting the economic well-being, world stature, and military defense of this nation. Educators have been condemned for squandering away the achievement gains which resulted from the post-Sputnik educational competition with the Soviet Union and producing a nation of young people who cannot read, write, or compute well enough to function as members of a society sufficiently healthy to flourish in the world marketplace.

In response to widespread public perceptions of a massive breakdown in public education, a wide array of commissions and research teams has been convened to assess the nature and extent of the problem. The level of concern and amount of energy being expended in thinking about public elementary and secondary schooling are more intense now than at any previous time in our history. As a result of this display of concern, proposals have been put forward at the national, state, and local levels, setting out new standards to which educators, schools, and students should be held accountable in order to halt what one commission deemed the "rising tide of mediocrity that threatens our very future as a nation and as a people" (National Commission on Excellence in Education, 1983). These proposals have been offered by both laypersons and by members of the education professions; a number of them have already been enacted into law or written into policy requirements. All are well intended and sincerely proposed. Not one of these proposals, however, takes into account the most fundamental variables in the educational process: the nature of the relationship between educators and their students and the extent to which students are actively engaged in the learning process. Without this perspective, the proposals for educational improvement are unlikely to accomplish their goals of improving student learning. The greatest number of these proposals are targeted at the American high school. This book reviews the context within which contemporary standards exist.

Two different concepts of standards have shaped the American high school, and the current wave of initiatives is in some ways a product of the tension between them. The standard against which the success of the educational enterprise has been measured for a century and a half is the democratic-egalitarian ideal of universal attendance. It has been largely responsible for creating a mass school system that is one of the world's most inclusive. In addition to the standard of universal attendance, American schools have occasionally been measured against a standard of high academic achievement. A segment of the current standards-raising movement appears to blame our national success in pursuing the first standard for our alleged failure to meet the second. Universal attendance, particularly the enrollment of lower-class, minority, and immigrant students (the most recent arrivals), appears to be held accountable for the conditions in high schools which result in low academic performance for a substantial minority of the students.

A review of the literature, however, suggests that the problem with academic standards is not limited to the "newer" students, although the problems may be most visible and discouraging in lower-class or inner-city schools. The problem of academic standards in the 1980s is one of low academic achievement in the vast majority of schools, even in wealthier small towns and suburbs. There appears to have developed an implicit "bargain" between students and educators in virtually all of our high schools, which results in a de-emphasis on academic learning and student disengagement from learning. This bargain is negotiated, albeit tacitly, between two parties, both of which have resources, but unequal power. This bargain determines the level of academic learning that takes place in the classroom. Although content and the acquisition of knowledge ultimately suffer, the bargain struck in most classrooms furthers its primary goal of making the relationships between educators and students more comfortable and less troublesome.

This book attempts to account for this bargain and for students' disengagement by focusing on the forces and pressures that shape the commitment to academic learning by adolescents and educators, and the organizational priorities and practices that reinforce and sustain the agreement to minimize rigorous academic coursework. We examine the bargain from several perspectives.

A vast majority of students think that there is no need to concentrate on the acquisition of knowledge in high school, and as a result, most have become progressively disengaged from the academic experience. For many students, the meaning of high school and the alternative options available for investing energy and time are such that there is little incentive to be heavily involved in academic learning. From the perspective of teachers and other educators, the bargain is made desirable because of the nature of the prevailing reward structure for educators and because of the authority conferred by the autonomy given classroom teachers. Finally, many organizational policies have played a distressing role in discouraging academic learning. Although unintentionally, many features and priorities characteristic of the vast majority of high schools encourage teachers and students to participate in the bargain in order to release tensions that could erupt into visible and intolerable signs of disorder.

This book analyzes current proposals to enhance educational standards in our nation's public high schools in light of the power and influence of bargaining in classrooms, which we define in the Introduction. It draws on two sets of proposals to improve high school standards: those made by blue ribbon commissions and educational researchers and those made and implemented by legislators, governors, and boards of education. It assesses standards-raising efforts which include the proposals set forth by the effective schools movement, proposals aimed at teacher competency, and those designed to impose greater controls on students.

As current standards-raising proposals were compiled and analyzed, it became clear that none addressed that element of the high school process which we had identified previously as the critical component in academic learning, the bargain struck between students and educators. Indeed, our conclusion is that in many instances the proposed reforms have not only failed to address the bargain, but may also in fact exacerbate its current consequences. Efforts to alter high school grading or graduation requirements, to reduce the distractions of extracurricular activities, or to be stricter in disciplining student misbehavior will not significantly increase student levels of academic achievement unless efforts are made to specifically assess and address the impact of the current bargain on learning. Academic achievement will not increase unless the conditions for fostering an entirely new agreement between students and educators are created. Similarly, efforts to improve the teaching profession will not significantly increase academic achievement among the nation's students unless those efforts are tailored to change the terms under which educators enter into a bargain. Unless a new bargain between educators and students is struck, the implicit learning contract in our nation's schools will not change and neither will our chance to achieve academic excellence for *all* our students.

▥ INTRODUCTION:
An Unaffordable Bargain

Americans have subjected their high schools to intense scrutiny and criticism over the past several years. The public is particularly distressed about evidence of declining academic achievement, reflected in the publicized deterioration of Scholastic Aptitude Test scores since 1963, the complaints of college faculty about their students' lowered intellectual competence, the disturbing conclusions drawn by the National Assessment of Educational Progress surveys which reveal that higher-order cognitive and reasoning skills among adolescents have eroded, embarrassing international comparative evaluations, and repeated insinuations that high school graduates lack sufficient skills to be productive as workers, consumers, or citizens.

The urgency underlying such concerns has precipitated a number of studies of schooling in the United States, most of which focus on the high school and its contributions to many real and imagined social and economic problems. Conducted by a variety of commissions, task forces, contractors, and independent scholars employing a broad range of research methodologies, these studies have produced results of varying quality and sophistication. These results and commission recommendations have spurred local and state initiatives in every region. Hundreds of commissions and task forces on educational excellence are active in the United States. The momentum is such that even the most ambitious efforts to capture and report the scope and range of school improvement activities are dated when released and are obsolete (except as historical documents) within several months.

The purpose of this book is not only to examine and summarize current initiatives and reforms but also to explore recent scholarship bearing on personal relations and organizational dynamics that determine what schools do and how role relations among students, teachers, and administrators are shaped by and affect academic standards. We focus on the groups ultimately most influenced by the initiatives, particularly students, but also teachers, and administrators.

1

We adopt this posture because although most improvement efforts and well-intentioned initiatives seek to increase student attendance, participation, and commitment, they do not appear to appreciate the changing place of high school in an adolescent's life. By probing the economic, social, and individual functions of secondary education, especially the meaning and utility of the experience to interested constituencies, it is possible to develop a more accurate perspective of the movement to raise academic standards. Reform initiatives that fail to address the context within which academic standards currently exist risk compromising their effectiveness, or, worse, may have unintended, potentially damaging consequences.* According to virtually every objective and subjective criterion presented in the recent literature, high school students today achieve less academically than their predecessors of 20 years ago (Astin, 1982; Anderson, B., 1983; Arnstine, 1983; Evans, 1983; The College Board, 1983b; Kemmerer, 1983; Levanto, 1975a, 1975b; Levine, M., 1983; Lerner, 1982; Peng, et al., 1981). Although the quantitative evidence is uneven and subject to varying interpretations, it is apparent that roughly comparative measurements of subject matter involvement and performance have declined steadily since the mid-1960s. High school students' scores on standardized tests have fallen (although there are segments of the populaiton whose performance has apparently begun to improve). They enroll in fewer challenging advanced basic academic courses and in more introductory, service, and personal development classes. They spend less time on homework and more time working and watching television. High school attendance rates have worsened. Over the past decade the U.S. graduation rate has declined in excess of four percent. Adolescents' higher-order reasoning and interpretive skills have weakened. High school students are more visibly disruptive, less committed to high school, and less engaged in academic activities. They appear to care less about their educational experience and have come to invest their time, effort, and attention elsewhere. Even such researchers as Laurence C. Stedman and Marshall S. Smith (1983), who caution against overreacting to the evidence of eroding standards, recognize that there may indeed be a crisis in education demanding immediate attention. "Certainly we cannot afford to be complacent at a time when half of our high school graduates take no math or science after 10th grade, nearly 40 percent of the 17-year-olds cannot draw inferences from written material, and only one-third can solve a mathematics problem requiring several steps." (p. 94; see also Hall, et al., 1984; Wolf, 1983; Holsinger, 1982)

---

*(The impact of students and teachers on academic learning is recognized in Sizer, 1983a, 1984a, 1984b; McNeil, 1981; Neufeld, 1980; Hampel, 1986; Kemmerer, 1983; Seeley, 1984; Duckworth, 1983; Farrar, Neufeld, & Miles, 1983; Powell, Farrar, & Cohen, 1985).

Many of those who have stressed the pattern of decline argue that achievement and standards have eroded because high schools now enroll a larger percentage of the adolescent population (Cohen, D., & Neufeld, 1981; Bakalis, 1983; Cusick, 1983). Secondary schools have both diversified and become universal, enrolling lower-class, immigrant, and minority youth who would not have attended high schools in the nineteenth century. In order to attract and retain these students, the argument continues, high schools have diluted their curricula and eased their academic demands. Some of the problems that schools are experiencing today *are* the result of universal attendance, and a portion of the standards-raising efforts addresses at least several of the fundamental consequences of universalism.

Much of the literature and many of the actual initiatives imply that the students themselves are responsible for declining standards. Many reform activities appear to presume that the problem can be remedied by getting tough; expecting and demanding more; diverting disruptive, disinterested, and indifferent students from the basic academic program into alternative tracks and schools; awarding them substandard diplomas; or forcing them out of school altogether.

Up to this point, consequently, the most visible standards-raising efforts have focused on the widely publicized lack of academic achievement of lower-class and minority students, those adolescents who presumably have found their way into high schools since World War II. In many ways, the recent arrivals have been identified as the problem. Minimum competency testing, perhaps the movement's single most popular thrust, is directed at lower-achieving students, a disproportionate number of whom are working-class, poor, black, or Hispanic (Dougherty, 1983). It is obvious to at least one segment of the standards-raising movement, in other words, that the fastest and most certain method of improving academic performance standards is to get rid of the low achievers, and that may well be the consequence, if not the intention, of many efforts.

Despite the persuasiveness and utility of the universal attendance perspective, even when compensating for its tendency to be abused, it is critical to look beyond the problems associated with student body diversification. One of the most troubling themes in the recent literature is the tendency of students from *all* social classes, children attending even the "better" achievement-oriented high schools, to be uniformly uninvolved in the acquisition of challenging academic knowledge (Goodlad, 1984; Sizer, 1984b; McNeil, 1982; Cusick, 1983). Illuminated by the National Assessment of Educational Progress surveys, virtually all adolescents have suffered a decline in academic achievement and higher-order reasoning ability (Anderson, B., et al., 1983; Anderson, B., 1983). The problem is increasingly visible among most adolescents: those attending predominately white, middle-class, academically oriented suburban institutions, those in inner-city schools, and even students attending many parochial and rural programs. It is not limited to the most recent arrivals, lower-class, and minority youth.

The standards-raising movement has failed to grasp the implications of the *general* pattern of declining academic performance. Virtually all adolescents, especially middle-class youth, have progressively disengaged themselves from high school, at least from its academic opportunities. They appear less committed to rigorous intellectual involvement, treating their academic responsibilities only perfunctorily. The place that high school occupies in the lives of adolescents is changing. Youth everywhere have begun to respond to a shift in the meaning of high school in similar ways, the cumulative effects of which have resulted in declining academic achievement and standards.

Responsibility for this decline is complicated. The achievement of adolescents depends upon their engagement in, and commitment to, rigorous academic work. The level of adolescents' commitment and particularly their opportunity and ability to be engaged in academic learning are shaped by individuals and institutions largely beyond their control. Prior educational experiences, the skill of their teachers, options that compete for their time and effort, their assessment of the eventual payoffs for sustaining engagement, and parental pressure, together determine the level of a high school student's commitment to concentrated academic learning. Responsibility, therefore, is shared. Any movement to raise standards in high schools must address and confront the prevailing pattern of general engagement and commitment if it is to have substantive meaning beyond raising superficial test scores, awarding differentiated diplomas, and placing alienated, disruptive students in substandard alternative programs, encouraging such students to drop out of school, or expelling them altogether.

To state this argument more explicitly, it is imperative that the standards-raising movement understands what has happened in the vast majority of high schools, to the relationship that teachers have worked out with their students, and most importantly, to be aware of the forces that shape and enforce currently existing standards. It is not as though the standards-raising movement will create and institute standards where there were none, despite the sentiments characteristic of segments of the movement. Standards already exist in high school, and there are good reasons why they are set at the level they are. Students, teachers, and the institutions they occupy together have adjusted to a complicated recent history. An arrangement has been worked out which ultimately compromises and de-emphasizes academic learning. This book explores this arrangement, this fusion of interests, in order to place the standards-raising effort in an appropriate context, and to reiterate the need to understand what is happening in *all* high schools, perhaps especially in ordinary, and even academically oriented, institutions.

Any effort to raise standards in high schools will face constraints shaped by the context within which the current standards have evolved. Although recent literature on schooling, much of which focuses on the secondary level, contributes substantially to our understanding of forces shaping access to and use of academic knowledge, its impact on virtually all state and local efforts to raise standards remains problematic. Prior to this era of the reports, attempts to improve standards were preoccupied almost exclusively with competency testing, particularly for students. The major studies released recently *have* broadened the dialogue dramatically and *have* informed the initiatives of many ambitious state and local commissions on excellence in education. They have expanded the arsenal of weapons in the standards-raising war well beyond competency testing and related evaluation efforts to include concern with graduation requirements, curricular fragmentation and the proliferation of electives, tracking and ability grouping, social promotion, absenteeism, teacher evaluation and pay, and the time available for academic engagement. Yet, many of the most penetrating and challenging observations in the current literature remain unrecognized, despite their powerful implications for any effort to alter the place and meaning of high school in the lives of adolescents.

In most high schools there exists a complex, tacit conspiracy to avoid sustained, rigorous, demanding, academic inquiry. A "bargain" of sorts is struck that demands little academically of either teachers or students. Many organizational policies protect and reinforce this arrangement, which governs classroom interaction, determines what teachers can require of their students, and shapes prevailing academic standards. This "bargain" is *not* an agreement between parties of equal power, stature, or responsibility. It is, rather, principally an adaptation that teachers and students make to the institutions which they occupy together. Each side brings to the arrangement experiences, aspirations, and options, both in and out of school, that make their respective behavior understandable and rational. The forces which have shaped and continue to perpetuate the fusion of interests that underlie the arrangement are rooted in a complex history. Teachers, students, and their institutions have responded to the changing meaning of high school in a way that has implications for raising academic standards, particularly for changing the level of engaged learning. It is, therefore, imperative that the current standards-raising movement understands how contemporary standards reflect these continous, interdependent and mutually reinforcing relationships if it is to have the impact on the mastery of knowledge that it seeks.

Several of the most revealing recent studies of schooling contain richly detailed, often painful, portraits of the bargain that constrains any effort to raise academic standards in high schools. It would be instructive at this point to consider an example of the impact of the bargain on a typical classroom, and then to examine the forces that affect current academic expectations and performance from the perspectives of students, teachers, and their organizations. The following illustration is drawn from Philip A. Cusick's *The Egalitarian Ideal and the American High School* (New York: Longman, 1983).

> In effect, the subject matter of a number of classes we witnessed was not so much art or drama or literature, but the personal relations between teacher and students. That makes sense. Even if the students did not care much about learning abstract knowledge, they were still quite decent and open to cordial relations with teachers. Since the teacher still had to keep twenty-five or so of them orderly for fifty or fifty-five minutes, then these cordial relations rather than the ostensible subject matter could serve as the basis for order. Given that, one could understand the sentiment behind the statements such as "you have to like the kids," "you have to get along with the kids," "we like the kids here."
>
> What was particularly interesting in this regard was that in more than a few cases, there did not seem to be any subject matter other than the cordial relations. Mr. P. always came into fourth period about five minutes late, whereupon he would take attendance, exchange some banter with the students up front, then ask them how they felt, or respond to a personal question: "Hey, is your hair getting thin?" "No, man, it's just that I combed it different. . . . Like it?" "Hey, whatsmatter? You look down." "Bucks lost, man, that's my team." "I didn't see the game—I had to do some work."
>
> On this particular day the junior class president came in selling candles to raise money. George, with a big grin as always, mumbled a little to the class about the candles being on sale. The teacher felt he was ineffective and spent the next few minutes giving George a lesson in salesmanship.
>
> "George, do these people know about your candles? You gotta tell 'em so they'll buy some. Come here."
>
> George did not mind, and smiling broadly he gave the whole box to Mr. P., who took them out, laid them on the lectern, bought one himself, told the class about their quality, their construction, and the uses of candles, and sold three. "See, George, you gotta present your product so your customers will want them." Then he got on the subject of selling and told of an announcer on the radio in Chicago when he grew up who got so excited about presenting his product, Hamm's beer, that he drank a whole case of it during one ballgame.

By this time the period was twenty minutes old and while he was doing these things, the students were in what might generously be called a state of disarray. The sixteen students were partly listening, partly sleeping, and partly talking among themselves. It was not just on December 14 that Mr. P. avoided teaching. He followed a similar pattern every day we were in his class. Even if he did have some academic work that he considered important enough to mention, he would immediately leave it if something else came up.

One day he started on railroad mileage. Another teacher walked in: "Hey, I fixed your TV." "Oh, excuse me," said Mr. P., and walked out. Twenty minutes later he returned and he told us that he wanted to talk about the increase in railroad mileage between 1830 and 1940, and while he was reading the graph from the book not one student was paying a bit of attention. The boys up front were talking among themselves about basketball. William plays varsity. Raymond and Robert were in the center of the room listening to his assessment of the opposition. George had left after his usual short stay. The girls on the other side were either looking out the window or sleeping. One was angered by an earlier exchange with Mr. P., who asked: "You been taking those pills again?" "I ain't taking no pills," she replied.

John, one of the white boys in back, was reading a magazine, and of the two black girls in the back one was reading a novel, the other, looking bored, turned and asked me who I was. When I told her she said, "Don't you get tired of sittin' in these classes?" "Do you?" "Yes, we never do anything in here," and she showed me some novels she was reading. Another boy on my right said, "I wish they'd burn all these books, then we could have school on tape."

All the time the teacher was talking about railroad mileage. Some had their books open but did not look at them. Others just sat and stared or talked to their friends. This apparently didn't bother Mr. P. No individual was getting singularly disruptive so he just went on until even he became bored and concluded quickly that although "America has a lot of problems it is still the best country in the world." (pp. 53–54)

When set at a low level, the bargain's essential features include: relatively little concern for academic content; a willingness to tolerate, if not encourage, diversion from the specified knowledge to be presented or discussed; the substitution of genial banter and conversation for concentrated academic exercises; improvisational instructional adaptation to student preference for or indifference toward specific subject matter or pedagogical techniques; the "negotation" of class content, assignments, and standards; and a high degree of teacher autonomy in managing the level of academic engagement, personal interaction, and course content. It is tempting simply to dismiss these practices as bad teaching. Perhaps when they result in little academic learning, they constitute the definition of bad teaching. If so, there is a great deal of bad teaching in American high schools. To condemn these practices simply as bad teaching, however, misses an opportunity to understand the organizational dynamics and fusion of personal and professional interests of all the members of the school community that in many cases discourage academic learning. The "bargain" or "arrangement" or "treaty" is a common theme in the qualitative literature that provides a number of clues about the formidable task confronting the standards-raising movement (i.e., Cusick, 1983; Sykes, 1984; Powell, Farrar, & Cohen, 1985; Richardson, Fisk, & Okun, 1983; Everhart, 1983; Lightfoot, 1983, pp. 143–44; Sizer, 1984b; Leonard, 1983; Owen, 1981; McNeil, 1981, 1982, 1984; Wegmann, 1974).

The provocative, if ultimately inconclusive, portrait of classroom life presented in the recent literature demonstrates the need for further research into the organizational priorities and dynamics that shape the conditions of academic learning in high school. Little is known, for example, about the prevalence of bargaining. Since it has surfaced as a common, yet generally undeveloped, devastating theme in the literature, it would be useful to determine its scope and distribution, its place in private schooling, and the extent to which it reinforces prevailing inequalities of social class, income, and race. If bargaining detrimentally affects even a large minority of classrooms, its implications for current and future reform initiatives are compelling.

Much of the following interpretation of the state of academic learning and the process of bargaining in high school is based on qualitative and ethnographic evidence. Although some of the observations reported in this literature have been corroborated by quantitative and survey research, caution should always be exercised when generalizing from evidence collected at a specific time and place.

The qualitative studies that inform this interpretation vary in scope and sophistication. Some were based upon thousands of hours of systematic observations and interviews in dozens of schools in different types of communities (i.e., Goodlad, 1984; Sizer, 1984b; Powell, Farrar, & Cohen, 1985; Boyer, 1983). Others examined several institutions intensively (i.e., Cusick, 1983; Lightfoot, 1983; McNeil, 1982; Neufeld, 1980). Still others reconstructed events in a single school, or reported on a narrow issue in only a few programs (i.e., Larkin, 1979; Jackson, 1981; Owen, 1981; Leonard, 1983; Peshkin, 1978; Wegmann, 1974; Cusick, 1973). Combined, these studies probe developments in all sorts of high schools and host communities, including elite, selective institutions, comprehensive suburban schools, inner-city and other urban programs, and small town and rural consolidated schools. This interpretation, in other words, does not rest on an isolated, exceptional, or idiosyncratic field study.

The richly detailed descriptions and reconstructions of classroom behavior presented in this qualitative literature disclose many similar patterns of interaction between teachers and students. The portrait of classroom life that emerges from this research is evocative, if not disturbing, in its implications for the current effort to raise academic standards in high schools.

It is not our intention, however, to leave the impression that all classrooms or schools resemble those discussed below. The literature also describes enviably successful classrooms, effective teachers, and deeply engaged, accomplished students. The "bargain" to limit academic learning is not set low in every classroom, or even in every school. In particular, our examination of student disengagement does not readily apply to several groups of students, although the evidence indicates that it applies to a significant proportion of the adolescents in the vast majority of high schools.

Specifically, disengagement is characteristic of at least three groups: 1) adolescents with extremely weak affiliative ties to schooling, visibly alienated or aggressively disruptive students, including those on the verge of dropping out; 2) indifferent students who actively resist the imposition of academic standards by challenging their teachers' authority, by diverting instruction away from content, or by attempting to negotiate easier assignments; and 3) adolescents who quietly and passively resist academic learning by offering minimal compliance in order to avoid jeopardizing their opportunity to pass a course or to graduate. The concept of disengagement does not include at least two other groups: 1) students who enjoy and thrive on concentrated learning for intrinsic reasons; and 2) adolescents who learn acquisitively but are motivated fundamentally by the extrinsic reward (the diploma, grade point average, class ranking, letters of recommendation) for demonstrating that they have acquired knowledge.

Obviously the percentages of students in the five or so categories differ by community, institution, and classroom. In the high-powered, academically elite schools (whether private, suburban, or urban) that routinely send 90 percent of their graduates to college (almost exclusively to four-year institutions, with 25 percent to the most demanding, selective liberal arts programs), relatively few students are actively or even passively disengaged. Their students may not love the pursuit of knowledge for its own sake, but their expectations and academic levels remain sufficiently high to make serious disengagement almost unbearable. A liberal estimate of the proportion of such students in the entire high school population is perhaps 15 to 20 percent. If the numbers of adolescent dropouts and nonattenders are included in the calculation's denominator, the figure would fall slightly. In contrast, the disengaged population probably exceeds two-thirds of the total number of high school students nationwide. Perhaps two-thirds of those intending to enroll in institutions of higher education do not have to concentrate on challenging academic coursework to be admitted, even to the better public universities.

The recent literature, therefore, strongly suggests that there are serious problems with academic learning and student engagement in most communities, even if a very small but significant minority of schools or students are not in deep trouble. It is one of the central purposes of this book to organize, analyze, account for, and interpret the clues about disengagement contained in the qualitative and quantitative research on high school and adolescence. In addition, this book applies the perspective gained from this analysis to an assessment of the current reform movement. Because the entire disengaged population, including the passive and active resisters, is large, overlooking these clues could lead the standards-raising movement, which heretofore has focused on the most aggressively alienated students, toward results that it does not intend.

PART I
Students

1 ◫ Student Disengagement and Academic Learning

During the twentieth century, adolescents have progressively disengaged themselves from their high school's academic experience, if they have not entirely abandoned its social opportunities. What they have done is not irrational. Like everyone else, adolescents care about the things that they have to care about, and they do not have to care about academic engagement very much. Few students must invest themselves seriously in a sustained fashion in high school. Instead, most tolerate the academic experience that high school provides and discourage their teachers from demanding much engaged participation from them. Students play a major role in setting the level of their concentrated academic engagement within a class, within a school day, and outside of school. For a variety of reasons, it appears that most students have decided to invest their time and energy elsewhere, in activities that reward them financially, offer them some semblance of adult responsibility, or treat them as valuable consumers. Other students have become involved in destructive or socially irresponsible activities.

It will do little good to blame today's adolescents, any more than their predecessors, for wanting to do no more than they have to do, or for resisting uninspired instruction and "education for its own sake." Those reform initiatives designed to reward students for attending school or to punish them for leaving are unlikely to guarantee that meaningful academic achievement will improve. Traditional incentives which once kept at least a large percentage of the high school student body modestly involved in academic work have eroded for both ideological and economic reasons.

The collapse of these incentives has left many classrooms filled with indifferent and disaffiliated students. Journalist George Leonard (1983) portrayed the reality of disengagement in several classrooms, led by dedicated, well-prepared teachers, in an integrated suburban high school near San Francisco. After visiting art and English classes in early 1983, he reconstructed the experience:

13

At one table a black boy with tired, dispirited eyes and lines on his forehead as deep as a sixty-year-old's was reading an account in the sports section of the morning paper about the University of California's miraculous last-second victory over Stanford. At another table a group of Hispanic boys were discussing a spectacular catch made by the 49ers' new wide receiver, Renaldo Nehemiah. "Man, he was open!" A pretty Oriental girl was reading an article in World Tennis entitled "Tennis Anyone?" At yet another table a mixed group of black and Filipino boys were discussing the boxing match in which South Korean boxer Duk Koo Kim had been fatally injured. A long-haired Filipino mimicked Ray "Boom Boom" Mancini's flurry of blows to Kim's head in the four-teenth round and Kim's futile attempt to rise from the canvas. "Nobody could have lived after that," he said. His remark was followed by a thoughtful silence, after which another boy said quietly, "His mother pulled the plug yesterday. She donated his kidneys."

For a few moments the room rustled with sound and movement. "Did anybody fulfill your assignments yesterday? I said I'd give you an extra twelve points if you did. Did anybody do it?"

Silence.

"Did anybody try?"

Two hands started up, then disappeared, like timid forest animals darting back into their holes.

"Well, keep it and show it to me. It's important that you try."

At the beginning of Nick's fifth-period English 2B class, the students straggled in reluctantly, with sullen expressions on their faces. Some of the boys sat down only grudgingly, as if this would be the last concession they would make for the rest of the period. Many of the girls immediately busied themselves with makeup. "I need a mirror," said a heavily painted blonde girl. "Anybody got a mirror?" A Hispanic girl two rows back furnished the mirror and the blonde began working on her eyelashes. "Before we start the next lesson," Nick announced, "I want to say a few words about the last one."

"Say a few words," a heavyset Samoan boy in the back row repeated in a loud, mindless, honking voice. No one paid much attention as Nick went over some common mistakes in the previous day's assignment. Now and then there would be a burst of restless talk or laughter. The Samoan recurrently repeated a phrase in the same loud, expressionless voice. For the most part, Nick ignored the outbursts and went on relent-lessly with the task of handing out dittos and explaining what the class members should be doing. Gradually about half of them settled down to a semblance of work. But the atmosphere was far from tranquil. (pp. 61–62)

Adolescents set their level of academic engagement for complicated reasons, including, most obviously, their earlier experiences with schooling and their families' and friends' posture toward academic learning. There are other less obviously direct forces that shape the nature and depth of an adolescent's commitment to, and engagement in, academic coursework. Like adults, adolescents sensitively assess the potential value of alternatives for investing their time and effort. They constantly attempt to determine the potential contribution to their lives of opportunities that compete for their attention and loyalty. The meaning of diplomas or other educational credentials, for example, affects adolescents' assessment of the potential payoff for investing their energy in academic pursuits. Although they probably cannot articulate it, youth are aware that historically this nation has pretended that the possession of a high school diploma represented the possession of a certain body of knowledge, when in fact it has symbolized no such thing—at least in the twentieth century— for the vast majority of graduates. They have responded to this unarticulated awareness by offering their educational loyalty in order to acquire the diploma through minimal compliance with whatever was needed to earn the credential. Ordinarily, this rarely required the mastery of difficult academic subject matter. Changes in the value of the credential, furthermore, have a fundamental, if unappreciated, impact on the nature of educational loyalty. The remainder of this chapter explores the tradition of academic engagement in the American high school.

THE TRADITION OF ACADEMIC ENGAGEMENT

Ever since the high school was well on its way to becoming a mass institution, certainly by the 1920s, adolescents have displayed little commitment to or engagement with academic learning. There exists no golden age of academic rigor with which to contrast nostalgically the contemporary American high school. Scholars have begun to acknowledge that the lack of higher-order reasoning and comprehension skills among high school students are not of recent origin; they have existed for some time. Stedman and Smith (1983), for example, have argued that high schools have never done an admirable job of educating the vast majority of adolescents. Emphasizing the striking degree of continuity over the past 60 years, they concluded that "our schools historically have failed to educate well a majority of our youth, whether this is measured by college graduation, the capacity to write a cogent essay, mastery of advanced mathematical and scientific concepts, training in literature and foreign languages, or the acquisition of higher-order reasoning and problem-solving skills" (p. 94).

The available primary evidence, including community studies and surveys of adolescent behavior and attitudes, confirms and reinforces the observation that relatively few high school students have been devoted to academic learning, at least since World War I. Like their counterparts of the late 1960s and early 1970s, students earlier in the century were preoccupied with social acitivities, romantic involvements, personal appearance, and sports. Few of the adolescents who swelled high school enrollment figures after 1915 were conspicuously committed to the academic opportunities that the experience provided. They attended principally because graduating improved sharply their opportunities for employment or higher education and, increasingly, because their friends attended and they welcomed the opportunity to enhance their stature among their peers by participating in extracurricular and social activities.

The Lynds (1929) captured the changing place of high school in the lives of Middletown's adolescents during the late 1920s when they observed that "today the school is becoming not a place to which children go from their homes for a few hours daily but a place from which they go home to eat and sleep" (p. 211). It was not the high school's academic program, however, that attracted the community's youth. Indeed, many parents bemoaned the transformation of Middletown's high school from a rigorous college preparatory institution to a social and vocational center, a process that had allowed adolescents to avoid a traditional, classical academic course of study and eased performance standards. "More than one mother shook her head over the fact that her daughter never does any studying at home and is out every evening but gets A's in all her work," the Lynds noted. "It is generally recognized that a boy or girl graduating from the high school can scarcely enter an eastern college without a year of additional preparatory work elsewhere" (p. 195).

Fifteen years later August B. Hollingshead (1949) explored adolescent culture in Elmtown. Based upon research completed during the early 1940s, and eventually published in 1949, his study called attention to the "cleavage" between academic and nonacademic or social activities in high school and emphasized the concern that Elmtown's youth devoted to the latter (pp. 125, 145–79). Like the Lynds in Middletown, Hollingshead found that the high school students were asked to do very little homework; few had to study more than "an hour or two a week outside of school hours" (p. 199).

The students who worked for wages in Elmtown tended to come from the lowest two social classes. Steady employment in this largely industrial community forced adolescents to sacrifice participation in extracurricular and social activities. Work was something that middle-class and affluent students were willing and able to avoid, since it was a mark of some status to receive an allowance from one's parents (p. 203). Similarly, those adolescents who were least committed to high school and were consequently most likely to drop out before graduation were from the lowest social and economic classes. More students each year understood that the high school diploma could improve their occupational and economic opportunities. Middle-class youth and wealthier adolescents, along with Elmtown's white-collar employers, recognized the increasing marketability of high school diploma. Hollingshead concluded that this credential "has come to be regarded as an index of a young person's capacity to enter white-collar jobs. The association between education, job levels, and prestige in the social structure is so high that the person with more education moves into the high-ranking job and the person with little education into the low-ranking job" (p. 289).

Susan Ellen Toth's (1978) eloquent memoir of her adolescence in Ames, Iowa, during the 1950s confirms the work of the Lynds and Hollingshead regarding the place of academic work in the life of high school students. Although somewhat more intellectually inclined than her peers or friends, Toth (who moved on from Ames to attend Smith College) spent her adolescence relatively uninvolved with academic subject matter and, like her counterparts elsewhere, was consumed with cultivating and nurturing personal relationships, the minutiae of acquiring social status, and the pursuit of entertainment.

Virtually all of the prominent field studies and surveys of adolescent attitudes and behavior during the 1950s corroborate Toth's recollections of the postwar era. A large-scale national poll, conducted through Purdue University, focused on the habits, knowledge, opinions, and aspirations of American teenagers during the early 1950s. The poll demonstrates the relatively inconsequential place of academic activities in the lives of high school students. When asked "What is the most important thing young people should get out of high school?" only 14 percent of the entire group surveyed agreed on the importance of an "academic background." Both adults and adolescents strongly emphasized the importance of "personality adjustment" (that is, knowing how to get along with people) over either vocational skill development or academic preparation (Remmers & Radler, 1957, pp. 129, 140). There was near unanimity across regions, social class, gender, and age on this issue; only those whose mothers had attended college and students in the West were slightly more committed to basic subject-matter mastery. This response undoubtedly reflected widespread popular commitment to the goals of the progressive and life-adjustment movements of the 1930s and 1940s, which broadened radically the public's view of the purposes of education (Ravitch, 1983b).

This devaluation of academic knowledge was reflected in the answers that students surveyed in the same poll gave to a series of "knowledge questions" in science and social studies. Overall, 40 percent of the high school students insisted that the earth was the center of the universe, a figure that reflected little evidence of improvement when the responses of ninth and twelfth graders were compared. Despite their slight preference for academic learning, students in the West did worse on virtually all of the subject matter questions: approximately one-half agreed that the earth was the center of the universe, one-fifth maintained that Lincoln had written the Declaration of Independence, and three-fourths stated that the earth's circumference was 125,000 miles.

In 1951, the Los Angeles public schools' associate superintendent tested the basic skills and fundamental knowledge of the district's children. According to *Time Magazine* ("Failure in Los Angeles," 1951), when the teachers and parents got to look at the results, they "yelped with pained surprise." Among the eleventh graders, 3 percent could not tell time, 4 percent did not know what letter preceded "M" in the alphabet, and 14 percent could not calculate 50 percent of 36. Those about to enter high school were equally disappointing: although almost all of the eighth graders could find California on a map, 13 percent could not locate the Atlantic Ocean, and 16 percent failed to find their home town. After the ensuing outcry following the local newspaper's headline, "330 of L.A. High School Juniors Can't Tell Time," the district's administrators commented tellingly that "if we work the kids, we get hell. If we don't work them, we get hell." Within the context of the 1950s, despite evidence of low levels of academic proficiency, the public—most parents and students—devalued academic subject-matter mastery relative to other more highly regarded life-adjustment functions.

Other studies on the importance of adolescent social relations and the impact of athletics and other nonacademic activities on the formation of status hierarchies during the 1950s and 1960s indicate that engagement with basic academic subject matter was not central to the lives of the vast majority of high school students. C. Wayne Gordon (1957) and James Coleman (1961), among others, unraveled the ways in which adolescents "used" the social opportunities that high schools provided to enhance their power, visibility, and status. It was an exceptional adolescent culture that distributed those things which mattered to teenagers, particularly social status, on the basis of deep engagement with academic coursework. Indeed, it was not uncommon for academically talented youth, particularly girls, to resist visible academic success. From such accounts, it is clear that the problem of student indifference or disengagement from academic learning in high school is not a product of the 1960s and 1970s, but one that has endured for at least 60 years.

THE WORLD OF HIGH SCHOOL: AN ORIENTATION

We recognize this long tradition of disengagement as well as acknowledge that indifference toward academic learning appears to have worsened over the past generation. The following analysis accounts for both of these patterns. The remainder of this part of the book, which focuses on the world of high school and lives of its students, addresses the causes and consequences of the lack of concern with, and commitment to, academic learning among adolescents from a number of perspectives. The roots of student disengagement are many and, like a vast number of contemporary social and political issues, are tangled and complex. To seek out and understand the causes of student disengagement from academic learning requires an inquiry into the factors influencing the school behavior of our nation's youth. Some of these variables involve the culture of the school, while many others concern the role of the school, particularly high school, in our society and the value, both real and perceived, of a high school education.

In particular, we see a number of major influences, in addition to those themes we have just set forth, which we feel shape the lives of students in high schools and govern substantially the extent to which adolescents are willing or perhaps even able to become engaged in the tasks of academic learning. The level of engagement in academic learning is influenced—directly or indirectly—by the extent to which receiving a diploma has educational, personal, or economic meaning to both its possessor and the world of work or further education, which must either accommodate or ignore the student. The demands of the nation's system of higher education also influence high school learners, even those who are not college-bound. These types of forces give powerful messages to adolescents about the reasons for staying in high school, for investing in the effort of schooling, for opting to make do and get by, or for dropping out, either figuratively or literally.

To understand the problems of our high schools, we are convinced that it is essential to examine those institutions that prepare our children for secondary education—the elementary schools. It is here that children have their first lessons not only in the basic skills of reading, writing, and computation, but also their first lessons in the ways of schools. Here, at the most impressionable age, youngsters are quietly and effectively taught the meaning of education, the rewards for and value of applying oneself to the distinctive task of school learning and performance. Here may be etched indelibly the attitudes for a lifetime.

Finally, and perhaps most obviously, to understand the problems of secondary education, one must explore what happens to students within the walls of their high schools. What do teachers and other educators have to offer to their students when the bells ring and classes begin? How rigorous is the educational endeavor offered students? Is the academic nurturing provided to one group of students applied in the same measure to all the others? What do we teach adolescents about the values of school learning and its contribution to life? How do we allow them to apply those lessons, acquired both advertently and inadvertently, to the tasks of schooling and to the other challenges they face?

The topics to be discussed in the pages that follow present a picture of the deep complexity of what is happening in our high schools and in the world in which our high schools must function. It is only when one looks at the complex world of high schools and the complexity of the re-lationship between those schools and the lives of the students who attend them that we can begin to grasp the true meaning—or lack of meaning—of any of the proposals to reform secondary education.

2 ▥ The Diploma

The high school diploma itself plays an important role in setting the level of a student's engagement with academic learning. An examination of its value and meaning as a credential, its role in motivating students, and its relationship to academic content or knowledge holds discouraging implications for the current standards-raising movement. Much of the discussion today, as well as many reforms, seem to be based upon assumptions suggesting collectively the following argument. For much of the twentieth century, the high school diploma reliably certified the possession of a specific body of knowledge and skills, commonly thought of as a high school education. This reliability was widely accepted through mid-century, when a gap began to emerge between the credential and the knowledge that it presumably reflected. The correspondence which began to erode during the 1960s severed almost entirely during the 1970s. As a credential, the diploma today has lost its credibility; it no longer validates the possession of any particular valued knowledge or skill base (see Hawkins, 1978; National Association of School Boards, 1976).

THE CREDIBILITY GAP

If this reasoning is correct, the current standards-raising movement can be seen as an effort to *restore* the diploma's credibility and integrity, to close that gaping chasm that erodes our confidence in the ability of high school graduates to know or do anything worthwhile. It assumes that the gap is of relatively recent origin and that students attending high school since the mid-1960s are largely responsible for its existence, because of their particular diversity, laziness, dullness, or whatever.

Certainly, students at any time have some responsibility for the scope, character, and level of their education. Students are not, however, solely responsible and are perhaps not even primarily responsible. Accordingly, there is another way of portraying the historical relationship between the diploma and the knowledge and skills that it supposedly certifies. This alternative interpretation casts at least a large segment of the standards-raising movement differently because it places responsibility for the dissonance on the schools as organizations and on the relative value of the credential in society rather than on adolescents themselves.

It is possible that the gap or dissonance has existed in roughly similar proportions since the high school was well on its way to becoming a mass institution and has only become slightly more visible over the past generation. Over the twentieth century the diploma may never have served as a credible symbol of content mastery. There *is* evidence that during the nineteenth century, when high schools were exclusive and devoted to the intellectual development of a small, homogenous elite, they served as meritocratic institutions based upon the academic content they delivered (Labaree, 1984a, 1984b). Throughout the early twentieth century, as a rapidly increasing share of the adolescent cohort attended and graduated from high school, the diploma continued to serve as a sifter and sorter. In contrast to the elite institutions of the nineteenth century, the twentieth-century high school performed this function not because it developed certain skills but because many adolescents did not attend and most did not graduate. The diploma performed a meritocratic function not because it certified the possession of an agreed-upon knowledge base but because it was relatively rare. The gap between the diploma and the "content" of a high school education emerged during the early stages of the evolution of the high school from an elite to a mass institution, probably by the 1920s.

The gap's existence was not particularly important, however, while opportunities were expanding for the children of immigrants particularly, and for whites more generally. Expanding occupational and economic opportunities subsidized the cost of the gap. The dissonance was tolerable and tolerated because the economy eventually absorbed virtually everyone with a diploma. No one found it necessary to probe too deeply into the content of a high school education, into the knowledge and skills that the diploma supposedly certified.

It is only during the immediate past that there has emerged strong pressure to reestablish the high school credential as a comprehensive, meritocratic, academic sorting mechanism based upon content, a function that it has not performed effectively since the late nineteenth century. Economic opportunities diminished during much of the past generation, beginning in the late 1960s with the war in southeast Asia, and were accelerated and aggravated by the unprecedented trade imbalances, federal deficit spending, and accompanying inflation rates of the 1970s. Although the economy has created millions of new jobs and employment opportunities recently have increased for many, wage scales for these positions are lower than those in the declining manufacturing sector.

Furthermore, most of the rapidly expanding fields—increasingly in the economy's low-paying and part-time service sector—require only modest skills and offer almost no meaningful opportunities for promotion or advancement. As a result, even though the economy can absorb most young adults (despite unemployment among young blacks in excess of 40 percent), it can no longer guarantee them upward mobility or satisfying jobs. Finally, to compound the disincentives problem created by this situation, relatively few of these jobs demand extensive educational credentials; although jobs are available, it is not necessary to have been a dedicated student to get them. So, in spite of the appearance of improvement, the nature of the occupational change has subverted motivation for school learning and attainment.

An ambitious effort to interpret the alienation, boredom, and indifference in an upper-middle-class suburban high school in the mid-1970s helps to clarify this point. Caught in a bind, youth understood that "education has become a meaningless exercise in necessity" (Larkin, 1979, p. 59; see also Seidman, 1980). The motivation for adolescents to attend high school through to graduation "is primarily negative and is not couched so much in terms of what rewards can be gained for continued effort, but what happens if one drops out" (Larkin, 1979, p. 60).

Within this economic context, coupled with near universal high school graduation rates, the standards-raising movement represents an effort to strengthen the schools' sorting function based upon the *content* of a secondary education. At least that portion of the movement directed at low achievers, who are disproportionately lower-class and minority youth, can be viewed in this way.

From this perspective, the movement's timing is ironic, if not cruel and unjust. It will undoubtedly punish adolescents who were unfortunate enough to enter high school just when we wanted to stop tolerating the dissonance between the diploma and the knowledge that we have pretended it represents. Aware of the danger of imposing "illusory" standards, David Seeley (1984) has observed that "we are finally talking seriously about academic learning for everyone. But, if we don't find a way of actually achieving this result, the new standards will become a crueler form of screening and pushing people out of educational opportunities, or they will be rescinded or watered down in the name of practicality" (p. 386; see also Levin, 1978, pp. 317–18).

It is impossible to address with confidence or precision the question of whether the gap between the high school diploma and the knowledge that it presumably certifies has changed over the twentieth century. No one has completed or undertaken the comparative longitudinal study of the relative value of the credential or the source of its legitimacy (either in terms of content or exclusivity) over time. The current complaints about the diploma's credibility have a familiar ring, however, which should encourage caution. A study of the high school diploma, conducted by the research division of the National Education Association in 1959—a poignant time in the nostalgic vision of a rigorous academic tradition—noted that

> critics of current high school education have attacked the high school diploma as meaningless, saying that in the past the diploma was awarded only to those who had demonstrated their ability to measure up to academic standards; now, these critics maintain, diplomas are given to almost anyone who attends high school faithfully for four years. ("High School Diplomas," 1959, p. 115)

For most of this century each generation has bemoaned declining academic standards in similar language. It has been an enduring problem, not one that had radically worsened in the past 20 years. Setting aside their faulty historical perspective, such critics have been largely correct: the separation of credential from content has occurred, but it occurred long ago. Although no one has studied the issue empirically, the existing pertinent literature suggests that ever since the high school abandoned its nineteenth-century mission to serve the elite, the diploma performed its meritocratic sorting and selection function largely based upon its relative exclusivity rather than upon its credible representation of academic content mastery.

Increasing numbers of adolescents aspired to attend and complete high school because the diploma could have a positive effect on their employment opportunities, as business increasingly rewarded each additional year of educational attainment. By the 1930s, at least, prospective employers were discriminating in favor of high school graduates. There is no evidence that their preference for youth possessing diplomas was based upon an assumption that high school graduates had mastered an academic content that made them preferable employees. It was the level of attainment alone that mattered; few high school graduates were called upon to demonstrate the value of the knowledge base that they possessed which supposedly differentiated them from their peers who had left school earlier.

Prospective employers may indeed have assumed that the diploma certified something, but it was more likely perseverance, commitment to a task, and responsibility symbolized by high school graduation than the mastery of a body of academic subject matter (Labaree, 1983, 1984a,b,

1986; Seidman, 1980; Levin, 1978). A recent national survey of American employers, conducted by researchers at The Johns Hopkins University, confirms this impression. The immediate employment opportunities of high school graduates were not affected by performance in academic coursework or the academic quality of the high school they had attended. Character attributes, particularly dependability, proper attitudes about work, and the ability to get along with supervisors and other employees, were vastly more important than either grades or course selection in job recruitment and hiring (Crain, 1984).

Randall Collins' (1979) imaginative review of the evolution of credentialing institutions in the United States recognized the relationship between the diploma and the content of a secondary education. "As the system elaborated," he argued, "the value of any particular kind and level of education came to depend less and less on any specific content that might have been learned in it, and more and more upon the sheer fact of having attained a given level and acquired the formal credential that allowed one to enter the next level (or ultimately to pass the requirements for entering a monopolized occupation)" (p. 93). Over the twentieth century it became "less and less important whether students learned any particular academic content at the lower levels or even if they were moved through without real examination at all. The occupationally relevant distinctions were pushed further and further ahead to the higher levels" (p. 118). Eventually students came "to move through schools largely by aging rather than by scholastic achievement" (p. 117; see also Kamens, 1977).

Since 1920, the value of a diploma has not been determined by the rigorous academic content that its possessors had mastered. One must return to the nineteenth century to find the "good old days" when high school students were deeply engaged in the acquisition of academic knowledge. Even then, the select few adolescents who were able to attend high school were rarely motivated by a love of education for its own sake or the intrinsic interest of the subject matter. They were motivated by the extrinsic value of a high school diploma in the marketplace. High school students, at least since the mid-nineteenth century, have customarily pursued their studies for fundamentally utilitarian reasons, a reality that has overwhelmed competing views of the purpose of schooling in this society (on the impact of utility, see Brann, 1979; Hurn, 1983; Hurn & Burn, 1983). When high schools were elite, exclusive institutions in the nineteenth century, the market value of the diploma was commensurately great, and as a result, teachers could exact extraordinary commitment and performance out of their students (Labaree, 1986). As high schools became more universal and the diploma became less scarce, the credential itself became devalued (Cohen & Neufeld, 1981). In a society that has marketed schooling—especially enhanced attainment—on an extrinsic or utilitarian basis, its ability to induce students to care about academic engagement and achievement was bound to deteriorate.

It is not our intention to leave the impression that nothing has changed since the mid-1960s. On the contrary, the captivating power of the high school diploma declined even further over the past generation, a function of its widespread attainment as well as of the decline in economic opportunities mentioned above, other options competing for the time and energy of youth, and other trends to be reviewed below. It is important, however, to avoid being seduced entirely by the *changes* that have affected the level of engagement and performance of high school students since the 1960s and to consider instead the pattern of *continuity* since the 1920s at least, which has characterized the relationship between the diploma and the presumed knowledge constituting a high school education. The gap that compromises the credibility of the diploma today is not a new phenomenon but is instead at least 60 years old. Not since the nineteenth century have we demanded (indeed, have we been in a position to demand, or even needed to demand) that the sorting function played by the credential correspond to the mastery of a specific body of knowledge or skills.

For a variety of reasons, the traditional rhetoric of utility that has motivated adolescents to care about the high school diploma and to devote at least some attention to the minimal levels of academic work necessary to win it has progressively lost much of its holding power. In part this is a function of the awareness of youth catching up to the reality of a devalued diploma, a process first visibly apparent in the black community during the 1960s (Smith, 1972). Although we have pretended that educational attainment, particularly promotion through the grades, was based upon the demonstrated mastery of cumulative subject-matter knowledge, children and adolescents have actually been motivated by the extrinsic promise of rewards for remaining in school (see Meyer, 1980). Recognizing the potential contribution that several recent studies of schooling have made to this discussion, Manuel J. Justiz, former director of the National Institute of Education, argued that

> our most fundamental educational credentials—the high school diploma and the college degree—are now based more on time studying various subjects than on attainment in those subjects. The proxy measures for time are credits: accumulate a certain number of credits, and you receive a diploma or degree. The drive to accumulate credits has undercut the very meaning of those credentials. (1984, p. 485)

Once the promised value of the diploma proves hollow, the rhetoric of the intrinsic pursuit of knowledge is exposed through a pattern of student disengagement and even defiance.

RESTORING THE DIPLOMA'S CREDENTIAL VALUE

Operating to a large extent upon the nostalgic view of the value and meaning of the formal credential, since the mid-1970s policymakers have been committed to restoring the "credibility" of the high school diploma as one of the primary goals of the standards-raising campaign. Indeed, proposals to restore the meaning of the high school diploma were the first initiatives in the current reform movement. The vision of the diploma's recent deterioration in credibility as a reliable educational, economic, and social credential can be traced to several specific sources. A federally sponsored study in the early 1970s concluded that one out of five adult Americans lacked the basic functional skills to read, write, or compute effectively (Hawkins, 1978; McClung, 1979). The media and opinion polls revealed increasing disappointment with the public schools' success in providing basic skill training, a concern captured by the phrase, "Why Johnny can't read" (Hawkins, 1978; Neill, 1978; Pedulla & Reidy, 1979; Haney & Madaus, 1978). Business leaders became increasingly distressed that public schools were not graduating prospective workers with the fundamental skills necessary to succeed on the job (Hawkins, 1978; Pedulla & Reilly, 1979). Students who progressed satisfactorily through school and received high school diplomas sought to enter the job market or institutions of higher education only to discover that they lacked the requisite fundamental skills to succeed in the "real world." Some of these students, after becoming aware of their educational deficits, took their former school districts to court, claiming that they were victims of negligent social promotion policies and "educational malpractice" (Pullin, 1982; McClung, 1979; Tractenberg, 1979; Nathan & Jennings, 1978; Wise, 1977; Pedulla & Reidy, 1979; Baratz, 1980; Haney & Madaus, 1978). Although none of these lawsuits succeeded, they had a powerful impact on the assumptions and understanding of policymakers, educators, and the public.

Such deep concerns about the lack of basic skills achievement on the part of high school graduates and their perceived inability to succeed in "real world" situations contributed to political pressure for accountability mechanisms to hold schools to standards that the lay public could easily measure and understand. A primary focus of this standards-raising effort became the high school diploma itself. As the National Association of School Boards stated to its membership in early 1976:

> If high school promotion and graduation have become routine in your district's high schools, chances are students, parents, and other citizens don't attach much meaning to a piece of paper that verifies the high school experience. . . . Restoring the credibility of the diploma may go a long way toward restoring public confidence in your schools. (National Association of School Boards, 1976, p. 4)

This "crisis of credibility" (Hawkins, 1978) provoked a response initiated for the most part not by educators but, instead, by politicians serving either as state legislators or as school board members (Haney & Madaus, 1978). Over the past decade politicians have launched campaigns on at least two related fronts designed to restore the diploma's integrity. The most common response has been to mandate the use of minimum competency tests to determine class placement or grade-to-grade promotion as well as exit examinations to award or deny educational credentials (Doughtery, 1983). In addition to, and occasionally in conjunction with, competency tests, states and communities have also begun to award "differentiated diplomas" designed to distinguish high school graduates who complete relatively rigorous academic courses of study from their counterparts, whose less successful secondary school careers are recognized with "certificates of attendance" or other diplomas lacking academic endorsements.

Minimum competency tests

Over the past decade, minimum competency tests (MCT) have become popular weapons in the arsenal of the standards-raisers. Their particular use in awarding high school diplomas is of paramount concern in understanding the impact of minimum competency testing on educational credentials, the characteristics of schooling at the secondary level, and the role of high school, both in the society at large and in the lives of adolescents. Since 1975, minimum competency tests have frequently been used to make critical decisions about individuals and to implement policy goals. State and local efforts to promote educational accountability increased the use of educational tests to evaluate minimum levels of student competency in basic skills performance. As of October 1983, forty states had initiated minimum competency tests and nineteen states had used tests to award regular high school diplomas (Pipho & Flakus-

Mosqueda, 1984).* In addition to testing to determine eligibility for diplomas, "promotional gates" testing to determine student eligibility for grade-to-grade promotion is employed in at least five states.**

The use of minimum competency testing, imposed most often from the state level, is for the most part a *political* rather than an *educational* reform effort (Haney & Madaus, 1978). It is, as Arthur Wise has described it, an attempt at "legislated learning" with little or no educational research to establish that such efforts were either viable, feasible, or offered a high likelihood of success in actually enhancing student achievement (Wise, 1979; Pullin, 1982).

Minimum competency testing proponents claim that the use of tests to make essential decisions about students, such as promoting them or awarding them a high school diploma, was necessary in order to eliminate the ills of grade inflation, social promotion, or the possession of "meaningless" high school diplomas and inequality in the delivery of educational services (Baratz, 1980; Pedulla & Reidy, 1979; Haney & Madaus, 1978). The movement appears to offer a simple solution to the problem of promoting both educational equality and at least some level of excellence, particularly in the pursuit of basic skills achievement. However, the levels of academic attainment sought in the programs are, as the name of the movement suggests, mere minimums. Furthermore, although the programs are highly results-oriented, they involve little social responsibility for the results. Instead, the programs' responsibility rests largely on the shoulders of students participating in the testing programs.

Far from being egalitarian, the movement is, as Cohen and Haney (1980) pointed out, a form of minimalist social welfare policy, a no-cost or low-cost form of window dressing which attempts to address the problems of status inflation created in a generation of students for whom a four-year college diploma was easily accessible. The minimum competency testing movement is, at base, an effort to restore the perceived social and economic meaning of the high school diploma in an era in which increas-

---

*The use of minimum competency tests to determine diploma entitlements or the type of diploma awarded has been implemented in Alabama, Arizona, California (local option), Florida, Georgia, Hawaii, Maryland, Mississippi, Nevada, New Jersey, New Mexico (diploma endorsements), New York, North Carolina, Ohio, Oregon (endorsements), Pennsylvania (honors endorsement), Rhode Island, Tennessee, Utah, Vermont, and Virginia (Doughtery, 1983; United States Department of Education, 1983a, 1983b).

**Arkansas, Louisiana, Maryland, Missouri, and Ohio, and several local districts, such as New York City (*Ibid.*; Barrett, 1982).

ing numbers of students have obtained access not only to the high school diploma but also to higher education and ultimately to higher rungs on the economic ladder (see Southern Regional Education Board, 1981). As we have previously noted, these efforts at restoration are, at least to some extent, misplaced, if for no other reason than the fact that there has always existed a gap between what the diploma is deemed to represent and actual knowledge of content.

The minimum competency testing movement implies that it relies upon a set of standards defined to be so minimal as to be both essential for successful adult life functioning and attainable by every nonhandicapped student. Results of the examinations indicate, however, that not all students are yet able to succeed in the new testing programs (Madaus, 1981; McClung, 1979; Pullin, 1982, 1983) and that when 100 percent success rates are either approached or realized, the standards for passing them are consistently increased (Haney & Madaus, 1978).

The impact of minimum competency testing on low-income, minority, and other educationally disadvantaged youngsters has been precisely what would have been predicted by looking at the success rates of those populations on previous educational achievement tests (Fisher, 1978). Educationally disadvantaged students, therefore, operate at a disadvantage when minimum competency tests are used to make significant decisions about their lives (Haney & Madaus, 1978; McClung, 1979). In addition, the new test requirements have resulted in substantial numbers of students dropping out of school in expectation of unsuccessful test performance or of disappointment or embarrassment on graduation day (Madaus, 1981).

In addition to the impact of minimum competency testing on racial minorities and economically disadvantaged students, the testing programs have also had a particular impact on another minority group: students with handicapping conditions. Since the mid-1970s, pressures to assimilate disabled students into the educational mainstream have increased because of the implemention of state and federal statutes mandating the provision of special education services. Like the mandates for desegregation of racial minority students, legal requirements concerning students with handicapping conditions have placed tremendous pressures on high schools to assimilate, educate, and grant certification to students those schools were often ill-equipped to serve. The pressure on high schools to accommodate and to certify such students and provide them with legitimate credentials has been alleviated somewhat by the new competency testing requirements which either exclude special education students entirely from participation in the testing program, fail to accommodate their handicapping conditions through the use of such tools as braille or large print versions of the test, or offer disabled students only the possibility of special diplomas (Fenton, 1980; Rosewater, 1979; Danielson, 1980; McClung & Pullin, 1978).

The failure to address, at least initially, the full implications of minimum competency testing is reflected graphically in the failure of many of the earliest efforts to provide mechanisms and funding for compensatory educational services for students who fail the examinations (Cohen & Haney, 1980; Haney & Madaus, 1978). Even when such compensatory or remedial education programs have been offered, there have been failures to provide guidance to teachers so that they might use test results diagnostically or modify their instruction or behavior so as to develop the skills and knowledge assessed on the test itself (Task Force on Educational Assessment Programs, 1979). Most dramatically, the inability of MCT programs to foster educational achievement is evident in the structure of most programs, which began to impose punitive sanctions on students for failing to succeed on the tests before a correspondingly appropriate curriculum had been implemented. Students taking the examinations were denied a fair opportunity to receive instruction in the skills and knowledge covered on the test before it was administered and sanctions for test failure were imposed (Madaus & McDonagh, 1979; McClung, 1979; Pullin, 1983).

Current research suggests that the process by which minimum competency tests are created and integrated into the curriculum, rather than the act of testing itself, determines the effect of testing requirements on learning (Klein, 1984). To a certain extent, where the skills and knowledge covered on the test are explicitly and publicly defined, the test can begin to define the instruction of conscientious teachers who wish to prepare students to succeed on the examination (Madaus & McDonagh, 1979; Airasian & Madaus, 1983). The testing mandate, therefore, can inadvertently define the curriculum for teachers. And, for students not previously offered adequate instruction in basic skills, minimum competency testing may compel the provision of instruction where it was not previously provided. Imposed at the state level, the test defines local curricula and intrudes into classrooms to an unprecedented extent. This shift toward greater state control of the curriculum has not been explicit, however, and is seldom addressed in the literature discussing minimum competency testing (Madaus & McDonagh, 1979). Further, it is notable that the imposition of implicit statewide curricula has often preceeded recent attempts by states to provide remediation for those who fail tests (Cohen & Haney, 1980) or to impose higher statewide course requirements for graduation. In the state of Florida, for example, at the time the diploma test was initiated, the only statewide course requirement for high school students was that a class in "Americanism versus Communism" be completed. It was not until seven years after the test-for-diploma program was initiated that the state moved to impose course requirements for graduation in the basic skills subjects, such as English and mathematics, covered on the minimum competency test (Southern Regional Education Board, 1981; U.S. Department of Education, 1983a).

The use of minimum competency testing to determine diploma awards or student placement has been accused of causing a shift in control of curriculum to the state level, forcing a decrease in enrollment among students who would have otherwise continued their high school careers, allowing resegregation of students on the basis of race or handicapping condition into remedial or compensatory educational classes, and reducing the number of high school diplomas awarded. Finally, one might well ask whether test-based diplomas now being awarded are in fact representative of real increases in academic achievement.

Minimum competency testing to determine the award of high school diplomas resembles the bait-and-switch advertising tactic, in which an inferior or less attractive item is substituted for the more desirable item at the point of sale. The product that attracts the attention and involvement of adolescents is an education that develops competencies needed for life. They are, in actuality, offered a score on a standardized paper-and-pencil competency examination, or a certificate of attendance. These are poor substitutes (Nathan & Jennings, 1978). Students are aware of this bait-and-switch, and it shapes their attitudes toward education since schools are allowed to continue to offer irrevelant curricula. In addition, it will be easier for "competent" students to disengage from learning when they observe that the "minimums" covered on the test become the maximum level of expectation (Pullin, 1982; Neill, 1978; Madaus & McDonagh, 1979; Levin, 1978; Labaree, 1983).

Critics have noted that where competency testing is used to impose control over student or teacher performance such efforts are unlikely to succeed. When these programs are imposed, they generally entail only organizational efforts and do not involve mandates or strategies for improving teaching or learning. Also, the success of such efforts relies heavily both upon student interest in pursuing the competency goals (which they may be encouraged to do if a diploma sanction is involved) and upon teacher willingness to adopt voluntarily the goals of the program. Increased reliance on simplified skills and knowledge is customary, given the limits of available test technology. Such narrowness in turn reduces student motivation. Finally, to initiate an outcomes-based competency definition of a high school education presents students with troublesome inconsistencies (Spady & Mitchell, 1977). If the high school exit test is set at a seventh- or ninth-grade level of difficulty, as are most such tests, why should students complete twelve years of schooling? If the high school exit tests measure "real life" competencies not ordinarily taught in school, as do most such tests, why should students waste their time in school when "real life" skills might more readily be learned at an after-school job or while shopping?

For those students most likely to lose their diplomas under a minimum competency testing program, the scheme becomes a form of "blaming the victim," the results of which have a negative impact on their attitudes toward school (Madaus & McDonagh, 1979; Cohen & Haney, 1980). Educationally disadvantaged, low-income, minority, and other students know that schooling has not been a successful experience for them. For many of these students, school is a painful and unsuccessful experience because of educational disadvantages that can be attributed to school segregation, second generation racial discrimination, inequities in the allocation of educational resources, and other social, political, and economic problems. For students whose test performance reflects such institutional and social structure problems, a positive attitude toward academic learning at school can hardly be expected.

Differentiated diplomas

In addition to competency testing, the current high school standards-raising effort became interested in implementing the practice, longstanding in some school systems, of awarding different types of high school exit credentials. Differentiated diplomas consist of the following:

- In systems requiring successful completion of a minimum competency test as a prerequisite for a diploma, students who fail the test but complete all other criteria for graduation are offered either certificates of completion, certificates of attendance, or diplomas upon which there is no competency seal or endorsement (Education Commission of the States, 1983b).
- Since the 1920s, New York State has offered Regents diplomas to students who pass honors examinations; a growing number of states, including Florida, have begun to award honors endorsements to high school graduates (National Association of Secondary School Principals, 1975).
- For a number of years predating the minimum competency testing movement, special diplomas or certificates have been awarded in some states to students with handicapping conditions who have attended special education programs. Expanded use of minimum

competency tests to award high school diplomas has increased the use of these special credentials for students with handicapping conditions in a least fifteen states (National Association of State Directors of Special Education, 1979; Rosewater, 1979).

- A number of systems are considering the use of special vocational/technical diplomas for students who do not pass through the regular academic curriculum but have instead successfully completed a program of vocational education. Some systems indicate on the diplomas a special high school attended or special courses taken.

- Many local and state boards of education have recently established two types of diplomas: those for students completing college preparatory coursework and diplomas with lower requirements for those students who are not preparing for college (Pipho & Flakus-Mosqueda, 1984).

- President Reagan and the U.S. Department of Education have implemented a President's Academic Fitness Award (PAFA) for graduating seniors who have a specified grade point average and score on a college admissions test, and who have completed national basic skill course requirements.

To a large extent, this increased interest in offering differing types of diplomas and certificates to students who have completed their high school experience is a reflection of the extent to which the current standards movement focuses upon the value of a high school credential. Differentiated diploma programs use student placement (into special education or vocational/technical education, for example) or student test performance (on Regents or competency exams) to measure the "value" of the education received.

The impact of these differential diploma programs upon student engagement in their high school experience may vary. For talented adolescents, the possibility of achieving an honors diploma in which the award is perceived as one based fully upon achievement and merit might encourage increased participation in the academic learning process. For students at the other end of the spectrum, however, differentiated diplomas may simply provide additional disincentives for learning. Students in special education or vocational tracks who, because of their program placements, have no expectation of a regular diploma have a substantial incentive to disengage from academic learning in school.

The problem of declining academic standards during the past generation is rooted in causes clearly more complicated than the devaluation of the high school diploma. The standards-raising movement, nevertheless, must recognize that in our society the level of an adolescent's academic engagement and performance depends in large part upon the payoff of a high school diploma: the extent to which it can be translated into a job that provides upward economic and social mobility, access to decent higher education, or other forms of status or opportunity that young people value. In a society that has earlier camouflaged its utilitarian use of schooling for individual economic and social advancement beneath a veneer of pronouncements about the intrinsic value of knowledge, it is not surprising that adolescents have responded as they have to the devaluation of the high school diploma in the marketplaces that concern youth.

The payoff for possessing a high school credential is not something over which schools have much control or influence. Other organizations determine the diploma's ultimate value as well as what skills and knowledge it is presumed to represent. Thus far, at least during the twentieth century, those organizations have provided incentives for students to acquire the credential but very little more. Only rarely have they provided valuable rewards for sustained academic learning or genuine engagement with exercises designed to develop higher-order cognitive skills. It seems unrealistic to expect the high school—just one segment of the sorting, training, credentialing, and placement enterprise—to shift the entire process on an unprecedented basis, from credit accumulation through minimal compliance to the mastery of challenging academic knowledge. Individuals are sensitive to the potential payoffs for investing their effort and time in one activity over another; unless the entire credentialing and allocation system converts its incentive structure, adolescents will remain skeptical about claims that the high school diploma means something or has a value they know it does not. Tinkering in isolation at the high school level with the diploma's role, meaning, and accessibility, without the willingness to address this skepticism with tolerance and imagination, will result in a punitive campaign against young persons who have accurately assessed the prevailing incentive structure and have invested their energies accordingly.

3 🕮 Content: The High School Course of Study

The formal, explicit "content" of a high school education is under fire. Virtually every major commission report, scholarly study, and state or local initiative criticizes the secondary school curriculum or course of study. Following is a list of some of the most glaring problems exposed or identified during the recent past.

- Knowledge is fragmented and incoherent; the concept of a "core" curriculum has receded or has been abandoned (Ravitch, 1981; Sizer, 1984b; Boyer, 1983; Cawelti, 1981; Newmann, 1980; Goodlad, 1984; National Commission on Excellence in Education, 1983; Adler, 1982; Bailey, A., 1983, 1984; Christenbury, 1979, 1983; Education Commission of the States, Task Force on Education for Economic Growth, 1983; Cusick, 1983; Education Commission of the States, 1983a; Dougherty, 1983; Peterson, 1983).
- Specialized, narrow, often trivial electives have proliferated (Ravitch, 1983b; Cawelti, 1981; Cusick, 1983).
- Course content is often determined by teachers acting in relative isolation and driven by their aspirations to develop classes based largely on their personal predelictions, hobbies, outside employment, disciplinary loyalties, and interest in attracting students in a competitive market, with courses designed to appeal to the adolescent's definition of "knowledge" and "relevance" (Cusick, 1983; Christenbury, 1980; Cromer, 1970; Kirschenbaum, 1969).
- Students occasionally exert unwarranted and detrimental influence over the curricular content of their high school educations (Cusick, 1983).
- However hastily developed in response to special interest group pressure, new courses displace basic academic classes (Ravitch, 1981).
- Instructional prioritites are confused and differ radically by district (Brodinsky, 1977; Goodlad, 1984; Boyer, 1983).
- Graduation requirements vary considerably by state and district (Education Commission of the States, 1983a; Fiske, 1983).

CURRICULAR FRAGMENTATION

The content of a high school education has always been relatively fragmented and diversified. In the nineteenth century the range of secondary schools was extraordinary in terms of student body caliber and aspirations, teachers' training and experience, and mission (since the progressive, cumulative educational ladder common today was not yet fully in place). As a result, this range resulted in great institutional diversity. However, despite such differences, which were aggravated by idiosyncratic college admission practices, the high school curriculum was generally oriented toward classical studies, mathematics, science, history, and geography. Students in different schools or those who aspired to different colleges might read and study different works of classical literature, perhaps, but the variety of subject matter was much narrower than today.

The process of curricular fragmentation became apparent during the 1880s and 1890s as vocational, home economics, and practical arts courses were introduced to augment the prevailing classical and basic academic courses of study. The introduction of nonacademic classes in part reflected a redefinition of the concept of equality of educational opportunity (Cohen, & Neufeld, 1981; Tyack & Hansot, 1981). Throughout the earlier nineteenth century, educational and political leaders argued that equality was enhanced when children from all social and economic classes were given the opportunity to enroll in the same courses together whenever possible. Such a vision buttressed the common school movement at the elementary level and its eventual extension upward through high school, although educational leaders came to reject this definition of equality late in the century. They argued, in contrast, that it was inherently undemocratic to force all children into the same courses, particularly to restrict their enrollment to impractical classical programs that discouraged many prospective students because of the subject matter's presumed uselessness. Equality of opportunity was redefined to defend the introduction of different curricular emphases for children, primarily adolescents, destined toward different occupations and futures. Manual training, vocational education, trade training, domestic science, and other practical "hand work" courses were developed and introduced to attract and hold adolescents who were assumed to be alienated from, and made uncomfortable by, unfamiliar and irrelevant "brain work."

By the early twentieth century, consequently, secondary schools throughout the nation were expanding their traditional college preparatory curricular program to include courses to help prepare some children to learn a trade, to prepare nutritious meals at low cost, and to be comfortably adjusted to their place in the labor force. The extent to which high schools actually accomplished these objectives is unknown, but the radical restructuring of institutions reflected this basic change in mission from serving the elite exclusively to accommodating the presumed interests and needs of the masses.

Our historical commitment over the twentieth century to attracting and holding all adolescents in high school has strongly encouraged—if not obligated—us to accommodate their interests and preferences for relevant experiences and classes. In addition to our strong interest in egalitarianism, our national tradition of valuing pragmatism, utilitarianism, and individualism has had a similiar impact on the evolution of school curricula. As Christopher Hurn and Barbara Burn have demonstrated, these values "have shaped our relative lack of selectivity, our lack of national examinations, and our suspicion of the traditional 'high culture' liberal arts curriculum" (Hurn, 1983, p. 8; see also Hurn & Burn, 1983). In contrast with most of the rest of the world, which has reserved prestige and esteem for subjects that are "distinctly, even defiantly, nonutilitarian," the United States has celebrated the extent to which education "provides skills and advances careers." American education, rhetorically committed to meeting the "needs" of students and society, has stood in marked contrast to the conception of schooling as an intrinsic good. This utilitarian mission, always at least marginally influential, gained legitimacy and authority during the mid-twentieth century as a symbol of the "progressive" agenda and "life adjustment" movement (Ravitch, 1983b). Our heritage of individualism also contrasts sharply with the inclination of other nations to rely on schools to develop a common body of knowledge, to transmit a common cultural tradition (Hurn, 1983). Together, these values have recently encouraged the fragmentation of school content both by stimulating the development of practical, immediately useful classes and by discouraging efforts to identify a unified, common intellectual and cultural tradition.

The process of curricular diversification continued steadily for several decades, accelerated at times by federal policy (including the Smith-Hughes Act of 1917), state mandates and fiscal practices (reimbursing local districts for adding driver education after World War II, for example), and professional ideology (a consequence of the *Cardinal Principals of Secondary Education* released in 1918 and the life-adjustment movement popular during the 1940s) (Ravitch, 1983b; Mitchell, R., 1981).

Despite the enticements provided by external funding, and the pressure to serve an increasingly diversified student body, the high school course of study remained surprisingly intact and undiluted at least through the 1930s. The vast majority of students enrolled in roughly the same courses. In this preconsolidation era, most high schools were too small or too poor to offer more than a handful of classes and were not yet so ruthlessly tracked that adolescents from all social classes did not take many courses similar in content and expectation. In the larger urban and suburban comprehensive high schools, some enrolling more than 5,000 students, the situation was different. Yet even large schools ordinarily offered only a small variety of classes in each academic department. Many had begun to group students by ability, eventually offering several sections of the same class, each attempting to cover comparable subject matter at a different pace and level. By and large, nevertheless, the formal high school course of study was still circumscribed (see, for example, "High School Graduation Requirements," 1959). Of course it is impossible to determine the extent to which course titles and descriptions actually reflect the content that students received, but within the limitations posed by the sort of evidence that was generated and preserved, it appears that the definition of a high school education was relatively much narrower in 1950 than it is today.

Several trends combined over the subsequent two decades to intensify the process of curricular fragmentation. First, in the tradition of the life-adjustment movement, which led to an expansion of practical arts and personal service classes during the 1940s and 1950s, federal and state policies that were combined with pressure from special interest groups increasingly mandated and/or subsidized instruction in traditionally nonacademic areas. These included sex education, consumer education, substance abuse education, and environmental education, among others. The actual time that high school students spend in classes in these areas is not really substantial, but if something must be eliminated from the curriculum for everything added, the cumulative impact of the introduction of nonacademic classes has become sufficiently evident to provoke criticism and resistance (Ravitch, 1981; Cawelti, 1981; Gray, 1980; Adelman, 1983; Graham, 1984a).

Second, and more significantly, the content of the basic academic disciplines has become far more fragmented since the early 1950s. The process has occurred for several reasons. Subject-matter knowledge became narrow and specialized in institutions of higher education, as faculty members were increasingly rewarded for conducting research on the frontiers of knowledge creation and preferred to teach the content they themselves studied. With the pace of the professionalization of university teaching accelerating after 1920, college professors were increasingly able to define and control more of the subject matter of their courses. Despite the rather feeble efforts of a handful of elite institutions to reestablish the strength of general education at the college level, by World War II the elective movement had permeated the vast majority of schools. College students were increasingly allowed to build their own higher education programs by selecting from hundreds, and eventually thousands, of different specialized courses, most of which were conceived and developed by individual faculty members based upon their own interests and professional commitments.

As more high school teachers completed college and were exposed to knowledge in highly specialized classes (indeed, they could rarely avoid it), their understanding of disciplinary subject matter changed. They came to agree with their professors that specialized knowledge was legitimate and ultimately concluded that it was appropriate to develop courses for high school students that resembled the classes they had taken in college. As a result, the number of classes designed around narrow topics or themes began to appear in high school curricular handbooks or catalogs. Particularly in language arts and social studies but also in science and mathematics, courses were developed and introduced that focused on a narrow segment of the field's subject matter. Resembling in some respects their collegiate counterparts, electives in high schools dealt with "World War II," "Nineteenth-Century Feminist Authors," "Child Psychology," "Film," or "Comparative Religions." These are several of the more credible examples of electives in English and social studies. Of course the subject matter presented in these courses could be demanding and could provide opportunities for intensive academic learning; their legitimacy as subjects worthy of study is undeniable. Coupled with prevailing course requirements that permit students to graduate after accumulating a specified number of credits in each basic discipline with little regard for the content learned, however, the proliferation of even rigorous electives undermined the opportunity for many students to study American history, world civilization, and European literature systematically.

The presence of many insubstantial, even trivial, electives in high school course handbooks compounds the legitimate knotty problems associated with the fragmentation of knowledge. The popularity of classes such as "Rock Poetry" (in which students listen to, decipher, and "analyze" the songs of their favorite performers), "Gourmet Foods," "Literature for Lovers," "Bookless Class," or "The Sixth Sense" encourage proposals for similar electives. Opportunities to study such subjects might pose only financial problems for school districts if it were not for the fact that their availability reinforces existing occupational and economic inequalities. Enrollment in the less substantial electives is not ordinarily random but is correlated with social status (Cusick, 1983, p. 46). Lower-class students and adolescents lacking strong commitment to extended schooling disproportionately populate such classes; indeed, many of the special interest electives were introduced to make school more bearable for students with weak affiliative ties to more formal education.

The stampede to introduce electives in the basic disciplines accelerated during the late 1960s and early 1970s as schools attempted to accommodate student concern for relevance. The earlier focus on rigorous academic seminars for advanced high school students that touched off the elective movement after 1960 often degenerated into an outright tendency to allow student interest to determine course content. Permitting adolescents to define elective subject matter led to further curricular fragmentation. High school students are notoriously fickle and faddish about their commitment to academic knowledge; this was particularly true during the late 1960s and early 1970s. This posture contributed to the movement to break subject matter into even smaller units. It became common, for example, for English curricula to consist of dozens of eight- or nine-week "minicourses" or "microelectives." By constructing short topical courses, schools could accommodate adolescents' fleeting understanding of, and dedication to, what they most wanted to know.

Supporters defended the specialized elective movement as a panacea for virtually all of the problems confronting teaching during the late 1960s and early 1970s. Specialized classes and packages of minicourses would stimulate and hold student interest; renew the dedication of teachers tired of or bored with traditional subject matter; appeal to teachers who shared adolescents' definitions of the knowledge most worth learning; improve attendance, motivation, and discipline; meet the needs of individual students; better serve the self-actualization goals of adolescents and teachers; allow for more local options; improve the schools' responsiveness to the claims of minorities and others neglected in the traditional curriculum; and make it possible for students to intensify their vocational training.

Weaknesses in the rationale and implementation of specialized electives were identified just as the movement was getting off the ground. Even sympathizers were critical of potential problems associated with curricular freedom of choice. More than one critic observed that electives, particularly in English, tended to minimize or curtail opportunities for students to hone their composition skills; most specialized classes devoted almost exclusive attention to reading and discussing narrow bodies of literature (Crabbe, 1970; Johnson, J. et al., 1976). Others challenged the appropriateness of the college model of specialized departmental knowledge and countered that high school teachers should make every effort to integrate the subject matter of their fields. The tendency of many electives to be grouped by ability and social class was identified (Crabbe, 1970). Gyves and Clark (1975) warned that the elective system was not a solution to instructional problems and cautioned that thinking of it in such a way could exclude alternative innovations from serious consideration.

Fueled by the "Back to Basics" movement of the 1970s, criticism of elective proliferation escalated dramatically. Beyond the problems already recognized, other commentators questioned the abdication of professional responsibility for defining academic content (Christenbury, 1979, 1983). Others observed that unstructured election permits peer pressure—always a strong influence on adolescent decision-making in any case—to force hasty or unwise curricular choices on some adolescents (Lucas, 1976; Cawelti, 1981; Heidelberg, 1971). Electives tend to be easier and contribute significantly to grade inflation (Brodinsky, 1977; Distefano, 1975). Too often narrow, specialized electives leave students unfamiliar with our cultural heritage (Ravitch, 1981, 1983a; Cawalti, 1981). Because of expanded staffing responsibilities, electives often drain the financial and personnel resources of a school district (Cheever & Sayer, 1982). And, of course, electives limit the opportunity to master basic academic knowledge (Ravitch, 1981; Christenbury, 1983; Sizer, 1984b; Boyer, 1983; Parnell, 1974).

Despite the criticism, and evidence of a modest retreat from the least defensible electives, high school students, when given a choice, continue to enroll in introductory, superficial, and inconsequential courses at the expense of fundamental classes in the basic disciplines. High school students have been given considerable freedom to design their own course of study. Until very recently the vast majority of states have left the definition of a high school education up to local districts. Few states require anything more specific than three years of English, two years of social studies, one year each of mathematics and science, and perhaps some exposure to health education, in order to graduate from high school with a valid diploma. Fewer states have defined the appropriate academic content, and local district requirements are rarely more specific. Ordinarily, high schools allow students to fulfill graduation requirements by selecting roughly 50 percent of their courses from a variety of electives in all subject areas. Furthermore, it is not uncommon for high schools to permit students to fulfill up to a third of the remaining basic educational requirements by selecting specialized classes in the core academic subject-matter fields. Few high schools offer a coherent academic program required of all students.

Unconstrained by meaningful graduation requirements, until recently most students have used freedom of class selection to design their own course of study. Even when curricular tracking restricts course selection (some would argue *because* it restricts choices), each high school provides a variety of "educations." The definition of a high school education has stretched to encompass whatever collection of courses any individual student might select. There are, in other words, nearly as many definitions of a secondary education as there are high school students (Cusick, 1983; Goodlad, 1984).

Students typically enroll in more personal service, development, and work-study classes than in the past and reject the basic academic subjects, particularly advanced classes in science, mathematics, social studies, foreign languages, and composition. Clifford Adelman's (1983) reconstruction of patterns of high school course selection from 1964 to 1981, based upon transcripts and schedules, suggests that over the past two decades students have received a less rigorous academic education. Despite the methodological problems associated with his effort to draw conclusions from differing data bases, there remains little doubt about the direction and magnitude of the changing pattern of course selection, even though the precise scope of the shift may be impossible to determine. Adelman found that 1) students enroll in fewer basic academic courses today than a generation ago; 2) students from all curricular tracks spend more time in, and receive more credit for, "personal service and development courses"; 3) students have abandoned the college preparatory and vocational tracks for the "general" curriculum, an educational "wasteland," which is dominated by survey, remedial, and personal service classes; and 4) the high school curriculum has become increasingly "diffused and fragmented" since 1965 (see also Fiske, 1983).

It is not uncommon for diverse, comprehensive high school course catalogs or handbooks to resemble those of colleges. A single institution might offer 35 different English classes and 30 social studies electives (Lightfoot, 1983, pp. 197–98). The superintendent of the Dallas system noted in 1983 that the typical regular high school in his community offered 320 different courses and that the alternative or "magnet" programs offered an additional 230 classes (Wright, L., 1983, pp. 6-7). Special interest courses were introduced to appeal to students of diverse backgrounds, abilities, and aspirations. This process of accommodation became particularly important as universal attendance and near universal graduation eroded the incentive effects of a high school diploma as an exclusive badge of status that virtually guaranteed opportunity. To attract and hold students who are skeptical about the value or advantages of completing high school, new marketing strategies have been developed that are designed to appeal to adolescents' definition of "knowledge" and their interest in social activities. This accounts in part for the expansion of personal service and development classes.

The graduation requirements that govern students in the vast majority of high schools make it possible for some seniors to avoid school almost totally. By the end of the eleventh grade, many students, the college-bound included, have nearly satisfied both the credit and content requirements necessary for graduation and need to take only a final English class and perhaps a health elective. Many district leaders have begun to complain about the increasing tendency of students to "waste" their senior year (Panwitt, 1979; New York State Education Department, Student Affairs Task Force, 1975).In Ann Arbor, Michigan, for example, until recently it was not uncommon for seniors who had taken full loads in each of their preceding academic years to enroll in two classes in the morning and have their school day completed by 10:00 a.m. (Stock & Hansen, 1983).

It has become increasingly common for upper-class students, particularly seniors, to enroll in work-study and cooperative education programs which provide job training, work experience, income, and academic credit. Such courses are popular among even the college-bound students because they provide opportunities to leave campus early in the day, to avoid academic classes legitimately, and to receive assistance in locating part-time employment.

CURRICULAR TRACKING

The detrimental effects of minimal or incoherent graduation requirements on the academic content encountered or mastered by high school students are severely compounded by the effects of curricular tracking. In most districts, those hundreds of individual courses offered in large high schools have been organized and sequenced to some degree. Even though many administrators deny it, the paths through which most students end up in the courses that they do are complicated by organizational preferences and prerequisites. Furthermore, the sorts of ability groups that are formed in elementary schools are perpetuated into high school, so that students of presumed different academic skill levels receive disciplinary content in very different forms, depending, for example, on whether an adolescent is enrolled in an advanced placement or a consumer mathematics class. These tracking and grouping practices have resulted in delivering different knowledge or subject-matter content within a single discipline or across the entire curriculum.

There are as a result, two basic types of grouping, or tracking, at the secondary level. There is a relatively straightforward extension of elementary school grouping practices whereby students are assigned to high, medium, or low ability tracks in basic subjects such as English, math, social studies, and science. In addition to this so-called "ability" or "achievement" tracking, there is a second type of assignment that is based upon the curricular group in which a student is placed. This "curricular grouping" classifies students according to the type of educational and career future that is deemed appropriate for a student (Rosenbaum, 1980). Under this classification scheme, students are sorted according to a determination whether they should be college-bound, whether they should be designated for a vocational or low-level commercial or technical job, or whether they fall into that broad band of students for whom "general education" is appropriate.

Placement in curricular tracks, or streams, has become fairly widespread in the United States, as has placement in ability groups within a single subject. Before secondary education became relatively universal, the important distinctions between adolescents were made on the basis of whether or not someone attended, or graduated from, high school. As education became more accessible, as attendance and graduation became more universal, the differentiation process was moved inside of schools: high schools themselves became internally differentiated by curricular track, and, occasionally, by ability group. Most nations have kept educational credentials relatively inaccessible; they allow only a small percentage of their populations to pursue education beyond mastering basic literacy and numerical skills. They continue to make important social and economic distinctions based upon simple measures of attainment. Egalitarian societies, including the United States, however, have responded to similar pressure to differentiate among individuals according to some presumed index of ability, industriousness, and aptitude by separating students within high schools. A massive assessment, guidance training, and placement machinery has evolved to help make these distinctions among adolescents, counsel them into appropriate programs, prepare them for differing postsecondary futures, and launch them with credentials of varying value into very different adult lives.

Placements into ability groups or curricular tracks, as critical as such assignments are, have been shrouded in mystery and intentionally obscured for generations. Neither historians nor sociologists have been conspiciously successful in determining how particular students end up where they do. Ability-group assignments more logically have been based upon performance on various ability, aptitude, and interest tests, as well as on recommendations from teachers in earlier grades or other classes. Curricular track placement, however, has been a process confused by the extent to which adolescents believe that they actually "chose" their courses free from any institutional coercion. Some districts have traditionally made curricular track assignments on the basis of a set of presumptions about the destinies of particular students, presumptions shaped undoubtedly by evidence of social class, race, parental occupation, and the experiences of older siblings. Other districts have used what appears at first glance to have been far more relevant criteria, including the assessments of guidance counselors and teachers, and the preferences of parents and the students themselves. From this perspective, curricular tracking appears to be more democratic than ability-grouping and is more likely to enhance student engagement with school.

The notion of "student choice" in these matters, however, is enormously complicated. Several scholars, including Rosenbaum (1976, 1980), have begun to clarify the reality of free choice in high school. His research suggests that many students, particularly those with parents who are indifferent or otherwise unable to negotiate the entire placement enterprise, are not prepared to make informed decisions about their track assignment or to make choices about individual course selection with an understanding of the eventual consequences of enrolling in one class over another. Rosenbaum has gathered evidence, for example, that demonstrates how uninformed many students are about which track they are in, about how they got there, about graduation requirements, about college admissions standards and credit expectations. He has presented examples of students in vocational and general curricular tracks who have little or no idea that their high school educational histories will accompany them throughout adulthood and will inevitably bar many of them from entering legitimate four-year colleges.

Regardless of whether the approach taken in a high school is based upon ability or curricular grouping, or some hybrid of the two, the impact of such classification and placement schemes is the same. Students in low-ability groups or in vocational, prevocational, or general curricular tracks of low status tend to suffer similar fates. In general they tend to be offered watered down versions of the academic curriculum or courses relevant only to specific vocational training (often on outdated equipment or for vocations that are essentially obsolete). Even teachers who offer the same course across all ability levels often report that they spend less time on actual instructional and learning activities when working with students characterized by lesser status or ability than they do in higher status courses and college preparatory programs. Textbooks are occasionally older, handed down after they are rejected as outdated for the advanced track students. Science courses for lower-track students, even when similar content is specified, may not include the laboratory sessions that are considered imperative for college preparatory adolescents. Homework assignments for low-ability or low-track students are notoriously lighter than those expected of high-track individuals, which would tend to make more time available for outside activities that consistently distract from involvement with school.

We recognize that placement in higher tracks causes problems for some students who suffer from emotional stress and anxiety because of the pressure to achieve academically in school. We understand as well that some lower-track placements make school more appealing to certain students, keep them reasonably engaged in their classes, and provide some opportunity for them to succeed with less demanding expectations and assignments. Although we acknowledge the ways in which such advantages and disadvantages might accrue to some students in different tracks, we are principally concerned with the distinctive nature and level of learning in tracked classes for the majority of students, and with the ultimate impact of track placement on access to knowledge and adult opportunities.

In most high schools, content in high-track classes tends to be oriented toward developing college preparatory skills and to focus on relatively high cultural topics and assignments, such as reading, analyzing, and interpreting standard works of classical and contemporary literature. In contrast, content in most lower-track courses is far more likely to attend to the development of utilitarian skills, such as filling out job application forms. Recent qualitative scholarship on placement and grouping patterns in schools reveals essentially two distinct educational worlds, one preparing students for college, the other preparing adolescents for the workplace at best, and for nothing in particular at worst.

Regardless of whether they asked teachers or students, researchers with the extensive "Study of Schooling" project, for example, received consistently different responses—highly correlated to track placement—to questions about instructional goals or learning outcomes (Goodlad, 1984; Oakes, 1985). Jeannie Oakes recently reconstructed the glaring differences in expectations and outcomes that they encountered in tracked schools across the nation. When asked, "What is the most important thing you have learned or done so far in this class?," a sample of high track students responded,

> learning political and cultural trends in relation to international and domestic events. . . . Greek philosophy, Renaissance philosophy, humanities. How to write essays and to do term papers. The French Revolution. HISTORY! . . . About businesses—corporations, monopolies, oligopolies, etc., and how [they] start, how they work, how much control they have on the economy—prices, demand, supply, advertising. . . . Learned about different theories of psychology and about

Freud, Fromm, Sullivan and other psychologists. . . . How to read a classic novel and be able to pull out details, and write a complete and accurate report. . . . [U]nderstanding the balance between man and his environment. . . . Learning to change my thought processes in dealing with higher mathematics and computers. . . . I have learned to do what scientists do. . . . To know how to communicate with my teachers like friends and as teachers at the same time. To have confidence in myself other than my skills and class work. . . . How to organize myself and present an argument. . . . How to express myself through writing and being able to compose the different thoughts in a logical manner. . . . [The] drive to search and find out answers to questions. . . . How to think and reason logically and scientifically. (1985, pp. 69-70, 86-88)

When asked the same question, a group of low-track students enrolled in "academic" classes in the same school answered:

How to blow up light bulbs. . . . Really I have learned nothing. Only my roman numerals. I knew them, but not very good. I could do better in another class. . . . [H]ow to act when at an interview filling out forms . . . [H]ow to write checks and to figure the salary of a worker. Another thing is the the tax rate. . . . I don't remember. . . . To be honest, nothing. . . . Nothing outstanding. . . . English is boring. . . . Job applications. Job interviews. Preparation for the above. . . . Spelling, worksheets. . . . A few lessons which have not very much to do with history (I enjoyed it). . . . [T]hat I should do my questions for the book when he asks me to. . . . Manners. . . . How to shut up. . . . [C]oming into class and getting our folders and going to work. . . . I have learned manners. . . . How to go through a cart and find a folder by myself. (pp. 70-72, 88-89)

These student responses are not surprising after becoming familiar with their teachers' instructional objectives. If teaching effectiveness is reflected in a close correlation between educational objectives and learning outcomes, most of the teachers interviewed by Oakes and her associates appear to have been fairly successful. When asked about the "essential learning" they wanted their students to take with them from class, teachers in the high-track courses responded:

Interpreting and identifying. Evaluation, investigating power. . . . Ability to reason logically in all subject areas. . . . Scientific reasoning and logic. . . . Self-reliance, taking on responsibilities themselves. . . . To think critically—to analyze, *ask* questions. . . . How to evaluate—think objectively. To think logically and with clarity and to put it on paper. . . . Confidence in their own abilities and sense of what it's like in a college course. (pp. 80-91)

It also appears that teachers in the low-track classes got at least much of what they wanted from their students:

> I teach personal hygiene—to try to get the students to at least be aware of how to keep themselves clean. . . . How to fill out insurance forms. Income tax returns. . . . To be able to work with other students. To be able to work alone. To be able to follow directions. . . . How to cope with frustration. . . . Life skills. Work with checking account. . . . Content—minimal. (pp. 82-83)

In summary, the larger Goodlad (1984) and Oakes (1985) studies concluded that teachers in high-track classes spent more class time on instruction, had higher expectations for their students, were better organized, spent far less time on behavior and discipline problems, and were less punitive toward their students. (On most variables, mixed-track classes were found to be more like high-track than low-track courses.) According to Goodlad (1984), the assignment of students to low-track classes predicted for them "diminished access to what increasingly are being recognized as the more satisfactory conditions of learning" (p. 156).

James Rosenbaum's (1976, 1980) reconstruction of the process and effects of tracking in a New England community confirmed this portrait of varied teaching and learning and access to highly differentiated knowledge in school by curricular placement. Furthermore, Rosenbaum has carried the analysis of the consequences of tracking one step farther than other scholars. In addition to offering students content of varying quality, value, and utility, which is an obvious intended result of differentiation, he has convincingly demonstrated that on some occasions track placement actually affects the cognitive development of students. He presents the dilemma of tracking not simply as one of providing access to different content but as one of aggravating tragically or compounding existing distinctions in academic ability. He found that placement in higher tracks actually improved the measured mental abilities of some students and, correspondingly, that a low-track placement actually worsened the test scores of other adolescents. After enduring four years of classwork in different tracks, consequently, the students were much farther apart on measured mental ability than they had been when they had been separated first in junior high school. Rosenbaum's findings are sad, even though they may not be all that surprising, given the evidence compiled by Oakes (1985), Goodlad (1984), Anyon (1981), and others regarding the cumulative effects of the nature of teaching and learning in different curricular tracks and ability groups.

Track or group placement also appears to determine the social cliques with which adolescents identify, the friendships they make, and the extracurricular and out-of-school activities they undertake. The acknowledged but largely unappreciated power of these relationships affects what elective choices students may make, the expectations that they set for themselves, and the reward structure within which they must find encouragement, appreciation, and dignity. Together these relationships can exact a painful toll on adolescents courageous enough to attempt, wherever permitted, to venture into classes rejected by their friends or to find solace in academic accomplishment when their peers value indifference or defiance to traditional achievement norms. Disconcertingly, low-track and vocational students tend to share low levels of esteem. Their self-perceptions are apparently heavily influenced by their track and group placement, even after controlling for such related variables as race, sex, social class, aptitude, and high school class rank (Rosenbaum, 1980). It is not surprising, therefore, to find such students more truant from school, more likely to be involved in disciplinary infractions and other rebellious behavior, and more likely to be suspended or expelled from school (Rosenbaum, 1980). Finally, because track and ability group placement is highly correlated to socioeconomic status and race, with blacks, Hispanics, Native Americans, working-class children, and the poor disproportionately assigned to low-ability and low-status tracks, such placement practices tend to reinforce prevailing economic, social, language, and educational inequalities (Goodlad, 1984; Rosenbaum, 1976).

THE MEASURE OF CONTENT

Aggravating the effects of these trends has been the way in which our schools have defined the "amount" of knowledge or content needed for graduation. Customarily, high schools require students to earn a specified number of "Carnegie Units" in order to receive a valid diploma. Adopted throughout the nation during the early twentieth century as a standardized measurement of secondary education, the Carnegie Unit came to represent, at minimum, 36 weeks of study in classes that met four or five times weekly in periods of 40 to 60 minutes in length (Shaw & Walker, 1981). The Carnegie Unit measure has governed the dispersion of graduation requirements since the 1920s (Nathan, 1976). Aside from the relatively recent use in some states of the additional requirement of successful performance on minimum competency examinations to establish eligibility for a diploma, accumulating a requisite number of Carnegie Units has become the basis for awarding high school graduation credentials.

Standards regarding the number and type of Carnegie Units required for high school graduation have varied considerably from state to state and, where state regulations have afforded latitude, from district to district (National Association of Secondary School Principals Special Task Force, 1975). As a result, a high school diploma awarded by one school district might not signify successful completion of the same units of study awarded by another school district within the same state or a district in another state (Nathan & Jennings, 1978; Spady & Mitchell, 1977).

Furthermore, from the definition presented above, it is clear that the Carnegie Unit represents the amount of "seat time" that a student must contribute in order to receive course credit toward fulfilling a district's graduation requirements. Carnegie Units do not measure or represent any specified amount or form of content, nor do they symbolize the mastery of any knowledge or the possession of any skills in particular.

Just as adolescents attend high school in order to secure a credential, they enroll in classes in order to secure credits toward that credential. This leads them to adopt a discouraging posture toward the courses they select and the class content that they must endure in order to acquire the necessary credit. In many instances, consequently, students interpret this definition of "credit" to mean that they can effectively limit their participation in school to doing only what is minimally required to earn the credentials that they value.

TOWARD COHERENCY AND INEQUALITY

In response to these warnings about problems associated with curricular fragmentation and the proliferation of electives, a number of states and communities have begun to implement reforms designed to restore some control over the content of a high school education. Thus far there have appeared at least four fundamental and distinct approaches to solving the problems with school knowledge: 1) modifying graduation requirements; 2) struggling to define and implement a "core" curriculum of basic (or "new" basic) subjects; 3) controlling opportunities for election; and 4) "enriching" the academic activities and opportunities of selected students, particularly those with demonstrated promise in mathematics, the sciences, or the arts.

Virtually all of the initiatives attempting to define the appropriate content of a high school education have conceptualized the problem as one of tightening graduation requirements by increasing the number of credits needed to receive a diploma, reducing the percentage of elective courses, and instituting some form of exit examination covering basic academic and survival skills. To some degree these actions will create core curricula by default. This has been the pattern because of the aggressive role that state departments of education have begun to play in the movement to raise standards. With but a few conspicuous exceptions, including New York, state departments of education have lacked the authority to specify course content. Instead, they have relied on their power to set minimal graduation requirements in terms of credit hours.

Spurred by the high regard paid the New York State Regents' Diploma, several other states are beginning to address the decentralization of course content issue by moving in the direction of developing state syllabi for high school subject fields. In 1981, for example, Texas identified the "essential elements" of 12 subject areas for each grade and has been working toward implementing relatively standardized syllabi in the following courses: English language arts, foreign languages, mathematics, science, health, physical education, the fine arts, social studies, economics, business education, vocational education, and Texas and U.S. history. Computer literacy is currently under consideration (U.S. Department of Education, 1983a, p. 78). Several other states are moving in the same direction, including California (in the limited subject areas), Delaware, Georgia, Illinios, Kentucky, Maryland, Rhode Island, Virginia, West Virginia, and Wisconsin (U.S. Department of Education, 1983a, 1983b;see also, Education Commission of the States, 1983). With the exception of the continued efforts of New York State to strengthen the Regents' requirements, these state-level efforts are in their embryonic stages. They are just now surfacing as proposals and will be working their way through the myriad special commissions, task forces, and state department committees.

Thus far it appears that there has been little headway made at the state level to grapple conclusively with the problem of defining a coherent body of knowledge that all adolescents would be expected to learn. The scattered initiatives in a handful of states are promising, but the tension and conflict that will undoubtedly surface when local and professional prerogatives are challenged have not been faced. Outside of New York, where there is a long tradition of, and machinery in place for, imposing definitions of the relative value of different knowledge, institutional and individual autonomy will surely pose barriers to the process of standardizing curricular content.

Although it will not lead to the universal standardization of knowledge, the movement at the local level to define a core course of studies or a general education promises some success. The literature on school improvement and the implementation of innovations reaffirms the necessity of pursuing such objectives at the local level (see, for example, Purkey

& Smith, 1982a). It is difficult to determine precisely the scope and nature of local initiatives in this area, but there have appeared a number of ambitious efforts to identify the most valuable knowledge and to integrate subject-matter content. For example, the Ann Arbor, Michigan, public schools have begun a reexamination of the fundamental question "What common learnings should all students be expected to acquire?" (Stock & Hansen, 1983, p. 4). Drawing upon the analyses that have informed the most substantive efforts to define the appropriate content at the secondary level (Boyer, 1983; The College Board, 1983b; Bailey, A., 1983, 1984; Goodlad, 1984; Adler, 1982; Sizer, 1984b), the Ann Arbor district, already one of the state's stronger, academically oriented systems, appears to have made great strides recently in redefining the explicit skills and knowledge to be required of all students (Stock & Hansen, 1983). In addition to the issue of curricular content, Ann Arbor's broad-based movement has considered the problem that will accompany any effort to integrate existing subject-matter fields (Cheever & Sayer, 1982), which the district's leaders have labeled "cross-disciplinary common learnings" (Stock & Hansen, 1983, p. 13). At this time Ann Arbor's high school content revision program exists principally on paper; it is in the process of being translated into action through the development of specific course objectives and syllabi and the monitoring of classroom activities.

Paralleling trends at the state level, it appears that relatively few local districts or individual high schools are confronting the thorny problem of the fragmentation of knowledge *within* a discipline or subject. There has been some momentum to curtail the growth of specialized electives since the mid-1970s, partly a product of the "Back to Basics" movement and partly a result of the financial contraction that has affected virtually all schools during the past decade. A number of high schools have pared down their curricula because they could not afford to offer as many narrow and specialized classes as they had during the relatively flush 1960s. Economic constraints have forced hard decisions about what is most worth teaching There is evidence that some teachers and administrators have responded responsibly to this combined ideological and financial pressure from communities to constrain the electives movement (Neufeld, 1980; National Association of Secondary School Principals, 1975; Borden, 1979, 1980). Because the number of courses listed in a catalog and even the titles of specific classes are not particularly reliable indicators of curricular content, however, it will take a great deal of research over the next few years to sort out the impact of this halting movement to reintegrate the secondary academic program.

A few communities are incorporating suggestions about "clustering" electives beyond their common or core general education subjects (Boyer,

1983; Stock & Hansen, 1983). This strategy could prove especially attractive to, and effective in, districts strongly committed to vocational, technical, and agricultural education, since the pressure to properly sequence and integrate curricula in these areas in order to enhance employment opportunities has become increasingly vocal (see, for example, Marvin, 1980; Rogers, 1980; Illinois State Office of Education, 1980). Nationwide, however, the potential contribution of clustering has not as yet been exploited.

Nor have many districts experimented with the organization of classes to nurture and protect opportunities for concentrated academic learning. At this time, the literature does not indicate that significant efforts are being made to reconceptualize the school day organizationally in order to create the uninterrupted blocks of time needed for intensive instruction that a number of the most prominent studies have recommended, such as those by Sizer (1984b) and Boyer (1983).

In addition to the tightening of graduation course requirements, the most popular effort to strengthen content appears to be enrichment programs, which have found increasing support and funding during the past two years. Roughly two-thirds of the states and an undetermined number of local districts have begun to implement plans for various kinds of institutes devoted to concentrated and intensive instruction and learning in several fields (U.S. Department of Education, 1983a, 1983b). Ordinarily sponsored by a state's Governor's office, these institutes, often located at university campuses, provide opportunities for highly selected and accomplished or promising students to spend at least two weeks in residential programs in the sciences, mathematics, and the arts. Several states have gone beyond the brief institute model and have patterned their efforts on the highly publicized "Governor's Schools" in different fields in North Carolina (U.S. Department fo Education, 1983a, 1983b). Large urban districts are experimenting with various "magnet" schools oriented toward the sciences, mathematics, technology, or the arts, modeled on the successful ongoing ventures in New York City in these fields.

The academic enrichment programs reported in the literature have been established principally for gifted and talented students. The competition for admission is intense. The institutes' popularity is undoubtedly rooted in their relative ease of establishment and low cost combined with the fact that they give the appearance of a timely response to the public criticism of weaknesses in specific subject fields, most notably the sciences, mathematics, and computer studies.

Although valuable for their participants, if for nothing else than the prestige of winning entrance, the enrichment programs are not designed to improve the academic learning of the vast majority of high school students. They probably will stimulate interest in these subjects on the part of adolescents whose abilities and industry place them just below the admissions cutoff point, but less capable or talented students will be left deprived and envious. Indeed, drawing away the most talented students and sending them to special classes, as is common with the academic magnet concept, will undoubtedly leave regular classrooms filled with only average and below-average students. This potentially dangerous practice could leave many schools without any high-achieving adolescents worthy of emulation who might encourage academic engagement among their indifferent and apathetic peers. Recent work on ability grouping and tracking, for instance, that of Oakes (1985), suggests the detrimental effects of this sort of separation. While it does offer some possible relief to the problems of fragmented curricular content, nevertheless, it will be dangerous to allow the academic enrichment programs to command unwarranted support or to permit them to divert attention from the fundamental task of developing a coherent course of studies for all high school students.

Similarly, current and projected content and curricular initiatives will probably only have a modest positive impact on the problems of academic learning and student disengagement. Local efforts demonstrate promise in forcing professional and community attention to the question of the appropriate content for a high school education and the problems with developing a coherent and acceptable course of study for all adolescents. Teachers can be discouraged from creating classes based largely on their own interests and commitments. In order to be responsive, teachers require individual autonomy, and some of the initiatives strive to balance professional responsibility and personal freedom so as to prevent teachers from idiosyncratically defining course or program content. It is unclear whether they will resolve the tensions inherent in this problem. More generally, the recent literature and initiatives have resurrected the dialogue about what is worth knowing, and about the propriety of a single high school offering a broad range of educations of differing substance and value. The popularity of these initiatives reflects public dissatisfaction with the traditional resolution of this challenging question that has guided secondary education for most of the twentieth century (Ravitch, 1983b).

Despite these possible positive outcomes, most of the content-oriented initiatives are not tailored to meet the challenges posed by widespread student disengagement for academic learning. Indeed, without careful consideration, the movement to institute a common core curriculum for all high school students regardless of vocational aspirations, interests in schooling, or ability, could aggravate existing levels of indifference and disaffiliation. Whatever the academic and cognitive costs of courses like "Girl Talk," or "What's Happening," (Cusick, 1983) their presumed "relevance" probably attracted and held a reasonable share of the student population. Without teachers comfortable with in-depth subject-matter content and the ability and enthusiasm to engage adolescents in learning, rigorous core courses (regardless of topics and themes covered) risk driving resistant and even many indifferent students into disruption and rebellion. Given the instructional experiences of most adolescents and their consequent classroom passivity, it appears that it is the "bargain" to avoid intensive academic activities that makes life bearable for many students and teachers. Any effort to disturb the prevailing equilibrium by increasing academic demands without improving teaching techniques will be greeted with a hostile reception and may ultimately exacerbate attendance and disciplinary problems.

4 ⚏ Student Employment and Extracurricular Activities

The commitment of students to academic endeavors is shaped by adolescents' options for investing their time and energy in a variety of competing activities, including employment, athletics, and socializing, as well as studying. This chapter examines the perspective of adolescents toward such alternatives and explores the impact of students' behavior outside of school on the nature of classroom engagement and the level of academic learning.

Student participation in the labor force or extracurricular activities involves difficult trade-offs for schools. On the one hand, there are a number of valuable rewards for participation that fall to adolescents and their high schools, which encourage virtually everyone, including students, parents, teachers, administrators, and school boards (as community representatives) to favor, if not demand, increased participation. On the other hand, extensive involvement with work and activities often detracts from academic engagement.

STUDENT EMPLOYMENT

In addition to electing more personal service and development classes, an increasing proportion of students, particularly juniors and seniors, are "electing" with their feet to leave school by noon or as early as possible for their part-time jobs, many of which demand a full-time commitment. The steady increase in student employment over the past generation reflects a reordering of priorities among adolescents, an effort to move their educational experiences more to the periphery of their lives.

According to the most thorough study of labor force participation by adolescents, the proportion of employed males aged 16 to 19 enrolled in high school increased steadily from one-third in 1960 to nearly one-half by 1977 (Peng, et al., 1981, p. 17; Lewin-Epstein, 1981). A similar pattern is evident among young women: the proportion of employed females aged

16 to 17 enrolled in high school increased from 22.6 percent in 1960 to 39.1 percent in 1977, and the figures for females aged 18-19 indicate that the proportion employed grew from 27.9 percent to 45.6 percent during the same period. Employment among youth aged 16 to 19 who were not in school remained constant or declined among males, or increased slightly among females. During this period the unemployment rates for both males and females enrolled in high school increased sharply (by 30-50 % for males and by 100 % or more for females), suggesting that an even larger proportion of adolescents were actively seeking employment by the late 1970s, a further reflection of the accelerating commitment of high school students to working. Another study of four middle-class high schools in Wisconsin indicates that the majority of upperclassmen worked for wages at the time of the survey, and that when students actively seeking work were added to those with jobs, four out of five were involved in the labor market in some way (McNeil, 1984). Cameron Crowe's (1981) provocative portrait of "Ridgemont High" in 1979 reveals the consuming, central place of employment in the lives of adolescents.

This pattern of increasing labor market participation by adolescents since 1960 reverses a 60-year trend of declining employment rates for 14 to 19-year-olds. Between 1900 and 1930, the proportion of adolescents—students and nonstudents alike—who were employed fell sharply. Although the rates for nonwhites continued to decline steadily for the next quarter of a century, the proportion of white males and females who worked increased slightly during the Depression of the 1930s and leveled off through the 1950s (Lewin-Epstein, 1981).

Not only have the labor market participation rates for adolescents increased over the past generation, but students work a startling number of hours. Three out of four senior males surveyed who worked, for example, were employed at least 15 hours per week, according to the High School and Beyond Project; nearly one-half worked half-time (20 hours or more). Young women worked only slightly fewer hours: 70 percent worked 15 hours or more (Lewin-Epstein, 1981).

Most students in all curricular programs are employed, with college-preparatory students working only slightly less than adolescents enrolled in vocational and business tracks. Labor force participation, in other words, is common in all schools, although there are slight regional differences (with students in the South employed less consistently than their counterparts in the Northeast and Midwest). Middle-class and suburban youth have the highest employment rates, although the tendency of teenagers in rural and agricultural communities to work at home for no pay distorts their employment rates downward (Lewin-Epstein, 1981).

White middle-class high schools experience the lowest employment rates: the wealthiest students do not hold jobs because they do not need them, and the poorest adolescents do not hold jobs because they cannot get them.

Furthermore, students' work today is more systematic and institutionalized than that of their counterparts in 1960. A generation ago most of those high school students who were employed ordinarily worked as casual laborers. They babysat, mowed lawns, delivered newspapers, helped neighbors clean garages and basements, waited tables, performed odd jobs, and occasionally pumped gasoline. Today adolescents continue to perform casual labor, although not to the same extent, and such work is commonly restricted to younger students, aged 14 or 15, who cannot work for businessess without a great deal of inconvenience or who are barred from formal employment by child labor laws. Older high school students today work principally in retail sales: in food service or as clerks in department or clothing stores. In addition, many young women, particularly those enrolled in commercial tracks, are employed in clerical and stenographic positions. The nature of work performed does not differ significantly among students in different educational tracks. The same holds true for the type of community in which an adolescent lives, with the obvious exception of rural teenagers working on farms more often than their urban and suburban counterparts (Lewin-Epstein, 1981).

Students work for obvious reasons. They want income which employment provides, principally for discretionary items—automobiles, electronic consumer products, fashionable clothes, entertainment, travel—but also for college tuition. Many adolescents are seeking out marketplace experience by working for pay. Many prefer the sense of responsibility and autonomy that even dead-end employment provides, a sharp contrast to their experience in school, where they must ask permission even to go to the restroom. Indeed, a sizeable number of students indicated in interviews that their jobs helped them to escape the "dullness and boredom of school" (McNeil, 1984; also Berryman & Schneider, 1983).

The pursuit of income, respectability, and independence helps to account for *why* students want to work. The major factor underlying the expansion of adolescent employment since 1960 is the dramatic increase in the *opportunities* for systematic work. It is not accidental that employment rates have increased simultaneously with the emergence of the convenience food industry since the early 1960s. It should be recognized that such jobs are ordinarily temporary and do not offer many opportunities for promotion or mobility. Furthermore, although it is often overlooked, the expansion of government-funded employment opportunities after

1966 accounts for much of the increase in student labor force participation, particularly among non-white and poor adolescents (Lewin-Epstein, 1981).

Because student employment is increasingly common, it is important to consider its impact on secondary education. Many high schools have made a number of accommodations to working adolescents over the past decade, which have serious implications for academic standards (McNeil, 1984; Neufeld, 1980, p. 117; Farrar, Neufeld, & Miles, 1983). First, a large percentage of upperclassmen, particularly seniors, leave campus as early as possible in the day to work. In a suburban Detroit high school, two-thirds of the seniors and one-half of the juniors left school at noon to go to work (Cusick, 1983). An ethnographer who approached several high school administrators in southern Wisconsin was told that her observations of classroom behavior would have to be made during the early morning because most students vacated the school by lunch period (McNeil, 1984). There are, as a result, proportionately fewer upper-class students remaining on campus who are willing and able to subscribe to advanced, rigorous, in-depth classes. Most students prefer to enroll in introductory classes and easier electives and avoid higher mathematics and foreign language courses. This discourages the development of advanced classes because teachers interested in such work have to compete for the few eligible students committed to spending the entire day at school. As a result, there exists a countertendency to develop further introductory or relatively superficial classes that appeal to younger students. Many guidance counselors report that there is intense competition between departments and among individual teachers to have classes scheduled during the morning.

Second, and more importantly, institutional expectations are lowered and teaching methods are adjusted to accommodate student employment and the priorities for the investment of time and energy that substantial work commitment implies (McNeil, 1984). Homework is reduced because students complain that their work responsibilities interfere with their ability to complete assignments outside of class. Seniors report that they spend an average of three hours per week on homework outside of school, a figure that falls among students who work more than the average number of hours (Lewin-Epstein, 1981). Students who do not work spend relatively more time on homework, although not much more time (which suggests that schools reduce expectations across the board) (Keith, 1982). Reports indicate that students are given the opportunity to read during class time what few pages are assigned. Writing assignments are likewise brief, often limited to a single paragraph. Students, some of whom are visibly sleepy, are rarely required to discuss materials that they do not review during class or to make presentations based upon outside research. It is ironic that as homework is reduced, students reassess their schedules and find that even more of them can work, and can work even more hours each week (McNeil, 1984).

Many high school students read nothing academic outside of class and rarely complete homework even when it is assigned. Consequently, instructional methods are adopted that demand little active participation on the part of students. Almost without exception the major studies of classroom behavior reveal similar patterns in virtually all schools. Content is often simplified, reduced to lists, and delivered through lectures (i.e., McNeil, 1982; Goodlad, 1984; Sizer, 1984b). Workbook assignments are substituted for discussion. Of course, not all workbooks are worse than all discussion, but an important opportunity to actively engage students in learning is lost. Under these conditions, instruction reinforces the passivity that characterizes the involvement of many high school students.

Inevitably, as Linda McNeil (1984) and others recognize, expectations for academic performance are lowered when classrooms accommodate increasing student employment. It should be recognized, of course, that working for pay contributes a great deal to students and helps to make high schools more peaceful and streetcorners less crowded (see Heffez, 1979, for a more optimistic portrait of the contribution of employment). Indeed, surveys find that students who work a modest number of hours earn higher grades than those who do not work at all. Heavy work schedules, however, do exact a scholastic penalty, as students who work at a relatively young age or who work more than 30 hours weekly are more likely to drop out of high school before graduating. Any effort to raise academic standards, nevertheless, must consider the trade-offs that accompany high rates of labor market participation by students enrolled in high school, particularly as jobs limit opportunities to pursue subjects beyond the introductory stage and to be actively engaged in demanding pedagogical exercises, which develop higher-order reasoning skills.

EXTRACURRICULAR ACTIVITIES

A study of participation in extracurricular activities illuminates the issues of academic learning and the place of high school in the lives of adolescents in at least two fundamentally different ways. It is obvious that activities, including sporting and social events, assemblies, and dramatic and musical productions, all consume time, effort, and resources that might otherwise be devoted to improving achievement in academic classes. Studies of youth culture and community life from the 1940s through the early 1960s consistently reveal the importance of participating in social, athletic, musical, dramatic, journalistic, and other acitivities when school ended in the afternoon. In most communities such participation essentially defined adolescent status hierarchies, particularly for middle-class and affluent youth; more recently, working-class and minority youth have attempted to exploit the availability of activities, principally in athletics and the performing arts, in order to enhance their social and economic mobility.

Approximately one-half of the high school population currently participates regularly in extracurricular activities. A minority of students are deeply involved with perhaps five or ten major activities which consume hundreds of hours over the course of an academic year. Most of these hours are spent in activities that are organized after school or on weekends. During the 1970s, in addition, it became common for extracurricular activities to find their way into the school day; some schools even began to award graduation credit for participation in what are essentially extracurricular activities, particularly in yearbook, but in other fields as well. Observers of high schools comment that students are ordinarily excused individually and in small groups in order to plan, practice, rehearse, decorate, travel, perform, and cheer.

Not all adolescents participate in extracurricular activities, however. And since the late 1960s, relatively fewer high school students have participated in such activities, at least to such a degree. They prefer instead to work for wages in the afternoon or to spend time with their friends away from school. Like the pattern of increasing labor market participation by high school students since the early 1960s, this parallel movement away from deep engagement in extracurricular activities reflects a shift in the place of the entire high school experience in the lives of adolescents.

After reviewing both trends, in 1981 the author of the "Youth Employment During High School" report concluded that over the preceding decade there seemed to be "both a departure from school-based activities and a more central role for work among seniors" (Lewin-Epstein, 1981, p. 56). Opportunities to work and responsibilities for assuming a larger share of the expenses for their own upkeep could limit participation in extracurricular activities. Since participation has traditionally been instrumental in binding adolescents to their high schools, this could have the broader effect of causing youth to identify less with their high schools and instead contribute to the movement of the entire experience to the relative periphery of their lives. Some students have come to find that they have less opportunity to engage in extracurricular activities because busing, brought about by the school consolidation and desegregation efforts, takes them away from campus immediately after school. Regular and repeated moves, for reasons of divorce or economics, could have a similar impact. In addition, during the early 1970s, many school authorities reacted to the threat of adolescent violence arising from political activism, racial hostility, and criminal activity (on the part of students and outsiders), by reducing opportunities to participate in extracurricular activities. These administrators instituted five-period school days, eliminated lunch periods, and got as many youngsters off of the school grounds as early and as quickly as possible in the afternoon. Their interpretation obviously requires the attention of other scholars. There is little empirical evidence that such maneuvering actually undermined the involvement of adolescents with their high schools, but such explanations are understandable and seem to corroborate Lewin-Epstein's general argument.

Despite Lewin-Epstein's conclusion, the evidence of rates of participation in extracurricular activities is mixed and subject to varying interpretations. Although the High School and Beyond Project's statistical data indicate relative stability over the past decade, the figures reported probably mask an overall erosion of participation, particularly in the middle-class high schools (Peng, et al., 1981, p. 19). The range of dates that forms the outside parameters of the study, 1972 to 1980, is not useful for this measurement. By 1972, a number of high school students had already abandoned extracurricular activities, since one by-product of developments in the late 1960s was the tendency of middle-class and affluent youth to use *nonparticipation* in activities as a measure of one's status: popular students, particularly many ambitious college-bound adolescents, flaunted their lack of involvement and wore their refusal to participate as a badge of status (Lightfoot, 1983, pp. 141, 168; Owen, 1981). Using 1972 as a baseline underestimates the degree to which high school students have withdrawn from extracurricular activities.

It is also virtually impossible to determine the actual level of a student's engagement with extracurricular activities, to measure whether or not he or she is meaningfully participating. Interviews with suburban high school students conducted by Ralph W. Larkin (1979) in 1976 indicate the nature of this problem. The investigator found that "over the past several years" there had been a "precipitous decline in student participation in school-related clubs." One-third of the clubs had stopped functioning. The yearbook editor recalled that when his activities editor went to review all of the school's clubs he found that "none of them exist any more. No one cares." When the activities editor announced that yearbook pictures would be taken and arranged to have a photographer present, "there would be one kid there." He attributed it to apathy: "They just don't care." The editor added that "some clubs just exist for the fact of having a yearbook picture and are supposedly in the yearbook. But otherwise, they have no function. They don't do anything" (pp. 146-147). Other students would join "ghost" clubs for the purposes of padding their college applications. It has even been suggested, by Cusick (1973), for example, that many of the extracurricular activities actually consisted of very few "activities." Clubs existed on paper, and their photographs appeared in the yearbook, but the members did very little. The honor society membership could think of nothing more to do than organize a bake sale; another large organization sponsored a single event during the academic year. Respectable numbers of organizations and large membership rolls belied a reality of few events. The absence of much real activity allowed just a few of the most popular students to run virtually everything while the vast majority of students, even though their photographs may have appeared on ten pages of the yearbook, actually participated infrequently and then only superficially. The paper façade of a vigorous extra-curricular program obscured the disengagement of many adolescents. These observations corroborate quantitative evidence of a growing indifference toward activities on the part of many adolescents.

Larkin terms this pattern of withdrawal and disengagement "The Great Refusal." "When given the alternative of voluntary participation in school activities without coercion, students would rather not participate," he argues. Three of the brightest, most articulate students interviewed captured the essence of the deteriorating involvement or progressive disengagement of adolescents during the 1970s when they discussed what the interviewer termed the "collapse of community" that high schools experienced over the past decade. "Jed" remembered looking at his father's yearbook and could not believe the extent to which the students "got into it, you know, when he went to school. The Red Cross Club was standing there with their uniforms on with their little boxes with the red crosses on them. (Laughter) I couldn't believe it." His friend "Jan" replied, "That's just like another thing that goes along with apathy. Everyone like wants to get out of school as soon as possible." "Yeah," another friend, "Roz," added, "it's like a job." Jan: "The teachers, too." Finally, Roz: "Nine to three. And then, maybe there's a little bit of homework. Sticking around after school is just not done. After three o'clock the halls are empty, it seems to me" (pp. 151-152). Larkin paints an excessively dismal picture of the consequences of disengagement, but one that contains the kernels of an experience that has become uncomfortably common.

> Students have been freed from the constraints of continual adult surveillance and oppressiveness, and their private behavior is their own. Teachers and administrators no longer "hassle" Utopia High School students over such private behaviors as hair length, dress codes, facial

hair, or jeans for women. Drug use is overlooked, so long as it doesn't overtly affect the instructional program. Smoking is allowed, and the norm of reasonableness reigns. However, the problem is that this liberalization has occurred in a climate of alienation and estrangement. Rules are left unenforced not so much because of overriding concerns for the rights and privileges of students, but because it requires extra work. Instead of a group of autonomous individuals working toward common goals, the school has become divested of its communal spirit and has become a hollow shell where teachers and students put in time. Existence at Utopia High School has become dreary and devoid of life. (p. 152)

There is scattered evidence that the pattern of disengagement in extracurricular activities has begun to reverse slightly since the early 1980s (Lightfoot, 1983, pp. 133-141). Yet at this point the trend remains inconclusive. It is important to recall that one should not be left with the impression that all students have withdrawn from extracurricular activities. Nationwide, one-half participate. Yet, it also appears that disengagement is common and suggests a redefinition for adolescents of the meaning of high school.

THE PAIN OF CURTAILING WORK AND PLAY

Few school districts seem to have begun to address the negative effects of widespread employment and extracurricular activities. Texas, however, appears to be making an effort to confront problems related to these options for students. Although it is only in the proposal stage, there is a statewide initiative, led by industrialist H. Ross Perot, to diminish distractions to academic learning posed by intensive participation by certain youth in extracurricular activities, particularly the team sports of football and basketball and marching band ("Blowing the Whistle on Johnny," 1984). The state of Texas is moving to implement guidelines that have been initiated locally in several districts. Los Angeles and Milwaukee, among others, have recently experimented with enforcing minimum grade point averages and attendance rates for determining eligibility for extracurricular activities. The results thus far have been painful but illuminate the depth of the problems associated with diversionary activities. At Hollywood High in Los Angeles, for example, all but two members of the returning varsity football team were disqualified because of inadequate academic records; the 21-member band was similarly decimated, with 14 students ruled ineligible because they could not maintain a C average and the other seven ineligible for receiving one or more failing grades. The local athletic director observed that the new rule had "killed our program, and it's killed the spirit of the school" ("Blowing the Whistle on Johnny," 1984, p. 80). Whenever such efforts have undermined successful athletic teams or other popular school productions, the regulations have been either dismantled, rescinded, or circumvented; this price has proven too high to pay.

Similarly, Dallas, Texas, has begun to limit part-time student employment. The superintendent recently reported that the public schools no longer allow high school students to receive work permits "except when jobs are an integral part of their training or they must work in order to attend school" (Wright, L., 1983, p. 7).

If implemented successfully, such initiatives could improve the academic engagement of high school students by limiting their options for investing their energy elsewhere, or at least make their participation in activities outside of school contingent upon their successful performance in basic subjects in school. As yet, the literature does not disclose the effectiveness of the few efforts already underway to minimize the detrimental consequences of employment and extracurricular activities, although the national press has begun to report complaints about the negative impact of these scattered initiatives on attendance and dropout rates, as well as on participation in school functions and the success of athletic and musical groups. These sorts of strong critical reactions have led some district boards to rescind their earlier actions and eliminate minimum grade point requirements for extracurricular eligibility. Finally, little attention has been directed toward the counterpressure to increase adolescent employment, which could accompany the introduction of a subminimum wage for youth under 18 and its potential impact on academic standards and learning.

5 ≡ Elementary and Higher Education

Academic learning and performance standards in high schools are shaped by other educational institutions, principally by elementary schools and by colleges and universities. This chapter will examine the contributions that levels of schooling below and above high schools play in preparing adolescents to tackle challenging academic assignments, in shaping their posture toward school culture and knowledge, and in affecting their level of engagement with their courses.

ELEMENTARY SCHOOLING

High school freshmen learned to become students in elementary schools. The demands that secondary school teachers can realistically make of their students are significantly shaped by the skills, learning habits, posture toward school work, and aspirations that ninth graders bring with them to high school. Their experiences in the lower grades have substantial implications for the way that adolescents perceive and participate in high school. It is difficult to raise the level of academic content in high school when many freshmen read at the fourth-grade level, for example, or when a large share of an institution's resources must be allocated to remediation. Of the many ways in which elementary schooling might detrimentally affect academic learning in high schools, we have isolated three of the most important: 1) the habits of learning and attitudes toward school knowledge often developed in the lower grades; 2) grade-to-grade promotion practices; and 3) ability grouping and placement policies. These aspects of life in elementary schools directly affect adolescents' receptiveness of, and ability to engage in, academic exercises in high school.

The Habits of School Learning

On many occasions the habits of learning and posture toward school achievement developed in the lower grades diminish the inclination, ability, and opportunity of students to move easily into a secondary-level program designed to develop higher-order reasoning skills. John I. Goodlad (1984) and others who have spent time observing classrooms over the past decade have consistently commented on the widespread use of instructional techniques and materials which appear to affect detrimentally the engagement of youngsters in school as well as their ability to adapt to challenging, discussion-oriented classes in high school (Oakes, 1985; Anyon, 1981; Cuban, 1984a). For example, children whose passivity toward academic learning was nourished by isolated seatwork or workbook practice, common in many classrooms, might wallow helplessly in the demanding dialogues that a number of recent commentators, including Theodore R. Sizer (1984b) and Mortimer Adler (1982) have recommended.

A number of scholars have drawn consistently discouraging portraits of teaching and learning patterns in elementary schools. Although it is impossible to determine the prevalence of some of these practices, observers in a variety of communities report the existence of similar approaches to teaching young children. Ethnographic studies of elementary classrooms reveal, for example, an emphasis on isolated, individual, intensely competitive seatwork (see N. Johnson, 1985, p. 184), where by the third or fourth grade, children are severely criticized for helping one another or for talking together about a problem with the material. Teachers distribute worksheets to the students, who then work alone in an effort to get as many of the answers correct as possible, with what often appears to be little regard for the process of arriving at the right answer. When the worksheet is completed, the student takes it to the teacher for grading. If the child receives an acceptable minimum score, the teacher provides another worksheet, and the student returns to his or her desk to finish the next assignment. As long as a student makes apparent satisfactory progress, there are few interruptions in the procedure.

Researchers have found that such learning practices encourage children to strive for a passing score, for enough "right answers" to have a worksheet accepted. These children marshall all sorts of resources to pursue this goal, including guessing and other strategies which do not reflect the mastery of pertinent content. Indeed, the children regard the "content" or knowledge as essentially irrelevant; it is the correct answers that preoccupy them, not the learning that is presumably needed to arrive at the right ones. Norris Brock Johnson has captured this process vividly in his thorough presentation of life in a contemporary, rural, fast-tracked, fifth-grade mathematics class:

The teacher sits at his desk, reading, and waiting for the students to arrive. The fifth period math students enter in a quiet and orderly fashion, go directly to their seats, and quietly talk among themselves. Several students, especially the females, say hello to the teacher, but most sit down and quietly wait for class to begin. . . . The teacher closes the door, silently takes a roll, and posts the note outside the door. The teacher gives no assignments or directions, but on the way back to his desk merely says, "Get to work."

Students immediately begin working. Finishing their work, they take their papers to the teacher's desk to check the answer sheet, return to their desks to correct any mistakes, then take the paper back to the teacher. The teacher either points out other mistakes or approves the work by saying "Excellent or "OK." (1985, p. 238)

This seems to be where and how many high school students learn to approach school knowledge: they seek the credential rather than the knowledge itself. Now, for children in the elementary grades the concept of pursuing "credentials" seems unwarranted, except when "credential" is defined in the fundamental language of childhood: wanting to avoid a parent's look of disappointment or slap, wanting the teacher to draw a happy face or stick a little star of colored paper on an acceptable worksheet. For many young children, by the fifth and sixth grades, educational credentials are expressed in terms of such experiences. They have begun to differentiate between school knowledge and all of the other learning that they do, and become willing to substitute various sorts of performance scores in school for real learning, something which they tend not to do outside of school.

Such habits of learning and postures toward knowledge which are launched and encouraged in elementary school combine to make many high school students either unable to master or indifferent to mastering academic content. These habits lie beneath the revealing question, asked so often after the sixth grade, "Is this going to be on the test?" Because it is directed toward the high school, most of the current scholarship has deflected attention from the nature of learning that characterizes many elementary classrooms. But after reviewing a portion of the emerging parallel body of literature critical of elementary schooling, Gary Sykes (1983), formerly of the National Institute of Education, concluded that

at the middle and secondary levels, then, when students are expected to develop complex skills and to deepen mastery of subject matter, serious achievement problems clearly emerge. Yet the problem is in part rooted in elementary-level teaching. Prolonged, intense emphasis on drill-skill approaches to reading in the elementary grades drives out attention to comprehension, to the critical process of making meaning from the written work. (p.100)

Of course there are times when such instruction and materials are useful, particularly in the earliest primary grades, and contribute significantly to the eventual development of both basic and higher-order skills. Such warnings should caution us, nevertheless, against relying too heavily on techniques that encourage, develop, and reward habits or styles of learning that could impede the later acquistion of critical reasoning, problem-solving, comprehension, and discussion skills.

Promotional Policies

Promotional policies and practices in elementary schools have been roundly blamed for contributing to the crisis in academic achievement in high schools. Critics have indicted "social promotion" in particular as a major cause of the failure of high schools to meet society's goals for education. Selecting a promotion policy involves, in part, a choice between egalitarian and meritocratic values, as well as a choice between maximizing organizational efficiency and convenience on the one hand, and individual educational achievement on the other. A meritocratic approach to grade promotion in school is an ordinarily labor-intensive effort that attempts to base decisions exclusively on many thorough measures of individual academic achievement. The alternative of social promotion represents a more organizationally expeditious approach which sacrifices many of the available sources of information on individual achievement, relying instead upon more general measures of group development and learning.

Promotion policies and practices, however, involve more than choices concerning organizational efficiency and meritocratic values. Traditionally, the concept of social promotion was based upon educational theories that held that the social and emotional development of young people was of paramount importance. This goal was best served by maintaining educational placements that kept youngsters with their age peers—even if they were not performing at identical academic levels—so that they would not have to suffer the embarrassment of being visibly older and more physically developed than their classmates. In reality, the tensions among these competing goals have never been resolved decisively; frequently districts have tried to avoid conflict by compromising among them.

In the nineteenth century, before high school attendance became universal, American public schools uniformly relied upon various meritocratic promotional practices, many of which were based exclusively on the results of examinations. As high schools became increasingly universal during the first half of the twentieth century, traditional promotion policies were perceived as punitive and injurious to the emotional and social adjustment of children; social promotion schemes were increasingly substituted for the prevailing meritocratic approaches. Social promotion policies were also prompted by the expansion of "scientific management" objectives and techniques during the early twentieth century: merit promotion was not cost-efficient, since many students had to repeat one or more grades (Labaree, 1983).

The practice of social promotion spread quickly and until recently was a virtually universal feature of public education. This approach encouraged elementary schools to advance through the grades age cohorts rather than skill cohorts. This filled high school classrooms with adolescents of roughly the same age, but whose academic caliber, habits of learning, and general engagement with intellectual issues varied considerably. High schools, consequently, have had to find ways of accommodating an unprecedented diversity of students.

In the nineteenth century, meritocratic promotion through achievement testing had provided a positive incentive: upward social and economic mobility for the relatively small proportion of students attending high school and attaining diplomas. The current approaches to merit promotion have quite the opposite impact. Current merit promotion proposals and practices are often based upon exit testing rather than entrance testing, and the incentive system is negative rather than positive. Students are urged to do well on promotional tests or in meeting promotional criteria so that they can *avoid* being held back in grade or being placed in a low-ability group or track. The negative incentive approach being applied now also differs from the positive incentive approach of nineteenth-century meritocratic efforts because of the changed value of the high school diploma. As we argued earlier, in the nineteenth and early twentieth centuries, the high school diploma was a desirable goal for adolescents because of the upward economic, social, and educational mobility it offered. Now, however, the high school diploma's decreased value has reduced the positive incentives for continued academic involvement for many students (Labaree, 1983).

Contemporary critics of social promotion now see the practice as a measure that adapts the school to the student rather than the student to the school, a system that places students on an "academic dole" (Labaree, 1983). They argue that social promotion has diluted the overall academic attainment of all students by affording grade advancement to some children who may not have actually attained in the elementary grades the basic skills upon which they believe promotion should presumably be based. According to these critics, abolishing social promotion would contribute substantially to increasing the value of the high school diploma. Their proposed remedies for the elimination of social promotion take two basic forms: an outright end to any teacher use of social promotion recommendations, and the use of standardized norm- or criterion-referenced tests to determine grade-to-grade promotion and to determine initial kindergarten or first-grade placement.

Little empirical basis seems to undergird these new policies on promotion or exit/entry testing. There is no proven positive relationship between the new promotion policies and student performance (Labaree, 1983; Goodlad, 1984). There are, however, some inferences which can be drawn about the operating assumptions behind these approaches. As Labaree (1983) concluded, most of the current new promotion practices and proposals assume that low achievement is primarily attributable to an initial lack of motivation on the part of the student. When the only component of a new promotion policy is a test requirement, for example, the policy appears to hinge upon an assumption that the test will force students (or, particularly in the case of preschool testing, children and their parents) to apply themselves more diligently to the task of learning. These policies require no direct change in the variables that schools or educators contribute to the instructional equation, since the policies offer them, and ask of them, nothing new to work with which they did not already have other than the threat of an exit test.

Further, such presumptions about student motivation fail to take into account the extent to which low levels of motivation are, in fact, an understandable, rational, and justifiable response to a social, educational, and economic system in which there are often few meaningful internal or external incentives for educational achievement. To the extent that such factors as student socioeconomic status, racial discrimination, family history, test invalidity, or instructional breakdowns are the causes of low achievement, student motivation is irrelevant, and retention in a grade will not necessarily spur achievement gains. It is also true that students are themselves aware of the unfairness of making them primarily accountable for overcoming myriad problems contributing to low achievement when many, if not most, of those causal factors were influences over which they do not have, and never will have, any control.

Indeed, a punitive promotion policy may simply serve itself as a disincentive for learning. A narrative describing New York City's promotional gates policy, for example, quoted a student from a Brooklyn junior high, "The worse [sic] thing that has happened to me is getting left back in the seventh grade. My friends treat me in a different way. Every time I see my friends, I feel like I am too dumb to speak to them" (Barrett, 1982, p. 1). The same article indicated that the New York City testing program allowed students to retake at mid-year promotional tests they had previously failed. However, mid-year passage of the test, while it certified eligibility for promotion, did not lead to immediate promotion since the students were still deemed to be too far behind their age peers, this time because they missed out on the coursework covered by their peers in the first half of the year. The result in New York City, as described by outside evaluators, was one of "resentment and negative reaction" (Barrett, 1982).

The new merit-promotion approaches also conflict directly with well-known theories concerning learning and the acquisition of knowledge. The work of Benjamin Bloom, for example, conflicts directly with the tacit assumptions of those endorsing merit promotion. Bloom has argued that every (nonhandicapped) student can achieve mastery of the basics and that student failure to achieve is due to instructional failure to meet student needs, rather than student inability or unwillingness to learn (Bloom, 1976). Given that this is the case, there is no real purpose for promotional gates or entry testing. Teachers should be able to use their own classroom testing to determine student attainment and shortfall and to guide instruction so that by year-end all students have mastered grade-level skills.

While there is little, if any, empirical evidence in support of the use of blame-placing mechanisms, such as the new merit promotion schemes, in which students are made primarily accountable for educational failure, there is evidence that enhanced remedial instruction has a positive effect. Confirming what common sense would argue, the evidence indicates that remedial instruction has more direct effect on achievement than do promotion policies (Labaree, 1983; Goodlad, 1984).

Ability Grouping

The third feature of elementary schooling that affects the levels of academic engagement and learning in high schools is the practice of ability grouping. Increasingly called "achievement grouping," the practice of homogeneous group placement has become widespread at the elementary level. In some respects, ability grouping can be seen as a compromise between meritocratic grade promotion and social promotion, since moving identifiable groups of children through the grades is perceived to be more acceptable than promoting them *en masse* without distinction.

The practice of ability grouping begins as early as kindergarten and the first grade, when students typically are divided into three or more reading groups and may be assigned to one of two or three groups in arithmetic. Although there is some movement from group to group, membership in a high or low cohort tends to persist over the primary grades, and differences in achievement across the ability groups increase with each year in school. By the time students enter the fourth grade, pupils in the same class often range in academic achievement (as measured by tests) from four full grade levels in reading and to six grade levels in mathematics.

Ethnographic studies of elementary classrooms in which ability grouping practices are employed suggest that such placement patterns actually exacerbate differences in achievement levels and may aggravate student disengagement from school learning, particularlry for low-income and minority children. This research suggests that white middle-class, competent, hard-working teachers in racially mixed classrooms are not particularly sensitive to the circumstances of some children who must operate with situationally induced inattention patterns that may be dysfunctional to academic learning. Teachers attempt to encourage academic learning and reward academic competence in terms of traditional measures of success. Their students, however, find themselves enticed in the opposite direction, since often social acceptance by peers is offered to those who actively and passively resist academic learning tasks and activities. They find greater status and acceptance by demonstrating indifference and even hostility to school culture (McDermott, 1974). Ability grouping, which tends to strengthen and tighten peer structures over time, intensifies the disengagement from academic learning tasks of increasingly cohesive groups of resisters.

Grouping practices in the elementary grades have been clarified by Norris Brock Johnson in his recent study of a racially mixed consolidated school in the northern Midwest. His field notes, presented in great detail throughout the book's central chapters, reveal patterns of differential teaching and learning that appear to be consistently associated with group or track placement (Johnson, N., 1985). Paralleling the data gathered at the high school level by Oakes (1985) and Goodlad (1984), he found that high school students who had been in high-group classes in the primary grades spent more than twice as much time on work-related tasks as did their counterparts who had been in the low-group classes. Overall, he concluded, "high session children gain more exposure to behaviors and attitudes important to success in future West Haven classrooms" (p. 88). He found that the relationship between teachers and their students differed sharply according to session level: teachers in the low groups were as emotionally distant and adversarial as the teachers in the high groups were accepting and emotionally close. Emotional distance, he suggested, kept the low-session children "from fully embracing the classroom culture and society. Low group students are not concerned with pleasing a teacher . . . who does not accept them" (p. 122).

Distinctions among children that resulted in differential group placements became greater as they passed through the grades in the "West Haven" school. Johnson's analysis of the school's middle grades demonstrated that the district's policies increasingly presented "different categories of knowledge and sorts of information to different groups of children in different physical spaces" (p. 152). This process of increasing separation and differential instruction cumulatively altered the school's classroom demographics. In the middle grades he found fewer and fewer black males in the high groups, and fewer and fewer white females in the low groups (p. 156). By the fourth and fifth grades, students in the low sessions, now predominately black males, began to demonstrate clear resistance to traditional academic classroom norms and expectations. "Subtle tension and strain predominate in the low session," Johnson explained, "as if volatile pressures are being suppressed. Students resist the authority of the teacher, not so much by open defiance as by indirection (nonverbal threat gestures) and passive aggression such as restless fidgeting" (p. 174). His discussion of the fourth grade concluded with the disturbing observation that

> the low session . . . is characterized by the distinctive behavior of black males . . . as well as their spatial isolation . . . in the classroom, by passive student resistance . . . and lack of adherence . . . to customary classroom norms and values, and by an adversial pattern of relationship between the teacher and most students. (p. 205)

Some of these students would try to disrupt the attempts of others to learn, but the school responded with little imagination to "the unforgivable violation of classroom life" that such behavior represented. They skirmished with their teachers until a "subtle truce" was called. The young boys, whose peer group pushed them to build a life within, yet at odds with, their classrooms, would "linger on the periphery" of the upper-elementary grades, where they were offered a "waiting containment" game (p. 209). As soon as they were of legal age, they would drop out of "West Haven High School." Johnson's portrait of this school system illuminates most facets of the effects of ability grouping in the elementary grades and suggests the practice's implications for breeding indifference, alienation, and resistance among adolescents attending high schools.

HIGHER EDUCATION

At the other end of the educational ladder, few institutions of higher education in a position to do so exert pressure on high schools to demand more of their students. Neither colleges and universities nor accrediting agencies provide incentives for high school students to exert themselves academically. The reluctance of all but a dozen or two institutions of higher education to exercise incentives dates back to at least the mid-1960s when admissions requirements were lowered for ideological reasons (Sjogren, 1982; see also Walsh, 1979; Walberg, 1983). Many college authorities and faculty members were reluctant to "impose" a definition of the content appropriate to a secondary education on American youth. Their reluctance may have stemmed in part from the fact that most colleges had already abandoned their responsibility to determine what content knowledge young adults should possess. Over the preceding three generations universities had capitulated to faculty pressure to fragment knowledge along ever more refined lines and to students' interest in designing their own educations. These reinforcing pressures are reflected in the diffusion of the collegiate elective system over the course of the twentieth century (Rudolph, 1982; Kirst, 1983; Riesman, 1980; London, 1982). College faculty themselves have been less willing to discriminate on the relative value of different kinds of knowledge.

No longer willing or able to define a coherent undergraduate education, many college representatives hesitated to force a systematic definition of a preparatory education on high schools. As a result, they backed away from requiring college-bound adolescents to learn a specific, coherently developed body of knowledge. Relatively few admissions committees probe course content sufficiently to make the sort of pejorative judgments that would be necessary to change the situation. Since the mid-1960s, they have instead "recommended" that prospective undergraduates take so many years of English and social studies and so forth. They have not, by and large, resisted the high school elective movement, nor have they confronted the issue of the relative value of different subjects or of different content within a single discipline.

The effects of the ideological neutrality of college admissions practice of the past generation have been compounded by a passivity caused by a weakening demand for higher education since the early 1970s (Ferguson, 1982, pp. 3-4; Breland, 1976). Demographic pressures rooted in the shriveling adolescent age cohort have forced many institutions of higher education, particularly the less selective colleges but also a large proportion of elite institutions, to lower their admissions standards. As a result, even those admissions committees that seek to preserve standards are less able to demand that college-bound high school students enroll in a rigorous program of academic classes. They were understandably unwilling to alienate a large share of their prospective market by preserving "unrealistic" expectations or standards. Some other college would inevitably accept applicants who lacked a traditional classical college preparatory background. Student "consumerism," as it has been called (Riesman, 1980; London, 1982), has encouraged college faculty since the late 1960s to lower standards, dilute content, and ease grading practices, all of which have undermined much of whatever inclination to impose rigorous admissions standards institutions of higher education might have retained. These decisions were based largely upon standardized test scores, high school grades, and class ranking, which were thought to discriminate against minority and working-class adolescents in favor of white upper-middle-class youth.

Together, therefore, ideology and market conditions combined to erode the incentives that institutions of higher education could provide to encourage high school students to be seriously engaged in challenging, coherent academic classes. "As might have been expected the high school response to the less rigorous college curriculum was to make their program less rigorous, at least for some students," concluded Cliff Sjogren's (1982) recent analysis of trends in college admissions practices (pp. 17ff). Paul Salmon (quoted in McCurdy, 1982, p. 549), executive director of the American Association of School Administrators, has argued that "the high school curriculum deteriorated in large part because the colleges relaxed requirements." As soon as institutions of higher education "let off, the kids quit taking science and mathematics. It drove out of the curriculum courses that require sequentially more difficult study" (see also Adelman, 1983, pp. 22-31; Clark, B., 1985a). Grade inflation at both the high school and college levels through the late 1970s camouflaged a portion of the decline in standards. Adolescents increasingly recognized that they simply did not have to exert themselves academically in order to be admitted to and succeed at a decent, if not highly selective, institution of higher education. Consequently, to the extent to which college-bound students set the academic standards and expectations for their high schools, the movement away from a demanding secondary curriculum is understandable.

In his critique of the impact of college admissions standards and practices on the nature of secondary education, Donald Arnstine (1983) focused attention on our adolescents' devotion to protecting their grade point averages and class ranking. "Many high school students take just enough academic courses to satisfy college entrance requirements, but no more," he argued. "They avoid additional academic work for fear of getting low grades and thus endangering their chances of getting into college" (p. 14).

This preoccupation with grades is understandable if one recognizes that for college-bound youth, the high school diploma has value only to the extent that it facilitates admission to the college of one's choice. For such students, class rank and grade point averages constitute the real credentials they seek. These sorts of admissions criteria have been "instrumental in altering the entire climate of secondary schools," Arnstine concluded. They focus the concern of students on grades and scores "rather than on substantive matters in society, in the arts, and in the sciences" (p. 17). High school students, encouraged by ambitious parents, pursue that which is necessary for college admission: success in high school classes, not necessarily or even principally the acquisition of knowledge.

There are a number of reasons why college admissions standards might play an important role in determining the nature and level of the academic engagement of high school students. In many respects, the university created the modern high school, particularly those aspects of secondary education pertinent to graduation. More specifically, the "Carnegie Unit," commonly used to measure progress toward graduation from high school, was introduced early in this century as a by-product of the effort to establish pensions for college faculty members. The Carnegie Foundation for the Advancement of Teaching was intent on providing financial support for retiring "college" professors (Shaw & Walker, 1981). Because of the wide discrepencies among "colleges" at the time, the Foundation developed guidelines to differentiate legitimate institutions of "higher" education from academies and other essentially secondary schools and from even less reputable proprietary programs. The definition eventually agreed upon specified that a "college" was an institution that accepted students who had completed a minimum number of hours of instruction in "high schools."

This process essentially defined a "high school" as a program of study that included the opportunity to complete 14 Carnegie Units (each "Unit" was the equivalent of one hour per day per subject for an entire academic year). The respective boundaries between "colleges" and "high schools" were clearly drawn through this process: colleges admitted students who had completed at least 14 units or credits of study in high schools. The process of completing the differentiation process was slow but steady, as more and more college faculty members were brought into the Carnegie pension program and their employing institutions began to use more precise criteria upon which to base their admissions decisions. By the 1930s the various postelementary schools had sorted and sifted themselves into the formal hierarchical ladder that is common today (Rudolph, 1982).

During the late nineteenth and early twentieth centuries, institutions of higher education customarily admitted students on the basis of their performance on idiosyncratic examinations administered by college faculty members (Wechsler, 1977). Even while colleges standardized their expectations for prospective undergraduates, they retained a great deal of control over the *content* of the preparation that they demanded of applicants. Over the course of the twentieth century, in contrast, institutions of higher education have gradually relinquished their intitial absolute control over the appropriate content of a high school education, preferring to allow individual districts to set graduation requirements and to rely upon external examinations to determine acceptable pools.

Beyond lowering admissions requirements, colleges have taken additional steps that have detrimentally affected academic engagement and learning in high schools. For example, in response to perceived declines in the ability of entering students, many institutions of higher education began to offer remedial courses (sometimes for college credit) to help compensate for the learning deficiencies of entering and transfer students. Michael Kirst (1983), among others, has suggested that adolescents recognized that if remediation classes were available in college, they could lower their engagement in academic learning while still in high school.

Because the admissions requirements of colleges and universities appear to have strongly influenced high school academic engagement and achievement, it is not surprising now to see that a number of institutions of higher education have begun to tighten their acceptance standards. In addition to the efforts of several elite, selective colleges to specify more precisely their expectations for entering undergraduates, a number of state systems have informed prospective students, especially those expecting to graduate from high schools in their state, that adolescents will have far less latitude and autonomy to design their own secondary education in the future. Thus far the movement to raise college admissions standards has been modest at best, with California and Utah, among others, demanding that high school students interested in attending their state colleges and universities must complete a program of relatively rigorous academic classes (Sjogren, 1982, p. 23; Kirst, 1983). California has even specified that several of these classes be taken during the senior year, which is often filled with insubstantial experiences designed to avoid challenging advanced subject-matter-oriented courses, or to earn an income from part-time work-study jobs, or to protect grade point averages.

It will be revealing to see whether or not such aggressiveness on the part of higher education will actually influence the engagement and achievement of high school students. There are reasons to be skeptical about the extent to which even promising efforts by college admissions committees will improve academic standards at the secondary level. Burton Clark (1985a, 1985b), for example, has cautioned against expecting too much improvement in high schools from tinkering at the college level. Among other constraints, he suggested that today high schools in the United States tend not to be "upwardly coupled" to colleges and universities. Instead, they are "downwardly coupled" to elementary schools in terms of governance, funding, administration, and status. This powerful linkage ties their expectations and objectives less to the institutions above them on the educational ladder than to the institutions below them. From the evidence presented in this chapter, therefore, it seems essential to appreciate the extent to which secondary reform cannot be undertaken in isolation from either the elementary schools which develop academic skills and attitudes toward school learning or the institutions of higher education which affect the motivation and expectations of at least a substantial segment of the adolescent population.

6 ▥ Attendance and Discipline

The process of disengagement is often quiet and passive. Many students who come to school do not attend class but instead wander the corridors and grounds for part or all of the day in search of experiences more interesting than those available in scheduled classes. Many students who attend classes sit passively at their desks, stubbornly refusing to finish homework assignments which they are often permitted to complete during class, preferring instead to attend to other relatively unobtrusive non-school matters: personal grooming, card playing, reading (novels of adventure, romance, or of children with supernatural powers), gossiping, writing notes when direct conversation is impossible, or just tending to their lives. Schools ordinarily tolerate, if not welcome, much of this silent, almost sullen withdrawal.

WITHDRAWAL AND DISRUPTION: A PROBLEM OF SHARED RESPONSIBILITY

Not all evidence of disengagement involves behavior that is so quiet and passive, however. Schools have also had to respond to students who are openly hostile and disruptive, who threaten teachers and other students with violence and humiliation, and who refuse to attend school altogether for brief or extended periods of time. Declining school or class attendance and rising discipline problems pose serious conflicts and trade-offs for our schools. Although educators argue that parental and student indifference and lack of involvement are their most serious problems, the public remains convinced that insufficient discipline on the part of students is the most distressing problem challenging our schools. President Reagan best reflected this view when he stated:

> American schools don't need vast new sums of money as much as they
> need a few fundamental reforms. . . . First, we need to restore good, old
> fashioned discipline. In too many schools across the land, teachers can't
> teach because they lack the authority to make students take tests, hand

83

in homework, or even quiet down their class. In some schools, teachers suffer verbal and physical abuse. I can't say it too forcefully. "This must stop." (cited in Cabinet Council on Human Resources, 1984, p. 1)

Silent withdrawal and actual disruption are debilitating problems in many high schools. They consume the time and resources of administrators and compromise the ability of classroom teachers to deliver content. At issue, however, is the nature and extent of these discipline problems and the impact proposed reforms will have not only for those who live and work in schools but also for social and economic issues central to schooling as it has evolved in this country. Measures meted out in response to misbehavior in school have serious effects on students, or educators and, ultimately, on society. Yet many of the responses to student misbehavior fail to see it as a symptom of disengagement from schooling. Thus in this chapter we argue that efforts to reform school disciplinary practices which do not take into account the underlying causes of such disengagement are likely to fail and may instead even promote further detachment from learning.

Whenever school administrators are asked to rank the most serious kind of misbehavior in their schools (DiPrete, et al., 1981) or to describe the most troublesome day-to-day problems in the administration of secondary schools (Thompson & Standard, 1975; DeLeonibus, 1979), absenteeism consistently outranks any other form of problem.* There is good reason for this: Since the 1960s, absenteeism increased dramatically and then levelled off at high levels (Meyer, et al., 1971). Moreover, despite the attention focused on the nation's largest cities, the increase in absenteeism is not limited to a few urban centers. It has become a national, not a local, problem (Birman & Natriello, 1978).

Even when students come to school, it can be difficult to get them into class. For example, although Detroit's public schools recently reported an absence rate of 20 percent, teacher attendance figures indicate that in fact nearly 30 percent of their students will be absent from class on an average day (Teachman, 1979). This means that the average Detroit high school teacher might have nine students absent from a class of 30 every day. Worse yet, different students are absent on different days, which means that continuity in instruction is seriously impeded, as teachers either have

---

*For other studies that show absenteeism is a major problem, see Chobot & Garibaldi, 1982: Wilson & Singer, 1982; Sentelle, 1980; Birman & Natriello, 1978; Brimm, et al., 1978; Kingston & Gentry, 1977; and Levanto, 1975a, 1975b.

to backtrack to help the previous day's absentees catch up or have to abandon substantive content entirely.

Absenteeism from school or from class clearly means that students are not learning. But absenteeism also means that students are roaming the halls or community, often getting into more serious trouble. Cusick (1983) found that groups of students in the building but not in class "caused the most trouble. They were the ones who were in the halls and lavatories, and the parking lots, who fomented the fights and assaults, and who showed up at the end of the year with the zero grade point average" (p. 27).* Absenteeism, consequently, becomes not only an educational problem but also a social and economic problem.

Following absenteeism and class-cutting, the next most common discipline problems include tardiness, disruptive behavior, verbal abuse, failure to do homework assignments, and drug or alcohol abuse (Hollingsworth, et al., 1984; Cusick, 1983; DiPrete, et al., 1981; Chobot & Garibaldi, 1982; DeLeonibus, 1979; Thompson & Stanard, 1975).

Although serious in and of themselves, the magnitude of problems of physical violence and vandalism compared to the incivilities described so far is small. The National Institute of Education-sponsored Safe School Study (*Violent Schools—Safe Schools,* 1977), which documents the forms and extent of violent student misbehavior in high schools, asked:

> Are crime and violence in schools more prevalent today than in the past? The evidence indicates that while acts of violence and property destruction in schools increased from the early sixties to the seventies, both increases leveled off after the early 1970's. Safe School Study data are consistent with these findings. Principals' assessments of the seriousness of violence and vandalism in their schools for the years 1971-1976 showed no overall change and some improvement in urban areas. For the offenses usually summed up in the terms "violence" and "vandalism," then, the data from these studies do not indicate that the situation is growing worse, and there are some hints that it may be getting better. (p.12)

In fact, more recent research by Paul Smith of the Childrens' Defense Fund, using unpublished 1982 Census data, shows that between 1977 and 1982 the number of personal claims of violence in schools had dropped 4 to 6 percent. The proportion of all personal crimes of violence committed

---

*Similar findings have been reported by Davis, 1975, Kingston & Gentry, 1977, and Teachman, 1979.

in school compared with other forms of misbehavior fell from 6.4 percent to 4.9 percent (Interview, April 9, 1984).

The reasons for attendance and discipline problems are many and complicated. A child's home environment can be influential. For example, research conducted in a large Connecticut high school found that students who lived with both parents had a lower rate of absenteeism than those who lived with one parent (Levanto, 1975b). DiPrete et al. (1981) found that students living in families with both parents or guardians in residence had better behavior records than other students and that students whose parents almost always knew where they were and what they were doing had much better conduct in school. As Clark (1983) persuasively argued, however, family structural characteristics by themselves do not explain attendance and discipline problems. It is the influence of families on children's behavior, attitudes, and knowledge needed to survive in school that is more significant. In this ethnographic portrait of ten poor, black, one- and two-parent families in Chicago (with high-and low-achieving children), he found the most important indicators of school success to be embedded in family habits and interactions rather than in the structural characteristics of poverty and single parenting.

Peer groups and cliques have an equally powerful influence on student behavior. Absenteeism rates are likely to be higher in schools where the students do not value attendance than in schools where they do (Birman & Natriello, 1978). Such evidence could also account for variability in rates of absenteeism within a school: students who belong to cliques whose members do not value school attendance will have higher rates of absenteeism than students belonging to cliques whose members do. Finally, unrecognized learning disabilities or handicapping conditions, poor self-esteem, and frustration with earlier school failures all contribute to absenteeism and discipline problems (Hyman & D'Alessandro, 1984).

Despite these important factors, the problems of attendance and discipline can not be entirely explained by placing responsibility solely on students and parents. Teaching practices can encourage disruptive behavior. In describing the findings of his three-year study on student discipline, Henry Lufler argued that, "while teachers often say that the discipline problems are the result of poor homes or unhappiness in the larger society, we attribute most discipline problems to in-school factors" (quoted in Currence, 1984, p. 8). Unruh (1977) blamed teachers' behavior for problems with classroom discipline, pointing explicitly to their lack of subject-matter knowledge, instructional objectives, and planning; their failure to involve students in goal setting; their poor relations with students; and their inability to control classes. The *Violent Schools—Safe Schools* study demonstrated that student suspension rates were higher in schools where teachers were not interested in the students, where teachers believed that students were not competent to solve their own problems, and where teachers exhibited racial bias in their teaching practices (Wu, et al., 1980b). Boring classes, lack of teacher responsiveness to students, and lack of respect for students' rights and cultural backgrounds have also been identified as major contributing factors to discipline problems (Lufler, 1978).

Inconsistent school policies and practices also encourage absenteeism and student misbehavior. Cusick (1983) observed that in spite of routines to handle the steady flow of discipline problems, administrators tended to react idiosyncratically to students. Teachers reported that this administrative inconsistency made the job of classroom discipline more difficult. In a three-year study on student discipline, Lufler (quoted in Currence, 1984) corroborated Cusick's indictment of arbitrariness and whimsical disciplinary practices.

> The most common mistake made by administrators and teachers is the failure to have an even and fair enforcement of school rules. For example, we found teachers excusing the misbehavior of students whom they considered to be college-bound, while students they did not see as being college-bound were punished more frequently. And, of course, those students perceived that unfairness; they perceived that they were subjected to punishments when other students were not. That created further misbehavior.
>
> You have some teachers proceeding on the assumption that a great deal of discipline is needed both in the classroom and in the corridors, and you have some teachers who are operating on the assumption that you don't need that much. So some teachers enforce certain rules, other teachers do not enforce those same rules, and that leads to an uneven disciplinary regime where different amounts of order and autonomy are maximized by staff based on their personal feelings. As a consequence, the acts that students might commit, either in a classroom or outside the classroom within a school, are either punished or not depending on the philosophy of the teacher who observes the event. (p. 8)

In-school factors can also be interpreted to mean the cumulative effects of poor teaching and policies of social promotion, both of which are rooted in instructional practices. Students who arrive at high school three to four years behind grade level in reading and math often suffer from poor self-esteem and frustration with schooling. Such students are likely to become severe discipline problems in high school or even dropouts. Disproportionate suspension rates for minority students, for students from low-income families, and for males raise similar questions about in-school factors, particularly when studies show that such students are suspended far more often for discretionary or "friction" offenses than are their peers (Campbell, et al., 1982; DiPrete, 1981; Children's Defense Fund, 1974; Williams, 1978; Garibaldi, 1978; Mizell, 1978; Wu, et al., 1980b). Discipline rules in many schools are so vague that it is common for both classroom teachers and administrators to have a wide range of options available for describing the offense and recommending the punishment. One of the causes of racial disproportions in the rates of disciplinary exclusion arises from the fact that some white educators are more likely to perceive the misbehavior of black students as serious disciplinary infractions when they would tolerate the same behavior on the part of white students. Moreover, the same rule infractions by white and black students often result in the imposition of more serious punishment for blacks. Finally, there is much that schools consider misbehavior on the part of black or other minority students that is simply cultural difference. For example, many minority students have been punished for refusing to look their teachers in the eye. For some minority children, looking a person in the eye is a mark of disrespect they have been trained to avoid (McDermott, 1974; Erickson, 1984).

Not only do students, their families, teachers, and administrators help to create attendance and discipline problems, but so does the community. This is especially true with respect to serious misbehavior, e.g., rule violations that could also constitute criminal activity. School crime does not occur in a vacuum; there is a strong correlation between neighborhood crime and school crime. Hyman and D'Alessandro (1984) substantiated this point by demonstrating that the more crime, unemployment, and violence that existed in a school's neighborhood, the more likely were its teachers and students to be victims of violence in school.

Another community influence on the school's ability to deal with student misbehavior is the public's egalitarian commitment to serving all children in schools and the political reality of local control of school finances. Both surface in this vignette supplied by Cusick (1983):

> There was also the pressure to keep the parents happy and the students in school. It happened that year in Suburban High that some boys damaged some teachers' cars, and when they were confronted by an assistant principal, responded by threatening that person's adolescent son. One would think that such behavior was unacceptable, but when it was talked out with the principal, they promised "not to do it again" and everything was dropped. Overall that was the way such things were handled. If such an incident were pressed it might result in poor publicity for the school and resentment on the part of the boys' parents, who were

voting taxpayers. If they were expelled, the school could lose the state aid. Perhaps most important, expulsion of such students would violate the staff members' own perspective that the school should serve the egalitarian ideal by serving the needs of all the students, even those who appear to need most some improving of their behavior. One does not serve those "needs" by throwing them out of school. (p. 40)

Finally, assertions have been made that court decisions on the constitutional rights of students may have inadvertently contributed to disciplinary ambiguity that results in misbehavior. Lufler (quoted in Currence, 1984), however, attributed inconsistent and neglected discipline practices to fears more imagined than real:

Courts have increased the insecurity of teachers as they deal with the average discipline problems that take place within the school. . . . As we surveyed the teachers we found a great deal of misunderstanding about what the courts have said, and an overwhelming pattern of overestimating the extent to which courts have told teachers what they can and can't do within the classroom. A few basic decisions in the area of school discipline, like suspension hearings before students are suspended from school, in teachers' minds have been viewed as permitting students to have lawyers when they are about to be suspended from school. So there's this pattern of exaggeration. What that has done is cause a lot of teachers to get out of the business of disciplining students. To a certain extent, courts have become alibis, used by teachers who don't wish to discipline students. (p. 18)

BLAMING THE STUDENTS

Students, teachers, administrators, and society all share responsibility for the existence and severity of attendance and discipline problems. The responses to problems of attendance and discipline, however, focus almost exclusively on the student, both as the source of the problem and as the entity which has to change in order to solve the problem.

Beginning in December, 1983, President Ronald Reagan and Terrel Bell, then Secretary of Education, initiated a series of measures designed to focus public attention on the problems of student behavior. A special work group chaired by the deputy undersecretary of education released a lengthy memorandum on the issue to the public in January, 1984. The work group concluded that school crime and disruption have increased dramatically in recent years. To counter such developments, they proposed punitive methods of dealing with disruption and announced administrative support for legal cases to increase the authority of teachers and administrators to discipline students. The memorandum cited the following example of appropriate discipline:

> When Joseph Clark was assigned as principal to Eastside High School in Paterson, N.J., he found teacher assaults, students carrying guns, drugs being bought and sold on campus, and sexual intercourse in the school's corridors and bathrooms. All that has changed. . . . What complex program did Joseph Clark use to bring about a learning environment at Eastside? During his *first week* as principal he expelled 300 of the school's 3,000 students. The word spread like wildfire that anyone that even looked crosseyed would answer to Principal Clark. Back in my day we called that kicking a certain part of the anatomy. (Williams as cited in Cabinet Council on Human Resources, 1984, p.13)

There are several important flaws in this view of student behavior. First of all, as the earlier review demonstrated, while physical violence and vandalism are educationally distractive, they are not as serious as absenteeism, in-school truancy, and classroom disturbances; the former may even be declining. Second, any effort to punish educational misbehavior through use of exclusion must be seriously questioned, for if a student is not in school, the chance that he or she is learning is substantially reduced if not eliminated entirely. The approach's most serious flaw is its one-dimensional focus: it assumes that students are the problem and that increased coercion can promote greater student engagement. This assumption, however, confuses engagement with passivity, which is more likely to result, along with increased dropout rates, in-school suspensions or expulsions.

In the wake of federal efforts to change schools, more than a quarter of the states have taken steps to improve attendance and discipline in local school districts. For example, individual states have increased the age for leaving, decreased the age for entering, increased the attendance rates required for state aid eligibility, instituted new sanctions for use against parents, guardians, or students for failure to attend school, mandated that school boards develop policies on attendance, and developed model attendance policies for school board consideration (United States Department of Education, 1984; "Changing Course," 1985). Several states have enacted statutory changes that mandate new specific attendance requirements which must be fulfilled for students to receive academic credit (Pepe, et al., 1985).

Only a few states have used positive incentives or an educative approach to attendance problems. In contrast with the approach taken elsewhere, Washington state's legislature provided $300,000 to the state superintendent for grants to local school districts to develop innovative programs to decrease the incidence of dropouts (Bridgeman, et al., 1984). In a similar vein, Pennsylvania launched a statewide campaign to increase parental involvement in the problems of attendance, discipline, and homework ("Changing Course," 1985).

Similarly, the response of local school districts to federal and national initiatives appears to be limited. Although *A Nation at Risk* (National Commission on Excellence in Education, 1983) recommended that several districts develop attendance policies with clear incentives and sanctions as well as firm and fair codes of conduct, one survey of school districts in Louisiana found that such recommendations "had only a minor, direct impact on Louisiana school districts within the first year after its public release" (Wimpelberg & Ginsberg, 1985, p. 189).

While the recommendations of *A Nation at Risk* may have had little or no impact at the school or district levels in the areas of attendance and discipline, this does not mean that even before the report school districts were not seeking new answers to old problems. During the 1970s and early 1980s especially, a number of initiatives were undertaken to improve attendance and to reduce discipline problems. Before describing them, however, a caveat is in order. No data other than informed speculation exist to show the magnitude of such initiatives compared to traditional disciplinary practices. In general, we argue, the prevailing pattern of alternatives in high schools for dealing with problems of attendance and discipline continues to be narrow in scope and modest in scale. Depending on the misbehavior, a student is admonished, sent back to class with a note, kept for the remainder of the period, switched to another class or school, told to attend a meeting with the teacher, notified that his or her parent(s)/guardian(s) will be called, sent to a detention room after school, suspended briefly, or expelled. Programs such as in-school alternatives to suspension enjoyed some popularity during the late 1970s and early 1980s but now are probably declining, since many were funded by federal Emergency School Aid Act funds that were placed in bloc grants and then used for other purposes (Moles, 1984). Some students are placed in vocational education tracks or alternative schools in response to discipline problems, but the exact numbers cannot be estimated.

Some schools have gone beyond prevailing practices to exempt students with good attendance from final examinations, to lower grades or withhold course credit for excessive absences, or to increase efforts (including using volunteers) to contact parents at home or at work (Thompson & Stanard, 1975; DeLeonibus, 1979). These as well as traditional practices, however, still suffer from defining the issue solely as a student problem. Accordingly, it is the student who has the responsibility to come to school or class, not the school's to examine the curriculum, teaching practices, or administrative procedures as possible related causes for absenteeism.

From the perspective of content, one can also question policies that provide academic "rewards" for attendance. Schools that raise grade averages for students with perfect attendance (DeLeonibus, 1978) or excuse faithful attendees from all final exams may be conveying a message that what happens in school in terms of learning content knowledge is not as important as simply being at school and "serving time." Such an approach undoubtedly encourages student disengagement from learning.

Finally, putting the responsibility entirely on the student for attending such courses creates the possibility for students to bargain away their opportunity to gain content simply by not attending their classes. One typical discipline policy in effect in several rural and suburban school districts in Michigan, for example, relies upon the use of academic penalties as sanctions for unexcused absences from a particular class. Unexcused tardy arrivals in class, failure to sign out when leaving school, or failure of a parent to provide a written excuse acceptable to the school within two days of a student's absence may result in an automatic failing grade and removal from that class for the remainder of the school semester. By enacting policies that deny students course credit or result in suspension or expulsion, schools absolve themselves of responsibility for the in-school problems described above and shift the blame for failure to the student. For students already alienated from the schooling process, the policies may in fact work to reward disengagement by encouraging students who did not want to be in school anyway to stay away.

Many adolescents regard suspensions from school as vacations. In contrast, such disciplinary alternatives as in-school suspensions could symbolize a far different perspective on the value of academic learning. In-school alternatives take a wide variety of shapes and forms. In the only comprehensive review of in-school alternatives to date, the National Institute of Education (Garibaldi, 1978)) found three major types: "time-out rooms," "in-school suspension centers," and "counseling and guidance programs." Time-out rooms, as their name suggests, are places, usually classrooms, where students are assigned to "cool off" for a specified time (one to three periods a day). Usually placement follows a disruptive incident in the classroom. Rooms are staffed by one or two individuals who function as counselors or activity monitors. Some programs require the student to complete academic work assigned in class; others just have the student reflect on the prior incident. Reassignment policies vary, with administrators often making the determination, but in some cases responsibility is delegated to the classroom monitor. Time-out rooms are generally located away from the normal flow of school activity and peers, to reduce distractions and to serve as a punitive deterrent (Garibaldi, 1978).

In-school suspension centers are extensions of time-out rooms. Here a student may spend as little as a day and as much as a semester (most are short term, from one to three days). Typically such programs are staffed by a minimum of three persons who monitor academic work, provide guidance services, and maintain contact with the home. In some cases, academic work assigned by teachers is supplemented by instruction from center staff. Although such units vary with respect to their restrictions, usually contact is limited between students sent to the center and regular students (Garibaldi, 1978).

The third type of in-school alternative to suspension is specifically designed to provide guidance and counseling. Because the focus is on counseling, the amount of time spent by students depends on the seriousness of the misbehavior, the length of the daily counseling session, and the success of the therapy. Therapeutic models vary, and staff sizes are generally small and separate from the regular counseling staff (Garibaldi, 1978). Only two formal evaluations of such programs have occurred. The first of these, conducted by the National Institute of Education, (Chobot & Garibaldi, 1982) reached findings that were at best inconclusive. The evaluators found a lack of meaningful, measurable program objectives. District staff expressed "satisfaction" with their programs or had "strong feelings" that their programs were accomplishing their objective but could not support their perceptions with any convincing data. The researchers noted that "when something new was tried there was no attempt... to determine whether it worked any better than the one it replaced" (p. 327). The study also noted limited parental involvement in the programs, variations in the extent students in the programs were assigned academic work, little meaningful counseling or follow-up of students, and no data that out-of-school suspensions had been reduced.

The second evaluation of a pilot in-school suspension program in Maryland (Montgomery County Public Schools, 1981) found that while out-of-school suspension rates went down, overall suspension rates went up when in-school suspensions were counted. More serious offenses were still punished by out-of-school suspensions, and minorities were disproportionately suspended. Although students and teachers reported feeling the program was effective, students with more serious suspension records did not. Less than one-half of the students in the in-school suspension program completed their assignments. Finally, recidivism rates were higher than in the out-of-school suspension program.

Unless one is willing to accept self-reports of success stories (Garibaldi, 1978; Sweeny-Rader, et al., 1980; Sentelle, 1980; Davis, 1975), evidence regarding in-school suspension programs is ultimately mixed. Although efforts may be sincere to find meaningful alternatives to out-of-school suspension, such programs risk being nothing more than "holding tanks" or counseling units to adapt the child to the school.

Mizell (1978) proposes a set of goals for such programs which remain relevant today since they go beyond punishment and control and suggest that school officials have an extensive responsibility to educate rather than simply to penalize students.

> In-school suspension alternatives should be developed for the purposes of: (1) helping the child; (2) identifying and remedying the root problem(s) responsible for the real or perceived commission of a disciplinary offense; (3) helping the student develop self-discipline; (4) gaining knowledge about the factors contributing to discipline-related problems, and initiating preventative measures to reduce those problems; (5) eliminating the use of out-of-school disciplinary suspensions for all offenses except those which clearly threaten the security of the school community; and (6) providing a framework within which school personnel can work to achieve the first five goals, while enabling the majority of the students in the school to continue to participate, without interruption, in the school's instructional process. (p. 137)

In short, the use of in-school suspensions does not have a substantial likelihood of success in keeping students in school and actively involved in school learning unless the approach is carefully tailored to address the problems of student disengagement.

A variation in the same premise behind in-school suspension is the use of public alternative schools for students who do not succeed in conventional schools because of attendance and discipline problems. Arnove and Strout (1977) estimated that programs for disruptive youth comprises one-third of existing alternative programs in the U.S. They added that all forms of alternative schools reached only one to two percent of school children. The goal of programs for such youth is ordinarily to create a set of conditions conducive to warm interpersonal relations, academic success, positive images of the future, and enhancement of self-concept. According to Arnove and Strout (1978a), "features of alternative programs instrumental to the achievement of these conditions include small, intimate schools with a low student-adult ratio, individualized instruction, competent and caring teachers, specialized personnel to provide counseling and social devices and a pragmatic vocational thrust" (p. 3).

Some programs, however, often exhibit a number of negative features: labeling and stigmatizing, housing a disproportionate number of minority students (leading in some cases to racial isolation), diluting academic preparation (that is, no science courses, rote learning, low teacher expectations), leading to menial and dead-end jobs, high student turnover rates (80 percent in some schools), and too little done too late for students with the most serious problems (Arnove & Strout, 1978a).

What are the implications of poor attendance and disciplinary infractions that can have serious consequences for efforts to enhance involvement with academic learning? Consider the consequences for a classroom teacher who has only a third of the class present during a two-week unit, as happens in many classrooms. Make-up work needs to be assigned, and previous lessons must be reviewed (taking up valuable instructional time and boring the students who were present). As Teachman (1979) noted, such efforts may help the student who is sometimes absent and who will do the make-up work, but they have almost no effect on the chronically truant student who is absent too often to ever catch up. Small wonder in such classrooms that the "bargain" is struck in favor of social relations and that the memorization of lists takes the place of meaningful content. Although the decline in violent behavior by those who attend school is heartening, this does not mean that tardiness, classroom disruptions, and failure to do homework exact no serious toll on the level of content learning in schools. On the contrary, the widespread occurrence of rudeness and incivility signal a lack of respect and involvement in learning which can have a devastating effect on teacher morale. Lortie (1975) persuasively argued that teachers derive their rewards principally from interpersonal relationships with students, not from salaries or promotions. The lack of student respect erodes the most meaningful rewards in teaching. This affects enthusiasm and engagement in the classroom and has consequences for bargaining between students and teachers: troublesome students are allowed to sit in the back of the room and ignore the lesson so long as they tacitly agree not to disrupt the class too often. The teacher attempts to focus what energy remains on the rest of the students, ignoring those in the back.

The current one-dimensional focus on the student as the problem and the present emphasis on coercion are not likely to promote greater student engagement. For example, is it likely that an environment for positive learning will result from expelling ten percent of the student body in a week's time, as happened in one high school (cited above)? Will it result from a policy that "makes attendance in all classes, even the boring ones, mandatory," as Teachman proposed (1979, p. 205)? In practice, there may not be any effort to create a "bargain" between teachers and students that emphasizes content, but rather an effort to remove students from the classroom so the bargain can be struck at a higher level with those who remain. For those who are removed, their education has ended.

It is instructive to compare the findings of a 1979 Phi Delta Kappan (PDK) commission on schools with little or no discipline problems with the findings described earlier on alternative schools serving disruptive students. The commission found that in relatively trouble-free schools disciplinary codes were the result of input from students, teachers, and administrators; problems with student-behavior, such as fighting, were seen as symptomatic of other problems; faculty and staff viewed school as a place for students to experience success; emphasis was placed on positive behaviors and preventative measures rather than on formal rule enforcement or punishment programs; and the principals were strong leaders in the sense of making their positions clear and influencing staff without being either tyrannical or Machiavellian (Lasley & Wayson, 1982).

According to Arnove and Strout (1978a), many alternative schools for disruptive students provide a "warm, supportive learning environment, with a low student-adult ratio, competent and caring teachers, individualized instruction, extensive counseling and support services, student participation in decision-making, and discernable connections between the programs and opportunities for advanced education or integration into the work force" (p. 31). Administrative leadership is also critical to the ultimate success or failure of such alternative schools.

When considering student disengagement, we see that the two ends of the spectrum—conventional schools with few discipline problems and successful alternative schools for disruptive youth—have something worthwhile to teach the vast number of schools in the middle which experience considerable attendance and discipline problems, and to policymakers intent on imposing simple solutions. Effective attendance and discipline policies seem to acknowledge that discipline is not simply a punitive process but an opportunity to educate for self-improvement as well. In short, philosophical orientation, organizational arrangements, adequate funding, and community support are hard to come by, certainly more so than "good old-fashioned discipline," but they seem to hold the promise of engaging students and teachers more effectively in the learning process.

PART II
Teachers

7 📖 Teachers: Autonomy and Quality

Academic engagement and learning for the vast majority of students suffer as they do principally because many teachers and schools neither demand nor reward sustained, deep engagement with fundamental subject-matter content and the development of higher-order reasoning skills. Teachers, other educators, and many organizational policies ultimately must shoulder primary responsibility for current problems with academic learning and standards. Although students participate in "bargaining," they do so with individuals and institutions that shaped their commitment to learning in the first place.

This chapter examines the bargain in terms of the teacher's role. It considers the effects of the reward structure for teaching on the nature of social relations in the classroom, the impact of professional autonomy on the context within which academic standards and achievement evolve, the efforts of teachers to shape their conditions of work, and the quality of the teaching force.

SOCIAL RELATIONS

Teachers depend upon their students for much of their sense of success, accomplishment, and satisfaction, a circumstance that has been noted and thoroughly explained by sociologists of education for decades (Lortie, 1975; Feiman-Nemser & Floden, 1986). Teachers must come to terms with what students desire to know, with students' definitions of knowledge. There have been few rewards for either students or teachers deeply committed to the mastery of challenging academic content. Students entering high school have had little positive or enjoyable experience with intensive subject matter. For many reasons, adolescents are commonly preoccupied with life events and opportunities that have little to do with academic coursework as it has been traditionally conceived. For these reasons students may not want to care about learning content that professional educators believe is worth knowing and often use their veto power over learning to divert classroom attention away from concentrated academic exercise (Buchmann, 1981, 1982; Cohen, D., 1983, 1984; and Cusick, 1983, 1973).

As a result, teachers manage their dependence upon students in many undefined and unarticulated ways. The best teachers find ways of engaging their students in meaningful and worthwhile learning, despite the effort of many adolescents to resist such exercises. They resolve the universal tension between their dependence upon students for occupational satisfaction and their professional responsibility to maximize the learning of even defiant students in favor of the latter. This is what makes them the best teachers. There are not many examples of such teachers in recent literature, but there are some (Lightfoot, 1983; Cohen, D., 1983; Cusick, 1983; Sizer, 1984b). Fundamentally, nevertheless, little is known about how these teachers have accomplished the most extraordinary task of getting an adolescent to care about something that is intrinsically hard, or about which there are few incentives to care, and indeed which must compete with many attractive and seductive options. The standards-raising movement has not concerned itself with these teachers to the extent that their accomplishments warrant, yet they have much to teach us. It does appear that most traditional variables pertaining to incentives (income, years of experience, tenure, per capita expenditures, autonomy, for example) do not accurately predict the existence of such teachers. There are a number of efforts to identify and celebrate "exemplary" teachers, but thus far this strategy has not taught us much about the prerequisites necessary to resolve the tension in favor of enhancing the acquisition of knowledge, except perhaps the obvious, that a good teacher must at least have mastered the disciplinary content of his or her field and have the skill to engage all the students in learning it.

The literature has been more concerned with those teachers who resolve the tension by accommodating their expectations and instruction to indifferent, disengaged, or defiant students. Such teachers cope with this tension by deferring to students. Since interaction with students appears to provide the most salient rewards in teaching, teachers often solve their interaction problems in ways that sacrifice or compromise the acquisition of academic knowledge (Feiman-Nemser & Floden, 1986). They cultivate and nurture good social relations in the classrooms at the expense of academic learning. Resolving the tension in this manner magnifies the importance of the social relations of the classroom. Teachers, particularly those who lack confidence in their mastery of their subject matter, or whose preparation or exposure to content is weak, are enticed into making peace with students through conversations and personal interaction unrelated to academic knowledge or appropriate instructional goals (see Owen, 1981, pp. 74, 78-79, 158-59).

The authority of even those teachers who are strongly committed to academic learning can be undermined by groups of powerful students. The ability of a handful of students to disrupt instruction, because of low-skill levels or other reasons, causes teachers to emphasize social relations in order to make everyone's life more bearable (Cusick, 1973; Lightfoot, 1983, pp. 143-144). Therefore, personal interaction between teachers and students, and among students themselves, can be allowed to shape or even control access to knowledge.

Preoccupation with personal relations in a classroom can impede academic endeavors in many ways. In order to maintain harmonious relationships, for example, some teachers negotiate with their students about a variety of issues that might promote or inhibit learning. One investigator (Wegmann, 1974) who observed and recorded more than 100 hours of such interaction and negotiation has described the process in detail. Working from his field notes and transcriptions of classroom dialogue, he has reconstructed the negotiation of assignments, examination content coverage, and even the "correctness" of individual objective test question responses in a dozen "academic" classes. He describes the interaction as a "process of mutually defining or managing academic reality" (p. 13).

In every case, students sought to minimize requirements, delay or postpone assignments, and receive the highest grades they could for the least amount of effort. Teachers attempted to ensure that the grades they awarded somehow reflected student performance, but the negotiation process often invalidated efforts to evaluate achievement (which could ultimately lead to grade inflation). The investigator was astonished by the frequency with which assignments were changed, for example, and that no one ever kept track of the confusing revisions. Everyone disagreed about requirements and due dates. As a result, teachers found it difficult to invoke their original standards or to hold students accountable who claimed to have misheard the final terms of the assignments. "What are we supposed to be doing?" was the most "frequent single question asked by students in high school classrooms" (p. 14). Since no one was ever able to answer the question satisfactorily or finally, it was common for the teacher to request that the students take out or turn in a specific piece of work, find that the students "as a group deny that any such work was assigned," accept this denial, and then proceed "as if no homework assignment was made" (p. 14).

Students asked one another about assignments in the corridors and over the telephone but were strongly discouraged by their friends from ever asking the teacher about homework, "lest he remember something they would prefer he forgot, or lest the questioning stimulate him to make an assignment he would not otherwise make" (p. 14). Because many teachers collected homework only intermittently, students became confused about the seriousness of assignments and challenged their teachers about their authority to expect a specific piece of work, again making it impossible for teachers to invoke "the completion or non-completion of the work as justification for the final course grade" (p. 14). Similar issues affected the administration of examinations and reduced the amount of academic learning that occurred, since the negotiation process always worked out in favor of the students. "How long need an answer be?" asked a student about to take an examination. "Although the test instructions call for twenty-five lines, will twenty be sufficient? It turns out that twenty will do" (p. 18; see also McNeil, 1981).

Such questions proceeded endlessly as students marshalled unimaginable resources to challenge incessantly, and often spuriously, their teachers' authority to impose academic standards. Teachers accepted unacceptable work, forgave confusion, and struggled constantly with students determined to impose their own definitions of knowledge on the class or at least to demoralize teachers who sought to preserve the integrity of requirements and expectations.

Such situations are excellent examples of "social traps," occasions when acting on one's immediate interests—making a classroom peaceful, perhaps—precludes, or at least mitigates against, the attainment of long-term objectives (Platt, 1973). These traps arise in almost all social relationships; it is almost always the natural inclination of all of us to take the path of least resistance, the easy way out, or the approach that will cause us the least discomfort in dealing with those with whom we live or work. Students and teachers are no different from spouses, lovers, or co-workers, all of whom share a need for the good fellowship and security that arise in settings in which cordial relations can, for the most part, be counted upon.

The satisfaction that accompanies the successful management of social relations in a classroom can delude teachers into believing that they are meeting their responsibilities when, in fact, attention to the immediate dynamics of personal interaction can be at the expense of the formal objective of maximizing academic learning. Like counselors and other human service professionals who must reconcile immediate interaction and formal and perhaps more long-term technical objectives, teachers can be tempted to focus on the management of social relations to the exclusion of academic endeavors. Orderly, smooth-running classes filled with contented, if not especially vibrant and engaged, students can offer the illusion of successful teaching, even when the acquisition of academic knowledge is sacrificed. Like others in parallel situations, many teachers would prefer to avoid the pain and even the implicit threat of personal humiliation that could accompany the imposition of assignments and commands on resentful students. Teachers and their students are often seduced into working out immediate process strategies that can provide personal rewards, while abandoning the potentially unpleasant consequences of focusing on academic content.

This helps to explain why teachers often adjust their expectations and modify their instruction in ways that ultimately lower academic standards. Expectations for student performance have been affected by this . Beyond the accommodation that some teachers have made to the expanding place of employment in the lives of adolescents, academic expectations for virtually all students have been reduced in order to attract all adolescents at a time when the devalued high school diploma has a hard time holding many students through the twelfth grade. Teachers apparently expect little, and demand less, of their students, especially outside of formal class time, but during the school day as well (Lerner, 1982). As noted above, teachers often cope by making the acquisition of knowledge "easier," less painful, and therefore less threatening, through unchallenging instructional methods: lecturing, assigning more seatwork, reducing complex conceptual problems to factual lists, diluting or omitting essential content knowledge, refusing to challenge students seriously, requiring little reading, minimizing writing assignments, changing instructional and classroom goals on the spot by attending to personal matters, or conversing with students. Together these accommodating strategies, labeled "defensive teaching" by one scholar (McNeil, 1981, 1982), help to keep the peace and appearance of tranquility but often at the cost of academic learning (see also examples in Owen, 1981, pp. 68, 72, 117, 154, 260-261; Davis, 1972; Cusick, 1983; Goodlad, 1984).

In addition to encouraging teachers to lower expectations and adjust their instruction in order to better manage students, maintaining social relations in the classroom also contributed to the pressure to pass all students along regardless of their academic performance. Social promotion serves to reduce classroom tension by easing demands on reluctant students and therefore allowing teachers to avoid confrontations over the mastery of required work. Because personal relations are critical to teaching satisfaction and classroom management, many students are permitted to pass through the grades by aging rather than by achieving. Since adolescents are motivated principally by the presumed extrinsic value of the diploma rather than by a commitment to knowledge acquisition, they find this arrangement acceptable.

ENTREPRENEURIAL TEACHING

Like everyone else, teachers exploit every opportunity to work out the best life that they can. They take advantage of whatever autonomy exists to shape their conditions of work and to integrate their work into the rest of their lives. The problems of curricular fragmentation and the proliferation of electives have been aggravated by the effect of the social relations in the classroom combined with the interest of teachers in shaping their conditions of work. In order to make their classrooms as harmonious as possible, high school teachers have regularly developed elective courses which they hoped would appeal to adolescents. General subject matter and specific class exercises have been designed to entice students into subscribing to certain classes. In many districts, especially those suffering declining enrollments, competition for students has become intense. In such circumstances teachers are encouraged to offer courses that somehow tap the interests of adolescents (Cusick, 1983). In high schools they learn in vivid and occasionally painful ways that intense academic work does not interest most of their students. Under the governing assumption that all knowledge is equivalent, that one course is as good as another, it is difficult for an individual teacher (and rare for collective groups of teachers) to defend a professionally defined, coherent body of knowledge.

Entrepreneurially inclined teachers, in an effort to integrate their work with the rest of their lives, often conceive, design, develop, and implement courses and programs based largely upon their own personal predilections, interests, avocations, and outside commitments. They occasionally parlay hobbies into formal courses or develop high school classes similar to those narrow seminars they enjoyed in college. High school electives, and the content of many basic required classes, have been shaped considerably by individual classroom teachers seeking to tailor their academic work to their other interests.

Cusick's (1983) discussion of the process through which teachers create curricula is particularly revealing. He cites several memorable examples of the ways in which teachers merge many of their personal and professional interests in courses that also allow them to manage the social relations of their classrooms and guarantee consistently large enrollments.

> A particular English teacher in that urban school who loved music put on musical performances and worked as a show promoter for some local agencies. He created an English elective called "Music as Expression," where he played the Beatles, street rock, the Beach Boys and all the music he liked in classes that were quite well subscribed by both

blacks and whites. The program consisted of listening to the music, then studying it and writing about the lyrics. He referred to his class as "relevant" and "interesting" and was very proud of having the "most popular elective class in this school." (pp. 80-81)

Other teachers redefined their institutional responsibilities in terms that enhanced their personal lives, often abandoning the assignments they were hired to complete. One suburban teacher employed for the purpose of offering four chemistry classes and a single course in physical science preferred the subject matter and students in his physical science course and quickly inverted the assignments, spending only 20 percent of his time teaching chemistry. Cusick found teachers who "deserted" their business math classses to develop entire programs in computer science and English teachers who focused their lives on building up electives in "Yearbook." The "endless number of candy, flower, bake, bagel, and tee-shirt sales" that he found in the schools he studied helped to provide the financial support for, and enhance the visibility of, the special classes and programs developed by "entrepreneurial" teachers (pp. 84-86; see also Neufeld, 1980). Some of these activities may have encouraged academic learning; certainly not all electives or narrowly or personally conceived classes are worthless. However, an idiosyncratically created curriculum has not been subjected to collaborative professional scrutiny. Furthermore, it is unlikely that rigorous assessments of course content will occur, given the fact that the specific content of courses is rarely examined carefully by building administrators, school district offices, or state educational agencies so long as summary "lesson plans" are submitted in the few schools in which they are still required and course titles can somehow be made to fit in with the curricular requirements of the state.

Some teachers, however, have been *forced* into an entrepreneurial posture toward their professional responsibilities because of the necessity for managing their time creatively. Teachers have less time available for teaching, due to a number of reasons. Economic pressures have forced districts to increase class sizes. Out-of-school commitments, collective bargaining agreements, and extra-duty contracts for athletics and other extracurricular activities eliminate the after-school time teachers have available for students. The high student-teacher ratios present in most high schools, particularly where teachers have subject-matter specialties and the faces in the classroom change every period, mean that most teachers are responsible for more than 150 different students a day. Spending even an average of five minutes per student per week grading papers, offering counseling, writing letters of recommendation, or doing the many other tasks we expect of our high school teachers means an additional twelve hours of extra work. Confronted with these constant and demanding obligations, it is not surprising that many teachers seize every opportunity to redefine their professional assignments so as to make their lives more comfortably integrated.

TEACHER QUALITY

The current reform movement has not been directly, but only tangentially, concerned with the effects of social relations and entrepreneurial teaching as they might be affected by the *quality* of the teaching labor force and those working conditions that affect the nation's ability to attract and retain talented teachers. Current school improvement efforts are potentially jeopardized by the quality and effectiveness of our teaching force. Improving academic engagement, achievement, and standards depends in part upon our nation's ability to recruit and retain talented teachers. The perceived desirability of teaching as an occupation affects the nature and scope of the labor pool from which prospective teachers are drawn. It also shapes the loyalties of practicing teachers. The public image and status of teaching, its economic reward structure, and working conditions in schools influence the career decisions of prospective teachers and the professional commitments of practicing teachers. To the extent that teaching is viewed as an undesirable occupation, its power to recruit and retain talented practitioners will remain limited, and the larger school improvement campaign will inevitably languish.

The caliber and commitment of the teaching force also have obvious implications for the prevalence of bargaining in classrooms, since teachers who lack confidence in their mastery of subject matter are more easily enticed into avoiding content. They are more willing to rely excessively on films, diversionary banter, recitations, workbook exercises, and other activities which substitute for challenging, thoughtful exchanges. They are less able to parlay perceptive student responses into effective content-oriented interaction.

Contemporary evidence about the state of the teaching force's academic qualifications—particularly regarding the commitment of talented faculty members to remain in the classroom—is distressing. Consider the following:

- Given the overall national decline in standardized test scores during the 1970s, scores for high school seniors and college students who plan to become teachers fell even more sharply on the SAT,

ACT, GRE, and NAEP tests (Weaver, 1978; Cooperman, et al., 1983; Lanier, 1986; Schlechty & Vance, 1983; Duke, 1984; Kerr, 1983).

- The National Longitudinal Study of graduating college seniors confirmed an overall decline in the quality of education throughout their four-year college programs. The SAT scores of graduating teacher education majors were lower than those of all other groups except for students in office/clerical and vocational trades (Weaver, 1979; Kerr, 1983).

- Fewer students are now even considering a career in education. Between 1972 and 1980, enrollments in teacher education programs dropped nearly 50 percent (NEA, 1981). This decline in teaching's drawing power may reflect a change in public attitudes toward teaching. In response to the question "Would you like to have a child of yours taking up teaching in the public schools as a career?" the Gallup Poll reported 75 percent answering "Yes" in 1969, 67 percent in 1972, and 48 percent in 1980 (Sykes, 1983).

- Teachers increasingly regret their decision to enter the profession. A recent NEA survey (1982) reports that of teachers sampled in 1981, 24 percent would probably not and 12 percent certainly would not enter teaching if they could start over again. By comparison, Lortie (1975) cites a 1967 NEA survey which reported comparable figures of 7.1 percent and 2 percent respectively. A Rand Corporation study suggests that the most academically oriented teachers are the most dissatisfied with the most salient working conditions in school, including salaries, autonomy, bureaucratic interference, and lack of administrative support (Darling-Hammond, 1984).

- Of those who take teaching positions, the most academically talented leave the classroom. Sometime between the fifth and seventh year, only about one-half of those who were intially employed to teach remain in school. In their study of retention rates for 1973-1980, moreover, Schlechty and Vance (1983) found that "there is a strong negative relationship between measured academic ability and retention in teaching" (see also Duke, 1984, p. 17; Darling-Hammond, 1984).

- Shortages of teachers in selected fields have already begun to affect the ability of many districts to offer appropriate classes in mathematics and science. These existing shortages will become more generalized over the next decade (Darling-Hammond, 1984).

In short, fewer students are interested in teaching as a career; those who are interested and enter teacher training programs have weaker academic backgrounds than those who major in other fields; those who graduate have even weaker skill levels than majors in other disciplines; teachers increasingly question their decision to enter the profession; and the most academically able abandon teaching early in their career. As Gary Sykes has suggested in his devastating profile of teacher quality, "it appears that at each point of choice including initial and final selection of a college major, the choice of an occupation, and the continuing option to stay or move on, the decision goes against teaching among the most intellectually capable" (1983, p. 102).

Of course there are caveats to this otherwise bleak picture. First, although today's teachers compare poorly with others who use a college degree as part of their professional preparation, when compared with teachers from an earlier era they appear more competent, at least in terms of credentials. In 1946, for example, only 20 states required a bachelor's degree for an elementary teaching certificate; by contrast, since the early 1970s, all states have enforced this requirement. Similarly, at the secondary level, in 1946, approximately 40 states required a bachelor's degree for secondary certification; by 1963, this was a requirement in all states (Stinnett, 1974, cited in Kerr, 1983, p. 127). Despite the progress made in enforcing certification standards requiring the possession of a bachelor's degree over the preceding decades, nearly one-half (41 percent) of the employed teaching force in 1948 had not graduated from college in many rural states in the midwestern, southern, and mountain regions ("Teachers in the Public Schools," 1949). In spite of the necessity to relax standards in order to accommodate the flood of students during the 1950s and 1960s, fewer than one percent of the teaching force lacked college degrees by the 1970s.

Second, although she acknowledged that research supports the general impression that "many persons pursuing careers in teaching are academically weak," Lanier (1986) has cautioned against concluding that teaching has lost its appeal to academically talented students. Teacher education, at least, if not teaching as an occupation, "does not fail to attract and retain persons of high ability," she argued. Approaching the issue of the talent flow into teaching somewhat differently from other researchers, Lanier has suggested that the occupation has continued to attract a reasonable percentage of the academically talented population (those who score in the upper quintile on achievement tests). Even though all occupations recruit from the most talented pool of candidates, teaching has continued to draw approximately 10 percent of the top scorers. Lanier hopes to focus attention on the question of

> what would constitute a reasonable percentage of the top quintile of college-educated persons that should pursue a career in teaching, assuming that society also wants bright and talented doctors, scientists,

lawyers, and other professionals. Judgments about reasonable proportions should be made explicit before researchers and policymakers comment on the apparent shortage of academically talented persons in teacher education. (Lanier, 1986)

Nevertheless, she recognized, "the lowest scoring subset of the college population seems to contain excessive numbers of prospective teachers." Teaching also appears to be attracting a larger share of the lowest achievers than in the past several decades, a trend which helps to explain "the genesis of the stereotype that those in teacher education are the least academically able" (Lanier, 1986; see also Nelson, 1985).

Finally, some who leave teaching may, in fact, do so as a result of finding themselves ill-suited for the profession, so their exit may be advantageous for teaching. Others may leave teaching, say, for administration, from a strong desire to exercise more responsibility. Since this form of ambition *per se* is not a sign of excellence in teaching, such upward mobility could be an asset to teaching by freeing such persons from the classroom (Sykes, 1983).

Such caveats aside, however, what are some of the causes of this bleak situation? Salaries, to begin with. Relatively low earning potential influences the appeal of teaching and affects the career decisions of practicing teachers. Although income potential appears not to be teaching's most potent recruiting device, those who defect from the profession and those who attempt to account for the high defection rates place most of the blame on low salaries. Nine out of ten teachers polled by the Gallup organization in 1984 held low salaries responsible for the decision of their colleagues to resign their teaching positions in favor of alternative employment (Gallup, A., 1984, p. 102). Problems with student discipline, the second most widely noted reason for defection, were cited only one-half as often as low salaries. Goodlad (1984) has argued that while salaries were not among the most salient reasons that the teachers he surveyed had entered teaching, low salaries had become the second most important reason for resigning. Other researchers agree. Wangberg, Metzger, and Levitov (1982), for example, found that much of the job dissatisfaction they had located among female elementary teachers was rooted in low, noncompetitive salaries. Whenever the quality of teaching is discussed, the low level of salaries compared with other professions is automatically assumed to be a major factor.

Moreover, to make matters worse, statistics show that after experiencing some relative improvement during the 1960s, teachers' salaries during the 1970s lost both purchasing power and ground to other occupations. While in 1970–1971 teachers earned 27 percent above the average full-time employee, by 1974 their salaries were only 12 percent above the average

(Freeman, 1976). During the rest of the 1970s, teachers continued to lose ground, dropping to an average annual salary of $19,269 in 1980–1981 from over $23,108 in 1971–1972 (adjusted to 1983 dollars). Through the 1970s, teachers' salaries lost roughly twelve percent in purchasing power due to their failure to keep pace with the ravaging inflation rates of that decade (Plisko, 1980, p. 50). As Kerr noted, "relative to education and social-science-based employment, engineering, the health 'industry,' and business have been gaining ground. Economically it would be irrational for the more able student to choose teaching" (1983, p. 128).

Pupil shortage is a plausible second reason for the decline in the academic quality of teachers. Beginning in 1969, a decline in the school-age population set the stage for a marked surplus of teachers. Weaver (1978, p. 546) argued that "as market demands for new graduates in a given field declines, the quality of the applicant pool prepared to enter that field will also decline." Talent follows opportunity, according to Weaver; the smart go elsewhere.

Changes in job opportunities for women represent perhaps one of the most significant reasons for the decline in quality of those entering the professional ranks of teaching. Concurrent with the common school movement of the nineteenth century came the feminization of teaching with its accompanying low status and poor salary conditions. To the extent that women had been expected to devote themselves to motherhood and homemaking, and had been discouraged or prevented from seeking employment in male-dominated fields, female talent was not able, realistically, to follow opportunity. The availability of women functioned as a cushion that enabled most school districts to avoid dramatically improving their financial incentives for teachers or modifying working conditions to make employment more attractive. Over the past generation, women have tended to take advantage of expanding employment opportunities in other fields and no longer constitute a reserve labor pool for the teaching profession. The hidden subsidy that talented women provided is now being withdrawn as attractive professional career options open to them. This change may fundamentally shape the developing teacher shortage of the late 1980s. The desirability of teaching as an occupation may be put to its most serious test as the withdrawn subsidy provided by women forces school districts to compete for labor in an increasingly open market.

That the intellectually most able women are indeed headed in new directions is suggested by Schlechty and Vance's (1983) study in North Carolina. They found that between 1973 and 1980 the proportion of relatively high scoring males did not change, but the proportion of females did. As Kerr (1983, p. 128) recognized clearly, "the merits of a beginning salary of $40,000 with a law firm far surpass what teaching might offer a bright, well-educated woman."

The careerless nature of teaching does not encourage or reward continued engagement or commitment. A uniform reward schedule based on seniority is largely insensitive to variations in talent and effort. Sykes (1983) argued that the lack of advancement opportunities coupled with the scarcity of rewards for excellence and effort create the following:

> the twenty-year veteran is indistinguishable from the neophyte and the typical salary schedule features a generally rising income slope, with the top-scale salary no more than double that at entry level. To advance, men move into administration or leave the profession altogether. Career mobility for women has been conspicuously absent ... with the result that women favor an in-and-out pattern, an accommodation to the birth of children and the demands of motherhood. (p. 110)

The deterioration of extrinsic rewards, however, tells only part of the story. Teaching's primary rewards have traditionally been intrinsic: derived from productive relationships with students, a sense of mastery over classroom processes, relatively high social status, a large degree of autonomy for interpreting and implementing educational goals.

In recent years, teachers have become vocal regarding what they find unattractive about working in schools, particularly those aspects of a teaching career that discourage so many of them to such an extent that they "vote with their feet" by resigning. Recent opinion surveys have clarified what practicing teachers regard as desirable and undesirable about their work. Teachers unanimously agree that although they contribute more to the general good of society than do members of any other occupation, their field now has virtually no status or prestige. Three out of five teachers in the most recent Gallup Poll (1984) ranked teachers ahead of all other workers, including physicians, lawyers, the clergy, politicians, and business executives, in terms of their contribution to the general public good (Gallup, A., 1985, p. 325). The teachers also ranked teaching last in terms of status, behind realtors, funeral directors, and advertising practitioners.

By contrasting the presumptions of teachers with the opinions of the public at large about the scope and value of educators' societal contribution, it is possible to see a part of the source of the teachers' disappointment with their relative status. Whereas 59 percent of the teachers ranked their profession highest in terms of contribution, only 29 percent of the U.S. public did so. Nearly one-half of the public stated that physicians and members of the clergy contributed most to society; teachers held a slight edge on funeral directors. The public, however, was willing to award teachers more social status than teachers gave to themselves. Nevertheless, the public agreed with teachers that the other professions were more prestigious and that teachers were about as respectable as local political office holders and funeral directors. For both teachers and the public in general, Gallup concluded that teaching was the profession with "the largest disparity between its status in the community and its contribution to society" (Gallup, A., 1985, p. 235).

Farber's (1984a, 1984b) analysis of the causes and effect of stress, burnout, and "wearout" among urban and suburban teachers corroborated the opinion poll's conclusions. The teachers he surveyed were almost unanimous in defending their positive impact on their students' lives; nearly one-half responded that they frequently dealt "very effectively with the problems" of their students, and another third claimed that they succeeded occasionally; fewer than one out of five responded that they "never" or "rarely" dealt with student problems effectively. Similarily, the vast majority of teachers agreed that they had accomplished many worthwhile things on the job. Suburban teachers were consistently (but only slightly) more confident than urban teachers about their positive influence and contribution (1984a, p. 330). In contrast, when asked about teaching's status, nearly 80 percent responded that they had never or rarely "felt satisfied with teachers' standing in today's society." Fewer than 20 percent answered that they occasionally or frequently felt satisfied with their field's prestige and recognition (1984a, p. 331).

The ability of teaching to attract and to retain talented individuals depends on the occupation's image and reputation in the larger society. The desirability of the job is dependent partially upon the respect that children and their parents bestow upon teachers. As historians, sociologists, and opinion pollsters have demonstrated, teachers in the United States have been subjected to ridicule for centuries. Ordinarily this lack of respect was rooted in the conflicting political roles that teachers might play in rural, isolated communities where it was a symbol of high status for local bullies to humiliate or torment a transient master recruited from the "outside" to keep school for a brief term. This disrespect may also have accompanied the assignment of incompetent, socially dependent individuals to the tasks of public service, such as schoolteaching, gravedigging, or bellringing. This tradition of hiring dependents of one sort or another persisted through the nineteenth century and probably resulted in particularly miserable appointments outside of the relatively better-educated New England states (Church & Sedlak, 1976). In the mid-nineteenth century, for example, president Joseph Caldwell of the University of North Carolina levied one of the most vicious attacks against the caliber of school teachers employed in that state:

Is a man constitutionally and habitually indolent, a burden upon all from whom he can exact support? Then there is one way of shaking him off, let us make him a schoolmaster. To teach school is, in the opinion of many, little else than sitting still and doing nothing. Has any man wasted all his property, or ended in debt by indiscretion and misconduct? The business of school-keeping stands wide open for his reception, and here he sinks to the bottom, for want of capacity to support himself. Has any one ruined himself, and done all he could to corrupt others, by dissipation, drinking, seduction, and a course of irregularities? Nay, has he returned from prison after an ignominious atonement for some violation of the laws? He is destitute of character and cannot be trusted, but presently he opens a school and the children are seen flocking into it, for if he is willing to act in that capacity, we shall all admit that as he can read and write, and cypher to the square root, he will make an excellent schoolmaster. (quoted in Hofstadter, 1962, p. 315)

This situation continued through the nineteenth century and began to erode only after the feminization of teaching had replaced many unqualified males with women of far better character and ability. Eventually the arrival of large numbers of women from middle-class backgrounds, many with high school diplomas and even degrees from fledgling normal schools, improved the intellectual and moral quality of the prospective labor force in teaching.

During the era of the professional teacher, the sorts of problems of the nineteenth century probably encumbered few practitioners. In contrast, during the twentieth century, teachers often suffered a loss of respect because of perceived problems with the *status* and *legitimacy* of their professional knowledge.

In contrast with the stereotype of unable and inadequately trained teachers stands the image of teachers as symbols of culture and learning. Regardless of whatever criticisms might be levied against the preparation of teachers or their presumed academic ability, teachers have customarily possessed educational credentials superior to the population at large and have measured intelligence higher than the national average. In many respects, because of these circumstances, teachers have historically been considered to be members of the local intelligensia. During the pre-common-school era, in the age of the district school, many masters, even if they had no intention of teaching more than a session or two for tuition money, had respectable educational credentials, at least relative to many citizens. Even the young women who entered the classrooms later in the nineteenth century had educational attainments that surpassed the adult population in general. When most students tended to leave school after the eighth grade, teachers with high school diplomas or a year or two in a normal school were respected as representatives of the nation's elite.

As the average level of educational attainment for the nation as a whole increased over the twentieth century, so did the level of the professional preparation of teachers. The relative gap between the average attainment of adults and that of the teaching force has remained fairly constant over the past 70 or 80 years. Once it became customary for adults to have graduated from high school, after 1930 or 1940, it had become customary for teachers to have earned college degrees. As youth in general began to attend institutions of higher education, teachers increasingly earned graduate degrees. The tradition of secondary school teachers earning masters degrees in their subject matter broadened to include a growing percentage of elementary school teachers earning advanced degrees in education. The appearance of M.A.T. programs in the 1960s, designed to relieve the teacher shortage by easing entry into the profession by liberal arts graduates, also helped to elevate the educational credentials of the entire teaching force.

After World War II, however, a trend developed that eroded the basis for the image of teachers as members of the local intelligensia. Communities like Newton, Massachusets and Winnetka, Illinois, evolved that were populated by highly educated families, where adults with graduate and professional degrees—who owed their social influence and economic power to their exceptional educational attainments—tended to concentrate. Adults in such communities tended to view their teachers either as intellectual equals or even as academic inferiors. Much of the criticism of teacher quality after World War II originated in these communities, where local school authorities were regularly distressed by the educational credentials and the mental qualifications of prospective and practicing teachers (Church & Sedlak, 1976; Shanker, 1983; Lynd, A., 1953). Over the ensuing two decades public opinion regarding teacher competency spread to less educationally prestigious communities and neighborhoods because the elite suburban critique was dispersed through the media. By the 1970s, it was not uncommon for parents with relatively average educational credentials, inferior to those possessed by the vast majority of teachers, to challenge both the content and pedagogical authority of their children's teachers. Even though teachers have continued to possess credentials superior to those held by the adult population on average, the existence of highly educated northern, suburban, professional-class communities (the adults in which were often opinion shapers) has helped to undermine the educators' claim to status and respect based upon superior training.

The educational enterprise itself has unwittingly contributed to the ease and confidence with which many citizens challenged their teachers' knowledge base and instructional practices. For several decades, since the

1920s, educationists in teachers' colleges and practicing teachers themselves had increasingly accepted what was labeled the "life adjustment" agenda for schools. The "progressive" and "life adjustment" movements of the twentieth century celebrated practical, utilitarian knowledge in schools designed to introduce children to content and skills in the fields of health, vocational preparation, social adjustment, the effective use of leisure time, and so forth (Ravitch, 1983b). As this movement gained momentum and popularity during the 1930s and 1940s particularly, it began to have an effect on the public's understanding of teachers' knowledge. By the 1950s and 1960s, focusing instructional content on practical issues such as preparing for a date or brushing one's teeth spurred a national critique of teaching practices and watered-down content similar to the reaction that had originated in the elite suburbs.

As school knowledge became more "commonsensical," in other words, it began to lose its authority, legitimacy, and status. As what was important for teachers to know appeared to become democratically accessible to virtually every adult, it became easier to treat educational knowledge with less respect. This unintended by-product of the life-adjustment movement—the devaluation of school and teacher knowledge—eroded the profession's status, thus diminishing its appeal to many talented prospective teachers.

In contrast to their professional prestige, working conditions for teachers have improved somewhat since 1900. Teachers today enjoy more freedom and autonomy than their predecessors, and many have far fewer responsibilities and obligations associated with their work. Over the twentieth century, for example, teachers have come to enjoy a great deal of personal freedom. In contrast to their counterparts in the nineteenth and early twentieth centuries, the lives of teachers today are infrequently limited by the types of contractual or customary stipulations about personal behavior, political activity, and moral beliefs that were common in the nineteenth century, when inflexible and exacting conduct codes were often viciously enforced by administrators, school board members, private citizens, and even students themselves (Elsbree, 1939). Nineteenth-century teachers were commonly berated for drinking, lascivious conduct, and other personal activities. The lives of female teachers were constrained more severely than those of their male colleagues. Such conduct codes began to weaken in the 1920s (during a severe teacher shortage), and most were eliminated entirely during the 1930s and 1940s, particularly as organized teachers began to negotiate formal, uniform contracts. Some restrictions continued to persist, especially limitations on the display of political behavior and beliefs in the classroom. Most constraints on personal behavior gradually disappeared, however, even traditional prohibitions against marriage and motherhood for women. During the 1960s and 1970s, teachers enjoyed unprecedented freedom in most areas of their lives. Although some smaller and rural communities continued to impose as many proscriptions as they thought they could get away with (largely by recruiting "safe" teachers from nearby towns), polls of job satisfaction revealed that few teachers felt uncomfortable with the degree of personal freedom and privacy their positions allowed them.

In addition to the improvement in personal and academic freedom, many other working conditions have changed in ways that seem to have made teaching more desirable. Class size, for example, has shrunk steadily since the early years of the twentieth century, when enrollment increases consistently placed 40 to 50 students with each teacher. To the extent that class size contributes to teacher frustration or satisfaction, at least some improvement in working conditions has occurred.

Furthermore, other sorts of benefits have made teaching more secure than it once was. Tenure provisions, for example, have effectively protected many teaching careers against efforts to end them. Tenure and other benefits, including retirement opportunities, professional leaves of absence, workmen's compensation, and predictable working conditions stipulated by contracts, have become so common that it is difficult to recall when few teachers had any protection against the prejudices and whims of employers and voters, or against illness and infirmity. Such benefits have contributed to the appeal of teaching as a profession, especially after 1930, when access to such provisions affecting job and personal security began to become widespread.

These dramatic improvements in working conditions in schools, however, have come to be expected rather than cherished, and it appears that improvements in these kinds of conditions are not able to compensate for perceived losses in those rewards that teachers do cherish. Despite these substantial gains, therefore, in many other respects teaching has become progressively less desirable over the past generation, at least from the perspective of the prerogatives and rewards that teachers find most attractive.

It is essential to recognize that the circumstances have worsened from the *perspective of classroom teachers,* and that at least a portion of the deterioration has been associated with explicit efforts to change teachers' attitudes and behavior: to improve the learning of students whom teachers had traditionally neglected, for example. Some erosion of autonomy and discretion (at the system, school, and classroom levels) has been intended by public policy designed and implemented (sincerely if not always wisely and sensitively) to stop teachers from continuing to teach as they always had taught.

From the perspective of traditional classroom practice, teaching has become less desirable over the past 15 years. The instrinsic rewards in teaching, which grow from contact with students and a sense of pride in student achievement, appear to have become less common for the majority of teachers. Fewer find solace in rewarding relationships with students (Wangberg, Metzger, & Levitov, 1982). Some teachers attribute this problem to their conviction that their students' behavior has worsened over the past 20 years. As demonstrated above, virtually all of the evidence collected on absenteeism, student disengagement, and even intimidation confirms this conviction. Yet teachers have always had to deal with indifferent and hostile, disruptive students. There has been no nostalgic "golden age" of academically committed, deeply engaged students (Doyle, 1978). During the generally placid 1950s, for example, some teachers complained of delinquency and disruptiveness, but their critique of student misbehavior included few indications of serious problems. An opinion poll probed the convictions and experiences of teachers across the nation regarding the behavior of their students in 1956. While adolescents were then receiving devastating critical press through popular movies, magazines, and the radio, the teachers surveyed agreed strongly that their students did not behave as badly as their portrayal in the media. Fewer than ten percent of the teachers stated that the representations were fair and accurate; nearly nine out of ten claimed that the situation in their community was "not nearly" or "not quite" so bad as it had been portrayed. When encouraged to elaborate on their impressions, teachers scrambled to report to the polling organization about trends in Halloween pranks, since the vast majority had no other real experiences with delinquency.

These criticisms appear quaint when juxtaposed against the sort of problems that engulfed classrooms during the 1960s and 1970s, when the situation worsened considerably. For a variety of reasons, including the general erosion of social authority, the effects of increasing family disorganization, and even the impact of the children's rights movement, students have become less intimated by their teachers; they are less afraid to confront adults. Some threaten humiliation when faced with instructional demands. Many are visibly apathetic toward what teachers have to offer. School policies and administrator preferences have eliminated many teachers' most prized responses to student disruption. Removing problem children from classrooms is an option that has been purged from the repertoires of many teachers as administrators press them to resolve disruptive confrontations in isolation.

The administrative priorities that force teachers to handle all but the most violent problems alone in their classroom have encouraged teachers to "get along" with their students, even to the extent of sacrificing academic learning (Cusick, 1983). When faced with the dilemma of resolving their management problems or fulfilling their professional responsibilities to deliver content, many teachers have increasingly abandoned academic standards and expectations in order to keep their classrooms peaceful and their schools' corridors tranquil. Although there are examples of teachers who appear actually to favor this process of bargaining away academic exercises in favor of genial banter, personal conversation, and interaction with students, many teachers find the situation frustrating and discouraging.

Since teachers often derive their sense of professional accomplishment from the appearance of achievement and growth on the part of their students, such pressure to substitute "getting along with kids" for real academic learning jeopardizes their sense of job satisfaction. These particular teachers do not find diversionary talk with adolescents about yesterday's basketball game as professionally rewarding as playing an active role in the learning of engaged students. They resent being placed in this position of sacrificing learning for peacemaking. In other words, some teachers find unappealing the necessity of dealing alone with students they would prefer to suspend or expel, or of interacting with students in ways that seem to abrogate professional responsibility, since there are few intrinsic rewards to be earned through either practice.

Various interest groups have attempted to redefine the responsibilities of teachers and other educators. Through the political process, civil and handicapper rights organizations have mounted relatively effective campaigns to change features of school organization and aspects of teacher practice. Concerned that teachers had abused their professional autonomy in the past by neglecting the education of certain groups of children, public and private authorities largely outside of the educational establishment have devoted much of the past 20 years to designing, implementing, and enforcing mandates and regulations intended to entice and coerce schools and teachers to provide adequate instruction to all of their students, to equalize access to knowledge once all children had won (at least theoretically) access to schools. In order to satisfy the public authorities responsible for these mandates and regulations, many of which were accompanied by access to funds, school districts were obligated to cooperate in the monitoring and evaluation of the services and instruction they provided to targeted groups of children.

Similarly, as schools became more directly involved in the redistribution of opportunity in American society, they assumed responsibilities for housing, as well as delivering a variety of educational and social services (Graham, 1984b). Expansion of educational functions in particular accelerated after 1965, funded by the Elementary and Secondary Educational Act of 1965 and other social welfare legislation (including Public Law 94-142—the Education for All Handicapped Children Act of 1975—and Title IX of the Education Amendments of 1972, which was designed to promote gender equity in the schools). Expansion brought complaints from many teachers, particularly those at the elementary level, where most programs were targeted, who felt that they were being held responsible for accommodating the disruptions to their routines imposed by pull-out compensatory programs and for completing the paper work that was considered necessary to assure public officials that the targeted funds were reaching the intended recipients. Many new requirements for compensatory or special education programs, for example, were usually added as bureaucratic responsibilities on top of teachers' existing instructional loads rather than freeing time for the performance of the new responsibilities. State student assessment or competency test mandates dictated teacher use of time and instructional strategies even in situations where such requirements conflicted with educators' best professional judgments about the academic needs of their students. The sundry accountability campaigns, rooted in civil rights movements and in public concern for evidence of declining academic achievement, have angered many teachers who believed that too much of their time and energy was misspent on monitoring the effects of schooling rather than improving student learning (Farber, 1984a, p. 327).

Similarly, teachers have also expressed concern that they have had to assume this burden at the expense of their autonomy to exercise their professional judgment about who they teach, what they should teach, how they should teach, and to what performance standard they should teach. They have vocally opposed many of these obligations, particularly those which implied that the educational establishment had consistently failed to provide equitable opportunities for all children to acquire knowledge and skills of comparable value and utility. To "improve" meant that many teachers would have to accept responsibilities they preferred to relinquish to someone else, or to develop new skills that were often painful to learn, and which some hoped (if not assumed) that they would be excused from learning as the "equity" fad passed through and from the enterprise. Because it persisted, however, teachers have recently faced the necessity of changing their practices, at least to the extent that researchers proved themselves able to expose and root out the clever ways in which practitioners often circumvented mandates and regulations. As it became evident that the campaigns were not going to evaporate, as so many of their predecessors had, the chorus of complaints has grown louder.

In addition to the disruption and increased responsibilities that resulted from the efforts of special interest groups to target institutional and personnel resources on specific groups of children, teachers have also been asked to accommodate their instructional practices to the necessity of improving the academic achievement of their weaker students. A number of programs have been introduced recently to change actual teaching practice in order to address the learning needs of children who appear not to flourish in classrooms dominated by traditional teaching methods, such as whole-class teacher-led instruction and drill. For example, the use of individualized learning programs, designed to develop a sense of accomplishment and mastery in children, has increased over the past decade. Regardless of their effects on student performance, which are by no means clear at this time, these programs occasionally have the unintended consequence of degrading teacher-student interaction. Many teachers who use these programs complain that their role has been narrowed severely, to the point of just passing out worksheets and certifying the progress of their students (Gitlin, 1983; Bullough, Gitlin, & Goldstein, 1984).

This sort of effect, unintended or not, has accompanied the introduction or expansion of a number of campaigns designed to improve student achievement levels by constraining the abuse of teacher autonomy in the classroom. Federal and foundation efforts to develop and disseminate "teacher-proof" curricular systems or packages, for example, have been regularly condemned for their implicit assumptions about teacher abilities and effectiveness. Although most of these curricular and pedagogical reform campaigns have withered under the resistance of teachers determined to preserve their prerogatives over the definition of appropriate content and instructional methods, they have represented a significant challenge to teacher authority and autonomy and have been vocally critiqued as they were being passively circumvented.

The blatant challenge to professional knowledge and judgement represented by the curriculum and instruction improvement campaigns of the past generation symbolizes the extension of the deskilling process, the central dynamic of industrialization, to teaching and other white-collar, middle-class, professional and technical occupations. Like practitioners in other fields experiencing similar shifts in the locus of control out of the hands of individual workers, teachers have attempted to resist efforts to erode their autonomy and undermine opportunities for the exercise of professional judgment. This deskilling process has been underway for generations, as the centralization of managerial authority has proceeded steadily since the mid-nineteenth century. The process was accelerated by the feminization of teaching, which allowed imbalances in gender relationships to reinforce the efforts of administrators (male) to control the behavior of teachers (female). Teacher rebelliousness toward this process dates from the late nineteenth century and contributed to the organization movement among classroom teachers in cities throughout the early twentieth century.

Teachers gradually acquiesced in most efforts to centralize authority and reduce their role in formal curriculum development; however, this was due in large part, it seems likely, because their authority in the classroom was not fundamentally jeopardized nor was their ability to secure rewarding relationships with their students seriously threatened. Once they closed their classroom door, most teachers were able to redefine the curriculum in their own terms, within some limits to be sure, but most were still able to exercise enormous discretion to decide what to teach, who to teach, and to teach to whatever standard they wished. Most importantly, they were able to continue to devote themselves to those students who consistently pleased and rewarded them. In sum, they were able to control and manipulate the terms of their relationships with different students in ways that provided them the most satisfaction.

Recent efforts to deskill teaching appear to have struck at the heart of teaching's psychic or intrinsic reward structure. They have begun to interfere with the social relations of the classroom by preventing some teachers from interacting closely with their students, by forcing other teachers to devote themselves to students who reward them the least, to work with resistant and troubled children instead of the deeply engaged, academically aggressive students whose posture toward school learning is most like their own. Some of these efforts have been undertaken explicitly to improve and equalize access to school knowledge among traditionally neglected children. Their intention is to force teachers to modify their classroom behavior to enhance the learning opportunities of all students.

For a century, teachers have complained about what they were giving up, but, until recently, few appear to have left teaching because of their losses. They left for other reasons, including marriage or more lucrative employment elsewhere. Only during the past generation have teachers in sizeable numbers abandoned their schools in protest against being forced to give up that which they most cherish about their lives in classrooms.

From this discussion, it should be apparent that the concept of autonomy in teaching is ambiguous and complicated. Is teacher autonomy bad? Or, should we assume that increasing autonomy will solve our educational problems? The fact is, autonomy contributes to irresponsible and disastrous teaching, as much as it is essential to imaginative and effective teaching. Autonomy is clearly a concept that deserves sustained attention, lest it serve as either a scapegoat or a panacea during the next decade. Although available scholarship contributes substantively little to understanding or resolving the issues created by teacher autonomy, we would like briefly to explore the concept and its implications.

Many teachers have had the autonomy or independence to define and create content improvisationally or in isolation. They have had a great deal of discretion to allocate time and other classroom resources in favor of certain children while discouraging or excluding other students. They have been able to set their expectations for different children according to personal criteria, including pertinent information about demonstrated ability, but also based on irrelevant characteristics, such as race, gender, or apparent engagement with formal schooling.

Because teachers have often abused these forms of autonomy, a number of campaigns to restrict or limit teacher autonomy have prospered. The campaigns have called attention to the ways in which autonomy has aggravated and reinforced inequalities in the classroom, and how collegial or professional norms must play a stronger role in shaping the decisions of teachers. There are many decisions about what to teach, whom to teach, or what standards and expectations individual teachers should not make alone in their classrooms without a strong sense of professional responsibility and the guidance of professional standards. Teachers make decisions in these areas constantly. They display responsible autonomy when recognizing the dilemmas inherent in fostering the learning of a classroom of children. They demonstrate professional responsibility when reflecting on the tradeoffs they must make in deciding to work with one child over another, or with one group rather than another, or identify and use a particular diagnostic or teaching strategy with a certain student. Effective teaching depends upon such professional autonomy and the responsible exercise of that autonomy.

The question is not whether autonomy is good or bad, for it is both. This sort of question distracts scholars and practitioners, and particularly, policymakers, from appreciating the complexity of the concept of autonomy and leads to proposals that would leave teachers straight-jacketed, with little opportunity to exercise responsible professional discretion. Such proposals would inadvertently discourage effective teachers and accelerate their defection to other occupations.

Because of problems with rewards, autonomy, and working conditions, many teachers question the wisdom of sustaining their commitment to teaching. Roughly one-half of Farber's (1984a) teachers acknowledged that they would not enter teaching if they were in a position to choose all over again, a posture slightly more common among urban than suburban teachers (see also Wangberg, Metzger, & Levitov, 1982; Duke, 1984, p. 17).

This apparent willingness to leave teaching has become more wide-spread over the past generation. A National Education Association survey of teachers across the nation in 1956 revealed that both male and female teachers were satisfied with their career decision. When asked, "Suppose you could go back to your college days and start all over again; in view of your present knowledge, would you become a teacher?" three out of four answered affirmatively ("The Status of the American Public School Teacher," 1957, p. 38).

Such disparities clearly affect how these teachers and other adults assess the desirability of a career in education for their own children. Teachers are about evenly divided on this matter for their daughters: 43 percent would like to have their daughters pursue a teaching career, 46 percent would not. They were more prejudiced against a teaching career for their sons: only 31 percent approved, while 59 percent reacted un-favorably. The public appeared to approve of a teaching career for their children more consistently than teachers did. Nearly 50 percent agreed that they would like their sons and daughters to enter teaching (Gallup, A., 1985, p. 324).

For the larger public, a career in teaching for one's children has also lost some of its appeal over the past decade and a half. When asked whether or not they would like their children to become teachers, 75 per-cent of the public reacted favorably to the proposal in 1969 (at the peak of teaching's popularity); the approval rate appears to have fallen steadily ever since (Duke, 1984, p. 19).

There is some evidence, however sporadic and tentative, which sug-gests that, instead of actively leaving the profession, many high school teachers have progressively disengaged themselves from their academic roles and responsibilities. Like many of their students, some teachers appear to have moved high school more to the periphery of their lives. They adjust their work schedules and responsibilities to accommodate their families, hobbies, and, increasingly, other jobs. Absenteeism rates for teachers have worsened over the past decade. These generalizations must be considered speculative, but they clearly have serious implications for raising academic standards. Cusick (1983), who spent a great deal of time exploring the daily activities of teachers from several high schools, concluded that "just as one was free to decide what to do in the classroom, one was free to decide how important teaching was in his or her life, and how he or she would integrate teaching with other important life-elements" (p. 95). He found that "teaching was only one of a number of central roles" (p. 95). In addition to performing one or more demanding jobs at school beyond teaching, such as coaching or serving as a union representative, many teachers held full-time second jobs. They worked at the post office or the telephone company, or owned and managed a driving school or a tax accounting business. It is difficult to assess the extent to which such added responsibilities detracted from these teachers' ability or time or energy to maximize the academic achievement of their students, and one should not presume that a high school teacher should only teach. It seems reasonable to conclude, nevertheless, that the bargain or arrangement that often limits academic learning is affected by the place and meaning of high school in the lives of teachers as well as their students. Such actions by teachers are rarely reported in the literature. Their implications are so compelling, however, that it is crucial for researchers to examine critically the frequency, nature, and consequences of teacher disengagement (see, for example, Lanier, 1986).

TEACHER EDUCATION AND ACCREDITATION

Having examined both extrinsic and intrinsic rewards as possible reasons for the difficulty that most schools face in recruiting and retaining qualified teachers, it is appropriate to turn to the institutions responsible for preparing and certifying prospective teachers and the organizations responsible for monitoring the teacher education process. If qualified teachers are difficult to attract because of widely held perceptions of eroding and humiliating extrinsic and intrinsic rewards, perhaps teacher education programs and accrediting agencies can at least prevent schools from being overwhelmed by incompetent teachers with no other professional options.

The quality of the teaching force depends in part upon teacher education programs effectively performing their training and credentialing functions at both the preservice and inservice levels. Critics have faulted teacher education institutions for generations, indicting them for performing neither of their fundamental responsibilities adequately. Historically, particularly throughout much of the nineteenth and early twentieth centuries, the vast majority of teachers possessed a meager professional preparation. It was common for most teachers to be trained in regional, county, or local normal schools. These institutions, which were established initially during the common school movement of the mid-nineteenth century, were ordinarily two-year courses of study. Despite their popularity, the normal schools were not particularly reputable institutions (Hofstadter, 1962).

Data collected during the 1920s and early 1930s suggest that the educational attainment levels of school teachers began to improve after World War I. This may have resulted from improvements in working conditions and salaries which began to attract prospective teachers willing to endure the hardship of extended training. It may also have resulted from the opportunity provided by the teacher surplus of the late 1920s and early 1930s to strengthen admissions standards and raise hiring qualifications (Evenden, Gamble, & Blue, 1935).

Over the ensuing decades, the level of training received by teachers improved steadily. Studies of teacher preparation completed during the 1950s disclosed that increased state certification requirements had an immediate impact: by 1955, 70 percent of the elementary school and 97 percent of the high school teachers had earned bachelor's degrees (at least in the 34 states surveyed) (Armstrong, 1957, p. 280; Maul, 1956). In addition, the locus of teacher training was beginning to shift. The proportion of elementary teachers trained in regular colleges and universities increased from roughly 29 percent to 77 percent between 1931 and 1955, and among secondary teachers the comparable figure rose only slightly from 70 percent to 81 percent, since few high school teachers had been trained in normal schools and teachers' colleges in the 1930s (Armstrong, 1957, p. 281; Maul, 1956).

During the 1960s and 1970s the trend of enforcing higher certification standards, combined with salary schedules that rewarded advanced educational attainment, continued to improve the overall professional qualifications of the teaching force. In 1961, 85 percent of all teachers held bachelor's degrees; more than 99 percent possessed at least a bachelor's degree in 1976 (Grant & Snyder, 1984, p. 51).

Although the dramatic improvement in the educational credentials of teachers launched a campaign of self-congratulation among educators, other groups began to apply a different perspective on the issue of teacher quality. As bachelor's degrees from reputable universities became almost universal among teachers, at least those recruited after 1930, a number of critics began to call attention to the measured intelligence of prospective teachers and to contrast it unfavorably with the estimated mental ability of their counterparts who aspired to other fields, particularly the more traditional established professions and the burgeoning technical fields in engineering and science. There is a tradition of scholarship that has attempted to asssess the relative intellectual or academic ability of prospective teachers. One of the first notable analyses, by William Learned and Ben Wood (1938), argued that when contrasted with all college students, prospective teachers scored below average on achievement tests. Learned and Wood contrasted the scores of seniors in teachers' colleges with scores earned by high school seniors and cruelly and embarrassingly concluded that "many pupils surpass the would-be teachers" (1938, p. 340). Overall, the researchers argued that the situation was "deplorable" and maintained that they believed the evidence supported their conclusion that teachers "have inferior minds" (Koerner, 1963, p. 40; Learned & Wood, 1938, pp. 39, 43, 64, 351).

Subsequent research on the intellectual ability of prospective teachers routinely reached similar conclusions. Local studies appear to corroborate these national surveys of academic talent. A study of students in teacher-training institutions in New York State, for example, found that the average high school academic performance of the prospective teachers "exceeded only those of the group who dropped out of college with failing marks, and that the average academic aptitude of the teacher groups ... exceeded only that of the group who failed in college" (Bicknell, 1959, p. 25; cited in Koerner, 1963, p. 45; Wolfle, 1954). At more prestigious universities the pattern was similar. A sample of the Harvard–Radcliffe student body revealed that "very few students were attracted to teaching at all and that those who were attracted came from the lower academic ranks" (Koerner, 1963, p. 45; Handlin, 1957, pp. 22-23).

As a consequence, regardless of the legitimate qualifications of teachers, the public image of practitioners' intellectual attributes and their training has detrimentally affected the field's attractiveness to potential recruits and has made many employed teachers uncomfortable with their position. The reputation of teacher education programs across university campuses has made it difficult for talented students to justify pursuing a career in teaching, as their friends from the disciplines, their professors, and their parents press them to defend their choice of a career less demanding than that for which their presumed intellectual abilities qualified them, a career beneath their academic stature.

Prospective teacher education students have struggled with this status problem for decades. They were given some relief during the 1960s, when many talented youth appeared to have been attracted by missionary ideals associated with teaching. They were willing to discount the allegations of intellectual inferiority that surrounded the development of teacher training during the 1950s and 1960s. Some critics may have assumed that the involvement of talented youth would elevate the status of teacher education, even if it could not actually improve much of the real substance.

It may also have been that teacher educators found themselves in fortuitous circumstances during the 1950s and 1960s. Because of the serious shortage of teachers between 1948 and 1972, coupled with the rapid improvement in salaries and other benefits associated with teaching, it may have been that many more talented youth were attracted to teacher education programs. As long as the opportunity remained, youth with strong intellectual ability were willing to endure undistinguished training programs in order to secure increasingly desirable positions after they graduated.

When shortage turned to surplus during the early 1970s, and teaching's material gains secured during the 1960s vanished with the high inflation rates and economic contraction after 1973, some of the most talented youth abandoned education in favor of opportunities opening in other fields. Certainly this was true of many academically talented young women, who were discouraged both by the relative loss of opportunity in teaching and the simultaneous expansion of access to high status, high reward careers in other fields (even though the two developments may have had nothing to do with one another). Data collected by the National Center for Educational Statistics suggest that although many youths abandoned preservice (undergraduate) teacher education, the defection rate was greater among females. Overall, between 1971 and 1981, of all bachelor's degrees awarded, those earned by education majors declined from 21 percent to 11.6 percent. Among females, the proportion who earned degrees in education dropped from 36.1 percent to 17.5 percent (Feistritzer, 1983, p. 80). Precise evidence about the intellectual qualifications of those young women who defected from teacher education during the 1970s has not been made conveniently available, except in the work of Schlechty and Vance for North Carolina. Nevertheless, it is possible to infer, from the fact that the enrollment of females in other fields (at least quantitatively more selective and rigorous than teacher education) increased parallel to the decline in teacher education, that many talented women comprised a disproportionate share of the defectors.

Of course the problems with teacher education are not exclusively those associated with the academic or intellectual quality of its students. Teacher educators themselves, the faculties of teacher training and certification institutions, must shoulder some of the responsibility for the field's problematic image. There is a widespread misperception of the identity of teacher educators; most critics have commonly identified them as faculty members in colleges and departments of education generally, and teachers of pedagogy or supervisors of student teachers specifically. In reality, virtually all college and university faculty members who teach undergraduates are "teacher educators," since prospective teachers normally take between 60 and 80 percent of their preservice coursework in the liberal arts and sciences. Professional coursework constitutes only a small portion of each prospective teacher's program. Critics of teacher education, and the larger public as well, consistently fail to appreciate this and assume that the training of teachers occurs exclusively in colleges or departments of education (Lanier, 1986).

With obvious exceptions, on most university campuses professional teacher educators, in the popular, limited definition of the term, suffer in terms of status relative to their counterparts in the arts and sciences and most other professional schools. This status differential is often compounded by inequities in the formulas used to allocate university financial resources across departments and colleges. Such formulas consistently provide significantly less money to education faculties per student than to other professional schools and arts disciplines.

These academic status and funding inequities, and the popular image as well, seem to be based upon an unenviable portrait of the abilities, preparation, and contributions of teacher education faculties in particular and the teacher training enterprises in general. Identification with the elementary and secondary schools is something which institutions of higher education have done their best to avoid for generations. Graduate and research aspirations tend to set the norms in most institutions of higher education, and even faculty members who are only intermittently or tangentially involved in such activities are not enthusiastic about looking downward to the application of their disciplinary knowledge in the public schools. They prefer to pretend an association with higher status teaching and learning. Aggravating this widely shared perspective, held even by many teacher educators, is the fact that the training and careers of education faculty members have tended to differ from those of their colleagues in the arts and sciences. As sociologists have suggested, many teacher educators were former public school teachers, often from working-class backgrounds, who pursued and earned their doctorates in part-time programs which encouraged their fantasies about further upward mobility. Many disciplinary-based faculty members have been sharply critical of the graduate training received by teacher educators; they have claimed for decades that doctorates in education, even Ph.D.s, were awarded on the basis of insubstantial coursework and spurious scholarship. Once they receive professorial appointments, the critique continues, teacher educators conduct virtually no research and lack the intellectual resources to keep abreast of their fields but instead teach content-thin methods classes and observe practicing teachers. They are considered to be conspicuously untheoretical, preoccupied as they are with pragmatic and action-oriented issues and actually "devalue" academic pursuits. A number of researchers have confirmed the accuracy of this portrait; the presiding image appears to be justified, at least in the vast majority of the 1300 institutions that train and certify teachers. They have further speculated on the disturbing reciprocal influence between a teacher education faculty with such an image and the recruitment of academically talented students into teaching (see, for example, Lanier, 1986; Ducharme & Agne, 1982; Prichard, Fen, & Buxton, 1971; Conant, 1963; Borrowman, 1956).

Considering these trends, therefore, it is evident that teacher education programs have had some difficulty in protecting access to the profession. They have traditionally been willing to enforce only relatively minimal admissions and graduation standards, and the reputation of the training that they offer has had the effect of alienating many potentially talented teachers. Unfortunately, the presence of academically weaker students in many teacher education programs has also undermined their appeal to intellectually talented undergraduates. This has led to a troubling reciprocal relationship between teacher education programs and their clienteles. The ability of teacher education programs to raise standards and to offer more rigorous content is usually constrained by the aspirations and abilities of students in these programs; yet some students are attracted to, and others are repelled from, teacher education programs because of the status and image they have in society in general and on university campuses in particular. This relationship between the programs and their students has made it difficult to reform teacher training institutions substantially. And since the opportunities provided by the teacher surplus of the 1970s were not exploited by institutions of higher education to reform or to improve radically the education of prospective teachers, it is likely that the developing shortage of the 1980s and 1990s will make the improvement process even more problematic.

Theoretically, the agencies that are charged with the responsiblity of monitoring the performance of teacher education programs could have helped to strengthen the formal professional training of teachers by enforcing standards and practices that could serve to reserve access to teaching positions to those possessing reputable credentials. However, in a study of the accreditation practices of the National Council for Accreditation of Teacher Education (NCATE), Wheeler (1980) found numerous weaknesses which resulted in the accreditation of many inferior teacher training programs. Visiting team and council members generally looked to see whether a task or function was performed at all, not, as the NCATE standards required, whether it was being performed well. Many requirements in the standards were never evaluated, some were interpreted in favor of the institution rather than on the basis of actual program quality, and standards were applied inconsistently. These findings ultimately question NCATE accreditation as an indicator of quality. Wheeler's study also showed that the NCATE's effect on program quality was marginal, at best, given the weakness of the organization's influence.

These weaknesses are important because until the 1970s NCATE's accreditation standards set the minimum for state expectations, since states used NCATE accreditation as a basis for granting certification to teachers who emigrated from other states. Moreover, until the mid-1970s most state departments of education lacked sufficient staff to conduct on-site reviews of programs of education; this meant that they relied heavily on NCATE's accreditation decisions (part of NCATE's accreditation process involves an on-site visit). In fact, several states (Arkansas, Georgia, North Dakota, and Wyoming) continue to rely *entirely* on NCATE accreditation for certification, or accept NCATE accreditation in lieu of state evaluation (Flakus-Mosqueda, 1983).

While state departments of education have increased their oversight activities since the mid-1970s, there is nothing to show that their monitoring efforts have improved programs of professional education. In fact, the existing evidence suggests that in practice their standards are as low as NCATE's. As one part of his study of whether NCATE made a difference in improving the quality of professional programs in schools of education, Wheeler (1980) studied a sample of schools denied NCATE accreditation. He found that every program denied NCATE accreditation enjoyed state approval at the time of denial. As a result of NCATE's actions, only four of the sixteen state departments of education intervened, and then only to a limited extent. In the remaining twelve states, nothing happened. Programs remained approved, and teachers were graduated and given certificates to teach (pp. 192-93).

A U. S. General Accounting Office report (1979) has described in detail the weaknesses of three other national and four of the six regional agencies that accredit, on a university-wide basis, institutions that train prospective teachers. The GAO examined how and to what degree such agencies actually evaluated institutional policies and practices that affected students and the public as consumers or that influenced teacher education program quality, at least indirectly. In brief, the GAO found that one or more of the following abusive practices occurred in the schools it encountered: 1) questionable admission and grading policies; 2) use of inadequately trained teachers; 3) failure to offer listed courses; 4) lack of information for students or prospective students on attrition and graduation requirements; and 5) false or misleading advertising (pp. 24-35). Such abusive practices were judged likely to affect program quality.

If extrinsic rewards are weak, if intrinsic rewards are declining, if agencies responsible for training and monitoring the quality of teachers entering the profession fail to do their job, perhaps it is not so surprising that attraction and retention of qualified talented teachers are two major problems facing education today.

8 ☴ Teacher Reforms

One way to respond to the prevalence of social relations over academic content in so many high school classrooms, and to the increasing disengagement of teachers from academic teaching, is to address the caliber of the teaching force. But are teacher examinations, performance pay schemes, and changes in certification requirements effective ways to attract and retain talented teachers or to weed out the unqualified? Even more to the point, do they really hold the promise of a renegotiation of the bargain in favor of more academic content? Or are they simply weak proxies for solutions to problems that require more structural change? This chapter addresses such questions, first by examining new incentives and then by reviewing new requirements.

INCENTIVES

State and local school districts have taken steps to improve the quality of teaching by restructuring incentives in two ways: salary increases and expanded inservice opportunities.

English (1983-1984) argues that it is the average salary of different potential occupations that captures a prospective recruit's eye. If we need to draw better people into teaching, what would it take to make teaching more competitive with other jobs that require equivalent training? Odden (1984) suggests that it might take an increase of $10,000 in the average salary for all 2.1 million public school teachers—leading to an initial total cost nationally of more than $20 billion.

By mid-1985, a third of the states had appropriated increases for teacher salaries, primarily by raising base pay rates by 9 to 15 percent or by adding $1,000 to $2,000 to each teacher's salary. Such increases also served to improve the starting salaries of beginning teachers since they raised all salary levels. So far California is the only state to pass legislation increasing just the salaries of beginning teachers; one part of its $800 million reform package for the elementary and secondary grades would allow the state to reimburse local school districts for the costs of increasing beginning teacher salaries up to a maximum of $18,000 (U.S. Department of Education, 1983a).

Some local school districts undertook their own initiatives. For example, the Dallas Board of Education voted a tax increase to improve salaries for teachers; in Los Angeles, the school district raised salary scales for beginning teachers (U.S. Department of Education, 1983a, pp. 102-103), and in Houston, the school district proposed a three-part program affecting staff, students, and the community. The Houston Plan calls for beginning salaries to be increased from $16,000 to $21,000 and, by 1986-87, a salary of $34,000 for teachers with 10 years of experience (U.S. Department of Education, 1984).

In addition to attracting better recruits into teaching, higher salaries might also help retain good teachers in the profession. Goodlad (1984) found that while "money was not a major reason teachers gave for entering teaching, it ranked second as a reason for leaving" (p. 172). Goodlad speculated that "anticipating rewards intrinsic to the work, teachers begin with the willingness to forego high salaries. However, when confronted with the frustration of their expectations, the fact that they are paid less than the bus drivers who bring their students to school may become a considerable source of dissatisfaction as well" (p. 172). In other words, for teachers who experience frustration in their efforts to shift the bargain away from social relations to academic content, low salaries add insult to injury.

Are the salary increases, at least at the state level, really as significant as they first sound? For most states, increases widely reported as major accomplishments represent nothing more than ongoing practices that signify the availability of few real new funds for salary improvement. For example, in 1984 Alabama's legislature approved a 15 percent pay increase for teachers. What was not reported was that most of the funds for salaries are not raised locally, but rather appropriated by the state legislature and then allocated to school districts. Moreover, in 1983 the legislature refused to increase teacher salaries at all, so its action in 1984 represented only a 7.5 percent increase when considered over two years. In 1982 the percentage increase was 16; for 1981 it had been nothing. As one state department official put it, "If there had been no national study we would have gotten the same raise" (Interview, June, 1984). In Georgia, the state sets the salary scale for teachers (school districts can add supplements), so it is nothing new for the states to announce increases. Since the usual increase is 5 to 8 percent, the 10 percent announced by the state and heralded in the media is put in a different light. Given these examples, it seems that the increases have been inflated out of proportion to their actual value, particularly since teachers lost purchasing power in the '70s.

The argument for making teachers' salaries more competitive with other professions over a period of time is compelling. From a short-term perspective, however, it is understandable why states and local school districts would not act to increase average salaries if doing so would simply reward mediocrity. If the present corps of teachers is at least in part responsible for the state of American education, what guarantee will there be that doubling their salaries will lead to improved outcomes? It may be that those who budget teachers' salaries are caught in a "Catch-22" situation, between the need to see improved outcomes in the short run, and the need to substantially increase salaries over the long run in order to recruit into teaching persons who can improve outcomes.

Some of the resistance to increasing teacher salaries may also derive from skepticism regarding the professional nature of teaching. It can be argued that teaching is an easy field to enter and should not be compared with the $40,000 beginning salaries available to those few talented students who compiled outstanding undergraduate and law school academic records. Given the number of teachers (in excess of 2.1 million) and their relative lack of autonomy and individual contracting of work, teachers might be more appropriately compared with workers in the automobile or steel industries than with doctors or lawyers. Teachers, finally, only work 180 to 190 days a year; persons in other professions work many more. To what degree the public holds these views cannot be determined. Our research suggests that they are relatively commonplace among administrators in school districts.

Moreover, it has only been hypothesized that prospective teachers weigh average salaries of different potential occupations when making decisions about what field to enter. To a new recruit, the starting salary may be just as important or even more so than the average.* Although a quarter of the states have "increased" salaries for all teachers, and in so doing have raised the bottom rung as well, our earlier discussion showed that such increases do not appear to be as substantial as initially reported. Those few states that provided additional increments for starting salaries or focused specifically on this area (for example, California) are notable for their scarcity. In the future, teacher unions may well play an important role in actually "backloading" salary schedules (Monk & Jacobson, 1985), since, as one state official put it: "local unions have been able to increase the upper end of the salary scale in negotiations as they responded to their

---

*The issue of whether salaries play a role *at all* in teacher decisions to enter or leave the profession is a subject of considerable controversy and deserves more research attention. We believe the quality of the work environment plays the determining role in such decisions and that salaries are of secondary importance.

graying faculty. It's the beginning teachers' salaries that have lagged behind" (Interview, March 22, 1984).

In addition to salary increases which affect all teachers are performance-based pay schemes such as merit pay and career ladders which offer various financial rewards. Merit pay is a bonus paid to an individual for outstanding classroom teaching or to a group of teachers in a school whose students perform beyond expectation. Such awards are made on the basis of administrative evaluation or written examinations. Teachers receiving such awards remain in the classroom full time. In contrast, career ladders provide additional pay for teachers who assume responsibility for duties such as mentoring beginning teachers or developing new curricula, in addition to their classroom teaching. Opportunities for assuming such tasks customarily depend on promotion through various rungs on a career ladder from "beginning" to "master" teacher. A team of evaluators, ordinarily consisting of teachers and administrators, determines who will occupy each rung. While the merit pay idea initially caught the public's eye, only one state, Florida, has actually passed such a plan.* "Meritorious" teachers are rewarded in two ways: with $3,000 individual bonuses and with bonuses for teaching in a "meritorious" school. Eligibility for individual bonuses requires four years of teaching experience (at least two in Florida), performance in the upper quartile on a subject-area examination, and a performance evaluation. Awards are to be made to teachers receiving the highest scores on the performance evaluation (estimated to be 6,333 teachers for the 1984-1985 academic year) (Rodman, 1985; "Teachers Revise Teacher-Pay Scheme," 1984). It was not unexpected that almost immediately Florida's two teacher unions filed lawsuits to halt the implementation of the merit-pay system, arguing that the merit-pay scheme conflicted with the rights of teachers under collective bargaining agreements negotiated with local school districts. What was unanticipated was the discovery that the state's "Teacher of the Year" and one of the state finalists for the national Teacher-in-Space competition failed to qualify for merit pay because neither had scored high

---

*California, as part of its 1983 omnibus school reform law, created a financial incentive to reward schools for improvements in the academic performance of their students. Under the program, high schools can earn bonuses of up to $400 per student if 93 percent of a schools' seniors take the California Assessment Program (CAP) test and if the school's average scores improve compared to the previous year (Fallon, 1985). Since schools are permitted to use the money as they see fit (except to sign a long-term contract), teachers might not benefit and so for the purposes of this chapter this approach is not considered a merit program for teachers.

enough on their evaluations. In addition, none of the 50 teachers at Florida's Terry Parker High School scored in the top 25 percent on their evaluations, yet the U.S. Department of Education had honored the school in its Secondary School Recognition Program (Currence, 1985). Such results raised serious questions about the efficacy of Florida's merit program. Presumably, a primary goal of merit pay is the attraction and retention of the best teachers. However, with some teacher organizations so opposed to the concept that the program is being litigated, it is questionable whether its intended effect of bolstering the morale of practicing teachers is being achieved. Moreover, evidence that criteria for receiving merit pay do not correlate with more commonsense judgments of teacher merit suggests that the program, which had a powerful political appeal, in practice may fail to recognize the very people it was designed to reward.

None of the new merit-pay proposals recognizes the overwhelming impact of intrinsic rewards for practicing teachers. Although low salaries may be a powerful variable in determing who is attracted to the teaching profession, the merit-pay concept appears to be targeted more directly at veteran teachers. However, the literature indicates that for these teachers it is the satisfaction gained from such variables as interpersonal relations within the classroom and mastery of professional decision-making in daily work that are crucial. It is interesting to note that Florida, the first state to adopt a statewide merit-pay scheme, was also the first state to become heavily involved in the type of state-mandated instructional delivery systems inherent in the use of student minimum competency tests to determine high school diploma awards. These programs rest in large part upon the notion that teacher instructional autonomy must be substantially reduced because it cannot be trusted.

The idea of linking merit-pay bonuses to school-wide improvement efforts is being implemented in Florida as well as in communities in other states. School-based awards under Florida's plan work in the following way. Twenty million dollars is divided among the state's 67 school districts on the basis of student enrollment. Ten million dollars is awarded to the top 25 percent of the schools in each district, and such funds are earmarked for personnel in these schools. The remaining $10 million may be used to provide incentives to schools not judged "meritorious." Meritorious schools will be determined by student scores on state, regional, or national tests as well as other criteria developed by the local school district (Tregend, 1984a, 1984b). Districts in other states use similar criteria. In Richmond, Virginia, for example, schools that show the greatest improvement in achievement on standardized tests, attendance, and other factors receive a "school merit award" of four dollars to ten dollars per pupil. All employees of schools receiving such an award are given a "personnel merit award" ranging from one-half to three percent of their salaries. The Dallas, Texas, school district, during the 1983-1984 school year, spent $3 million in leftover tax revenues for bonuses of $1,500 to professional staff and $750 to support staff. Bonuses went to personnel in the 25 schools with the best teacher and student attendance records and the highest scores on the Iowa Test of Basic Skills (U.S. Department of Education, 1984).

To the extent that merit-pay plans rely upon student performance on standardized tests as a measure of teacher (or building or district) merit, most teachers know that they can significantly improve test scores of many students by either drilling them for the test or by teaching simple test-taking skills. Such efforts do not increase the extent of teacher or student engagement with academic skills acquisition but, instead, serve as another mechanism for beating the system.

If responses in Louisiana are typical for other states, however, merit-pay bonuses are not being considered seriously by most school districts. Wimpelberg and Ginsberg's (1985) survey of all school districts in Louisiana a year after the publication of *A Nation at Risk* (National Commission on Excellence in Education, 1983) revealed that more than 90 percent of the superintendents were not considering merit pay as a means to improve teaching.

The current momentum clearly favors career ladders over merit-pay plans. By February, 1985, 13 states had approved such proposals with two states, Tennessee and Florida, having developed their projects past the pilot stage (Bridgeman, 1985). The career ladder segment of Tennessee's ten-point "Better Schools Program" has an allocation of $50 million for FY 84-85. The five-step ladder pays annual bonuses ranging from $500 to $7,000. Although new teachers must join the program, veteran teachers may choose whether they want to enter the program and retain the option of backing out of the alternative or staying in the present system. Each step is rewarded by a monetary bonus which varies depending on the number of months the person works. Thus a career level III (master teacher) would receive a $4,000 bonus under a 10-month (standard) contract, $5,000 for an 11-month contract, and $7,000 for a 12-month contract. During those additional months teachers would have new responsibilities in the area of professional and curricular development (*New York Times,* Feb. 26, 1984, p. 15). Programs from probationary status through career level III and the accompanying salary bonuses are the result of performance evaluations that are competency-based and applied by evaluators (teachers and other school personnel who have undergone training and have been released for a year from their classrooms or other responsibilities for such purposes (French, 1984-1985).

To further stimulate states, local school districts, and other institutions to develop performance-based pay plans (merit or career ladder), the Education Department awarded 51 grants totalling $1 million on March 19, 1984 (*New York Times,* March 11, 1984, p. 14).

What potential do policies involving merit pay and career ladders (or performance pay proposals) have to improve our schools? In terms of economics, there is little to differentiate the two, since both rely on supplemental pay to a select number of teachers. The attraction of career-ladder proposals stems from their potential to avoid at least one of the more blatant possibilities for abuse inherent in the merity-pay concept. In response to initial fears that evaluations for merit pay would lead to administrative abuse as principals rewarded only compliant teachers, proposals for career ladders have promised to include teachers as meaningful partners in the evaluation process. In addition, the career-ladder concept has the added attraction of potentially enriching the profession by expanding the responsibilities of "master teachers" to include mentoring and curriculum development during the regular academic year as well as during the summer.

What about the potential of either approach to attract or retain quality teachers? Their greatest contribution will likely be in retaining good teachers, in part for financial reasons, but in part because of their potential for affecting the working conditions of teachers. It is here that the contrasts between merit-pay and career-ladder proposals are particularly sharp, according to those who have studied such ventures. The career-ladder concept offers a chance to alter fundamentally the instructional nature of teaching by providing creative outlets for teachers who are ready and able to assume new challenges. Instead of seeking outside employment to supplement income and to relieve routine, master teachers can presumably assume new responsibilities that break down the isolated nature of classroom teaching and alter authority relations within schools. In contrast, the merit-pay concept perpetuates and even aggravates continued competition and insularity.

Although the work environment for some teachers may be improved through career-ladder proposals, it remains open to question whether a system designed around individual competition and individual reward can actually promote collective organizational improvement for students and teachers alike. Effective schools (few as they are and as problematic to create) are characterized by their consistent focus and purpose. Effective teachers plan cooperatively, work collectively, and, above all, recognize their interdependence. The values that underlie career-ladder proposals are at best conflicting: new roles to promote a more effective work environment where cooperation and assistance play a central role, but recruitment and rewards are based on the selection of a small group of individuals. If it is true, as Susan Johnson (1984) warns, that "competitive reward systems encourage independence rather than cooperation and divert employees' commitment from group goals to personal goals" (p. 184), then the teacher "autonomy" and its implications for teaching so graphically described in the beginning of this book may simply be reinforced, albeit in new forms.

Of course, merit-pay plans, which deliberately increase the competitive nature of the workplace, have even more serious failings from this perspective. The competitive orientation and pejorative judgments that result are given by teacher unions as their basic reason for opposing merit-pay plans and their cautious views toward career ladders. For example, in criticizing Florida's merit-pay plan for teachers in meritorious schools, Jake Moore, a local union official, said they would not participate "in any plan that is inherently divisive, one that pits one group against another" (Tregend, 1984a, p. 27).

Arthur Wise and Linda Darling-Hammond (1984/1985) made these same points in their extensive study of teacher evaluation practices and raise a second, equally telling problem for either scheme: the evaluation methods and underlying criteria for determining who is a "good" teacher. "Performance-based pay schemes assume that differential rewards and sanctions will improve individual teaching and enhance the profession as a whole. They further assume the existence of teacher evaluation methods that can fairly and effectively differentiate among teachers" (p. 29). Neither assumption, they argued, is necessarily correct. Instead, the utility of performance pay relates directly to the value teachers place on the rewards themselves and on the credibility of the evaluation process on which the rewards are based. They found that "valued rewards and credible evaluation are more likely to emerge from a professional approach to teacher evaluation than from the more traditional, bureaucratic approach. Substantial changes in typical evaluation practices will have to occur if performance rewards are to be both definable and effective in improving teaching" (p. 29).

Such changes included improvements in evaluator expertise and the evaluation criteria themselves, so judgments can go beyond whether order is maintained to questions about how well a teacher plans to impart academic knowledge, accounts for student levels of development and prior learning, and achieves immediate and long-range goals of instruction. They also believed evaluation systems must be able to determine whether strategies and techniques actually meet the changing needs of

students over time, integrate different objectives, and foster the development of skills and abilities.

But short-term criteria must also be supplemented with criteria that
can only be assessed over a longer period of time. Thus they argued that
an effective evaluation design should include a longitudinal assessment of
teacher plans, classroom activities, and student performances and products so that judgments about relative competence instead of minimum
competence can be made. Such methods, in their opinion, require non-
standardized applications of differentiated criteria, since research on
teaching has demonstrated that effective behaviors vary for different
grade levels, subject areas, types of students, and instructional goals.

Recent experience in Florida and Tennessee should be unsettling for
those concerned about teacher evaluation, especially for "Master
Teacher" plans. Toch (1984) describes the following events in Florida:

> On January 26, a Thursday, Robert Graff, the principal of Morgan E.
> Fitzgerald Middle School in Largo, Florida, sat in the auditorium of a
> Tampa high school, craning his neck with 500 others to see one of four
> television screens played on the auditorium stage.
>
> The previous Friday, the state had directed its school systems to select
> administrators to help evaluate applicants for incentive pay under
> Florida's new master-teacher plan. Because of a tight time schedule,
> those chosen, the state said, were to take a preliminary test of their
> ability to rate teachers the following Thursday. Mr. Graff was not asked
> to be an evaluator until Tuesday, two days before the test.
>
> In the auditorium, he spent an hour straining to focus on the videotape
> that was shown of teachers working in a classroom and trying to analyze
> their teaching strengths and weaknesses. Then he took a one-hour
> examination on teaching skills. Mr. Graff and others will soon take a
> second two-part test to determine whether they qualify to be certified by
> Florida to evaluate master-teacher candidates.
>
> Mr. Graff called the state's handling of things in January as "hap-
> hazard," an opinion shared by others. (pp. 1, 14)

Toch also learned that in Tennessee the consultant, hired by the State
Department of Education to review the evaluation procedures to be used
in the state's master-teacher plan, had resigned in November, 1983,
because she felt the state was moving to implement the procedures
without first ensuring that they were reliable. "Because of the political

pressure they are under from the Governor and the Commissioner (of education) to get the system in place by September, they haven't been able to proceed with any kind of scientific rigor," Susan J. Rosenholtz, the consultant, complained. "It will be virtually impossible to develop reliable evaluation standards between now and then" (Toch, 1984, p. 14).

Questionable evaluation standards can lead to one of two responses by those more directly affected: withdrawal or increased lobbying to shape the requirements to benefit the largest number of its members. Perhaps that explains in part the success of teacher organizations in Florida in reducing member participation in the merit-play plan and the large numbers of teachers in Tennessee who have announced they are willing to pursue the "toe in the water" option, that is, the right to enter the system, back out later, and return to the present system. Interviews with union officials in both states show their clear intent in developing a system that benefits the largest number of their members (Interviews, March, 1984). Other reasons for participation could include the incentives, the realization that if they don't get in now, available slots will soon be filled up, and current public pressure. Beginning teachers have no choice in states and school districts where career-ladder or master-teacher proposals are being implemented; they are required to participate.

Although many questions remain regarding whether either plan will improve the likelihood of retaining qualified teachers, the important question remains: What effect will these proposals have on the bargain struck between teachers and students in every classroom? The merit-pay concept could affect the bargain negatively if compliant teachers rather than excellent teachers were rewarded or if the evaluation criteria were to become so watered down that all teachers could qualify for the highest rewards. Cohen and Murnane (1985), for example, found considerable evidence for this last point in their study of merit-pay plans that have endured over time and predate the current wave of reform. These school districts expanded the criteria to include such things as extracurricular activities, professional development, community service, and good relations with parents, thereby making such programs more politically palatable. In effect "merit pay" was redefined to mean extra pay for extra work, not excellence in classroom teaching, and more and more teachers received "merit pay." Moreover, even where excellent teachers are rewarded, staff morale could decline in part because of some teachers being passed over, and in part because many students and parents would seek classes from those deemed "meritorious" teachers rather than others. The advantage of the merit-pay idea, assuming excellent teachers are identified, however, is that such teachers remain in the classroom rather than leaving for other duties.

Career-ladder proposals could create in-school alternatives for creatively talented teachers, thus reducing the exit of such persons to other fields. Under certain plans, however, excellent teachers will leave the classroom at least part of the time to pursue their new roles of mentoring, curriculum development, and evaluation. Where this occurs, students in those classrooms will suffer. It remains to be seen whether school-wide benefits will outweigh such losses to students in those classrooms, especially given the individual orientation of incentives in such plans.

A third form of financial incentive is responsive to the career-option interest of some teachers. Market-sensitive pay (English, 1983-1984) means paying teachers in some fields, such as math and science, more money simply because there are fewer qualified teachers in those fields. Such a strategy recognizes the law of supply and demand and the principle of scarcity. By the end of 1984, only a few states and a handful of districts had such proposals under consideration (U.S. Department of Education, 1984, pp. 73, 96).

In contrast to the spate of salary supplements described above, most states have been active in providing aid for prospective teachers in selected fields in the form of scholarships and forgivable loans. By 1985, half the states had such programs. Many are designed to attract talented math and science students into teaching, but some have broadened their focus to include other teaching fields as well (Bridgeman, 1985). The typical program is one of forgivable loans up to a certain amount (usually $2,000-$2,500), provided the person actually teaches math or science in that state for a certain period of time.

Turning from financial incentives to efforts to improve the quality of teaching through expanded inservice activities, we see that the record, in general, shows new initiatives targeted toward specific content areas such as math and science for a limited number of teachers. Thus, during 1984, at least one-third of the states created summer institutes or inservice programs during the regular academic year in order to meet expected shortages in these areas because of increased graduation requirements. Costs were either shared between the state and local school districts, as in North Dakota, or borne entirely by the state, as in Iowa. At least one school district, Richmond, Virginia, is using its own funds to retrain existing staff to meet shortages in other areas (U.S. Department of Education, 1984; Flakus-Mosqueda, 1983).

Several states have passed laws mandating certain competencies (such as the District of Columbia's requirement that teachers hired since 1983 demonstrate computer literacy before receiving tenure), or requiring that local school district inservice efforts become more intelligible (such as Hawaii's requirement that inservice training advisory councils be established in all public schools). Such initiatives, however, have not provided funds to teachers or school districts (U.S. Department of Education, 1984).

A small number of other states have simply broadened inservice opportunities without mandating any particular focus, but such programs are still limited in the number of teachers they serve. Others have passed legislation to expand professional development opportunities for a portion of practicing teachers. California, for example, now funds up to five percent of the teachers in a school district with grants up to $2,000 each to improve instructional capabilities. Louisiana will pay tuition at any state university for teachers who have taught at least three years, have acquired tenure, and seek to further their teaching career. Vermont, in 1983, created an Inservice Institute for Professional Development to provide inservice opportunities for practicing teachers. Kansas passed the Inservice Education Opportunities Act in the spring of 1984 to promote professional development for teachers and administrators (U.S. Department of Education, 1984; "Changing Course," 1985, pp. 11-30).

Finally, during 1984, at least three states initiated or expanded ongoing programs in the area of school effectiveness (Minnesota, South Carolina, and West Virginia). Minnesota's efforts appear to be the most dramatic. According to Daniel Lorty, director of government relations for the Minnesota Department of Education, the new training program will promote the "development of building-level leadership teams." The state appropriated $330,000 for training such teams, $250,000 to pay for substitute teachers while the training occurs, $250,000 for the state commission to develop plans or models of effectiveness, and finally, another $70,000 for administrative costs incurred by the state department of education ("Lawmakers Continue Action on Education Reform," 1984, p. 15).

Given the costs involved in increasing teacher salaries and the difficulties inherent in significantly modifying the work environment, it is not surprising that states and school districts should turn to more narrowly focused initiatives such as loans, scholarships, and inservice activities to attract more math and science teachers and to upgrade the skills of those already teaching such subjects. In terms of improving the quality of instruction in schools, however, such programs promise only marginal increments at best, given the lead time needed to complete schooling, the voluntary nature of inservice opportunities for experienced teachers, and the trend of school districts to reassign teachers from elective areas to courses for which they are not certified. Meanwhile, market-sensitive pay which could possibly alleviate shortage more quickly seems to be floundering in the wake of resistance by some professional organizations (English, 1983-1984).

REGULATION OF THE TEACHING PROFESSION

Although most states and some local school districts have responded to various commission reports with a series of reform packages or proposals which have included incentives for teachers, their greatest effort to date has been in the area of increasing requirements and expanding regulations to reduce the number of poorly qualified people who enter teaching.

State activity has clearly defined the way. Moreover, while commission reports spawned new initiatives, state activity has been underway since the 1970s, indicating that concern over flagging student performance has a relatively longer history. What the commission reports and subsequent public response did was to trigger an expansion and upgrading of state efforts, which collectively increased the role states play in setting the qualifications for entering teaching and the requirements for remaining in the profession.

By 1985, nearly 70 percent of the states required prospective teachers to pass the National Teachers Examination or other competency tests before receiving initial certification. Nearly one-third (11 of 34) instituted such requirements since *A Nation at Risk* was published. In addition several states which had earlier mandated such tests responded by increasing test score requirements (Sandefur, 1983; "Changing Course," 1985). Moreover, 40 percent of the states now require candidates to pass a competency test for admission to a teacher education program. In addition, at least three states now require veteran teachers to pass paper-and-pencil teacher competency tests in order to retain their permanent certification. Veteran teachers in Arkansas must now take a basic skills test in math, reading, and writing. Those failing one or more areas must take remedial courses before retaking the test. In Texas, current teachers must pass a one-time basic skills test. Teachers in Alabama are also required to pass a test in their subject area fields ("Changing Course," 1985). According to Sandefur (1983), for all types of tests, one or more of three areas of knowledge are examined: basic skills, professional/pedagogical knowledge, or knowledge of major academic fields.

Competency tests have an initial ring of credibility about them which cannot be denied. No one wants our nation's youth taught by those who cannot read, write, or compute with facility. To the degree that these tests prevent such persons from entering or staying in the teaching profession or discourage others from even starting a teacher education program, quality remains constant. But concerns about the tests' validity, scope, and consequences have been raised. For example, G. Smith (1984) argued that "teaching has been operationally defined in the narrowest sense, a high score on a pencil-paper test (p. 7)."

Hyman (1984) continued this line of criticism by focusing on the National Teachers Examination (NTE) when he noted that its legal rationale rests on content validity as a measure of preprofessional preparation—a rationale that is limited, he felt, since it fails to measure skills needed in the actual job of teaching. The National Teachers Examination (NTE), he concluded, "only purports to test a prospective teacher's academic preparation." The only claim that the NTE was able to make was that some relationship existed between the tests and "the content of teacher education programs" (Educational Testing Service, 1984). He went on to argue that for an instrument which tested knowledge alone, rather than job skills, there was no positive relationship between the score on such a competency test and improved student learning. Taking a pencil-and-paper test, he continued, requires different abilities than teaching in a classroom. His argument is supported by the Educational Testing Service, author and sponsor of the NTE, which has stated that the test is not the best measure of competency for practicing teachers, for whom evaluation of on-the-job performance is a better measure of teaching competence. An intensive literature review by Pugach and Roths (1983) corroborated the ETS statement arguing that "as appealing as the common sense argument may appear, there is scant evidence to support the contention that performance on teacher competency tests is correlated with effective teaching. . . . In sum, the current literature fails to support the key assumption that there are tests available today which discriminate between effective and ineffective teachers" (p. 37). Finally, Darling-Hammond and Wise (1983) confirmed this assessment: "Although these tests are meant to screen out incompetent teachers, studies have not found any consistent relationship between scores on teacher competency tests and measures of teacher performance in the classroom" (p. 66). Proponents of competency testing counter that such links would be difficult, if not impossible, to establish under any circumstances, given the multitude of influences that affect student learning. However, serious questions about the efficacy of teacher competency tests can be presented, particularly in light of those tests, or portions of tests, that purport to measure professional knowledge in the field of education. Such tests generally focus exclusively on knowledge of vocabulary terms in psychology (usually exclusively behaviorist in orientation) and psychometrics, information of limited use to successful practicing teachers (see Jackson, 1968).

While arguments proceed over the scope and meaning of teacher competency tests, much debate has focused upon the consequences of such tests for minority students who aspire to become teachers. In a detailed review of the literature in this area, G. Smith (1984) points out that sufficient evidence is now available from states with several years' experience (as well as those that have completed initial validation studies) to indicate that disproportionate numbers of minority students are or will be screened out of teaching. For example,

- In Georgia in 1983, 34 percent of the black candidates passed on the first attempt, compared to 87 percent of the white candidates.

- In Louisiana in 1983, 15 percent of the black teacher candidates compared to 78 percent of the white candidates passed the NTE. In 1982, the two largest predominantly black institutions produced less than 40 of the 2,800 teachers certified in that state.

- Florida competency testing data released in 1983 showed a first-time pass rate of 90 percent for white teacher candidates, 51 percent for Hispanic, and 35 percent for black.

- In California, since 1983, new teachers, administrators, and other school employees such as librarians have been required to pass the California Basic Educational Skills Test (CBEST), developed by the Educational Testing Service. Nearly 66 percent who took the exam passed it; but only 26 percent of the black candidates and only 38 percent of the Hispanics did so.

- In Texas, projections for the first administration of its competency test (based on 1983 performance data and recommended net scores for 1984) indicate failure rates ranging from 80 to 87 percent for black applicants and 56 to 65 percent for Hispanic applicants on the various parts of the test (reading, writing, and mathematics).

Given actual and projected failure rates, the prospects for minorities in the teaching force become rather dim. Smith argued that the rate of minority employment in teaching may fall from a present 12.5 percent nationally to less than 5 percent by 1990 as a consequence of testing.

The issue is not whether unqualified minority graduates should enter the ranks of teaching (granted for the moment that "unqualified" means those who lack proficiency in basic skills and content areas as measured by the tests). Rather the issues are whether the tests are valid, how the preparation provided to such students can be improved, and what remedial steps can be taken to assist students who fail these tests in order to gain the knowledge needed to pass them. It is, in short, impossible to disregard the correlation between the leadership by southern states in mandating teacher competency testing, the subsequent high rates of minority failure, and the enduring legacy of segregation. As more states implement tests, the problem will likely spread beyond previously *de jure* segregated school systems to *de facto* segregated school systems, throwing in greater relief the failure of our educational system to develop instructional delivery systems that promote success by minority youth.

To receive initial certification in eight states, it is not enough to simply pass a pencil-and-paper test; an assessment instrument is also used to measure on-the-job performance in the classroom. Georgia initiated this movement in 1980 with its Teacher Performance Assessment Instrument (TPAI), which requires a year-long evaluation process before certification. According to Kearns (1983), a number of additional states are considering following the lead of these states. Serious questions, however, can be raised about the timing of such an evaluation. Since the first year is often traumatizing and critical for shaping the attitudes of teachers, considerable support and assistance by peers, administrators, and college of education staff are needed. Perhaps a more appropriate time for evaluation would be the second year, after an initiation to teaching has occurred in a supportive environment.

Such new requirements indirectly affect programs that prepare teachers. In addition to these requirements, states have directly sought to improve the quality of teacher preparation programs by mandating certain grade point averages for admission and/or graduation, increasing certification requirements for particular programs (South Dakota and North Dakota), specifying specific skills that must be taught (Alabama), raising standards for approving programs (Connecticut and Texas), mandating more field experience for students and faculty (Louisiana, Oklahoma, South Carolina, and California), and stipulating that high student failure rates on state competency tests will lead to program probation or removal of approval for all graduates (Alabama, Florida, Georgia, Missouri, and Tennessee) ("Changing Course," 1985).

While tightening up on graduates of teacher preparation programs, states have liberalized requirements for individuals who have not had courses in education but who want to teach. In some cases these "alternative certification" programs are designed to alleviate shortages in math and science; in others, the purpose is to alleviate need, regardless of area. In New Jersey, however, the scope is much broader than simply to address the effects of a teacher shortage; state education leaders have opened public school teaching to qualified individuals, even when a pool of certified teachers is available (Interview, March 2, 1984; see also Cooperman, et al., 1983).

Will "alternative certification" serve as an effective way to attract more qualified persons into the ranks of teaching? An answer to this question depends on one's assessment of courses in teacher education and whether they contribute to effective teaching or not. A task force created by the American Association of Colleges of Teacher Education (AACTE) argued that the research literature shows fully certified teachers tend to be more effective and more satisfied employees than those not fully certified (AACTE Task Force on Teacher Certification, 1984). The task force maintained that alternative certification proposals are part of a more traditional response to problems of supply and demand, the granting of emergency certificates. "The practice of granting emergency certificates," concluded the AACTE committee, "constitutes a denial of all that has been learned about sound instructional practice and would ultimately lead to a loss of what we know about the conditions necessary for effective teaching and learning" (p. 23). Among other things, the task force also recommended that "unless and until a fully certified teacher can be placed in a particular position, the school district should simply suspend classes for which that teacher is necessary" (p. 24).

Proponents of alternative certification are more skeptical of the benefits of courses in education and emphasize their concern for relieving shortages in critical areas, such as math and science. For example, the authors of the New Jersey plan argued that

> the professional literature indicates that there is little or no relationship between taking courses and succeeding as a teacher. Except for student teaching, such courses seldom provide prospective teachers with an opportunity to integrate and apply training in a practical classroom setting. In the areas of math and science, where there is a known shortage of teachers, we consistently turn away top college graduates because they have not taken a "methods" or other education-related course. (Cooperman, et al., 1983. For a similar view about the need for science and math teachers see also Boyer, 1983, pp. 183–185)

Regardless of which view of education courses one holds, the success of alternative certification will depend on whether otherwise qualified persons can be attracted into teaching. Historically, states have not had good records when they have deviated from the full certification route because of the low salaries offered, the particular need to be filled (such as staffing a specific urban school), or the ability of local unions to use emergency lay-off provisions to place laid-off teachers in positions for which they lack qualifications. Whether these problems can be overcome remains very much an open question.

Assuming, however, that such proposals will be enacted in one form or another, they may well have a long-term beneficial effect in another area, the quality of programs offered by colleges of education. To the degree otherwise qualified persons can be attracted into math, science, or teaching in general (as the New Jersey Plan proposes), pressure will be exerted on colleges of education to develop more rigorous programs of study, since their graduates will no longer enjoy a monopoly of job opportunities. Given the general level of mediocrity that prevails among colleges of education, this element of competition can only be viewed in a favorable light if one is concerned about quality teaching. As noted earlier, neither accreditation agencies such as National Council for the Accreditation of Teacher Education (NCATE) nor state certification bodies seem to be able to improve the quality of programs of professional education. By allowing market forces to work, competition might well force changes that "regulatory" bodies cannot.*

The problem of quality in teacher preparation programs may go deeper than simply entrance and exit requirements, competency examinations, and alternative routes to certification. This is why states have become more active in directly mandating mastery of specific skills and additional field experiences for students and teachers and threatening to revoke program approval if graduates remain as ill-prepared as they have been to date. While granting that considerable improvement can be made in existing programs, there is, however, a legitimate concern that perhaps the expectation that teachers can emerge from an undergraduate program fully competent to teach is to some extent misguided. Several states and teacher educators themselves have begun to look seriously at the idea that an additional year of training, at least, may need to be required if programs of teacher preparation are to fulfill the demands now placed on them.**

---

*In response to attacks by its own members, other higher-education organizations, and the withdrawal of several prominent colleges of education from the organization, NCATE in June, 1985, enacted a series of changes designed to improve its regulatory capabilities. The new standards and procedures, however, will first go into effect during the 1988–1989 school year after a 21-month grace period for institutions to make the required changes. Moreover, there is ample reason to question how much of a difference the new standards will really make. For example, one of the most contested new requirements will be that a student must have a 2.5 grade-point average (C+/B−) to be admitted to a teacher training program (Rodman, 1985).

**This is one of the proposals of the Holmes Group, an organization of education deans from a number of leading research universities. This group has developed a set of stringent standards for teacher-training programs which they hope to implement over the next decade and some are already experimenting with increasing the level of subject-matter mastery in their respective programs (Currence, 1985).

While states had been replacing permanent certification with renewable certificates for the past 15 years, a quarter of the states have recently made such changes, in part as an effort to improve the quality of teaching among experienced teachers. For example, in North Dakota the state replaced the former lifetime certificate with a two-year and a five-year renewable certificate. Renewal requires at least four additional college credits, two years of teaching experience, and three positive recommendations (U.S. Department of Education, 1983a). South Dakota's new requirements took effect in the fall of 1983 and call for continuous teaching for recertification of teachers and administrators every five years. Previously, advanced teacher and administration certificates were awarded after receipt of a masters degree and five years of experience (U.S. Department of Education, 1983a).

States have also sought to improve teacher evaluation policies by mandating that districts develop criteria for evaluation (often specifying performance-based standards) and evaluate staff annually. Since 1983, 20 percent of the states have enacted such requirements ("Changing Course," 1985).

For experienced teachers perhaps exchanging permanent certificates for ones that must be periodically renewed can be an effective way to encourage such teachers to upgrade their skills or to weed out the less competent practitioners. At the present time only a handful of states grant certificates that have no renewal requirements (Flakus-Masqueda, 1983), reflecting a long-term trend designed to improve teaching through increased certification standards. Unless substantial changes occur, however, it is unlikely that renewable certification will have much effect on the existing teaching force. The prevailing pattern among states with renewable certification is to require a certain number of years of teaching experience (usually three to five), additional course credits or degree, some inservice training where additional courses can count toward such a request, and positive performance evaluations. None of these efforts will necessarily enhance the classroom instructional effectiveness of veteran teachers.

Changes in certification requirements alone are unlikely to improve the quality of the teaching force very much (that is, weeding out incompetents or promoting continued opportunities for good teachers). Additional required courses are usually taken at teacher education institutions that are noted for their poor quality. Inservice training is generally resented by experienced teachers and viewed as a waste of time. Most states do not have performance evaluations, and those that do are in the process of developing more rigorous standards. Michigan provides a good illustration of the last point. Institutions of higher education recommend candidates to the state department for continuing certification. Candidates must have three years experience, 18 additional semester hours, and a recommendation from their school principal stating that the candidate is a successful teacher. Unless a principal specifically states that the candidate is not a competent teacher, it is assumed that the teacher is competent. Thus, for example, if a principal writes that he or she will not or cannot evaluate competency (as a way to avoid saying the person is incompetent), the institution must give the benefit of the doubt to the candidate and recommend continuing certification. The state department then accepts institutional recommendation and grants certification (Interview, March 24, 1984).

It is important to consider why the current wave of initiatives directed at veteran teachers so thoroughly ignores mechanisms already available for addressing difficulties with practicing teachers. Every state in the union has on the books laws allowing the discharge and/or decertification, for cause, of incompetent teachers. Paper-and-pencil tests of teachers, the use of teachers with no training in pedagogy, and many of the other reforms proposed do not provide any more information and, in fact, provide far less information than is currently available—or should be— through existing evaluations of teachers by their supervisors. Yet teacher discharge or decertification mechanisms are used infrequently. If there are as many incompetent teachers in the field as the reformers would have us believe, and if effective on-the-job evaluations provide the potential for the most direct evidence of teacher competence, it would seem logical that we would be better served by reforms designed to enhance on-site evaluations and to encourage the use of existing mechanisms for terminating teachers who do not meet these standards.

When certification becomes tied to career ladders, more change may occur, in part because dismissal for incompetence may become easier to implement. Tennessee provides an example of this. As of July 1, 1984, new teachers will enter a one-year probationary period, which, if successfully completed, will be followed by a three-year apprenticeship appointment. Local school districts are responsible for evaluating teacher performance during this probationary year and the final two years of the apprenticeship. The state assumes responsibility for the third year and final year of the apprenticeship. If promoted, the teacher enters Career Level I and secures a five-year certificate as well as tenure from the local school district. At the end of four years, the teacher undergoes an evaluation process which can lead to promotion to Career Level II and a second five-year certificate, to renewal at Level I and a second five-year certificate, or to rejection. If the last occurs, the district is required to dismiss the teacher. While

Career Level III is the highest that can be attained, the five-year evaluation continues for the duration of the person's career. Once having attained a Level II or III, it is possible to be placed back in a lower level after a negative evaluation (Interview, March 16, 1984).

Two questions remain, however; first, will such a system be implemented as planned, and second, to what degree will experienced teachers be affected? Under the plan, such teachers have the right to exercise the "toe-in-the-water" provision where they can try the system first. Depending on how this provision works out in practice, the effects of the career-ladder plan and new certification requirements could be limited and long-term at best.

Serious issues remain concerning teacher evaluation. The major contribution of the Wise & Darling-Hammond study (1984) can be summed up in the following way. Effective evaluation rests on multiple evaluations carried out by numerous individuals employing multiple and explicit criteria over a long period of time. Creating such a system requires considerable thought, negotiation, and funding. The design of such programs will vary depending on the local resolution of these issues. To expect more effective systems to emerge simply because states now mandate that teachers be evaluated or to expect that state-developed criteria will allow for the diversity needed to meet the needs of a wide range of school districts is to subject an extremely complex problem to an oversimplistic solution.

If the problem is how to attract and retain competent teachers, who is really going to bear the burden of the current wave of proposed reforms? The answer is the least organized and the weakest, in terms of political power: the beginning teacher. Indeed, the opposition of teacher associations to most of the reform proposals, particularly those aimed at teacher testing, has been substantially altered so that proposals directed at incoming teacher candidates are no longer opposed while changes aimed at veteran teachers are thoroughly resisted. State and local school districts have moved quickly to institute competency tests before issuing an initial certification (and the trend is to require a passing score on such tests before a student can enter a teacher education program); alternative routes to certification are being proposed which could open up teaching positions to those who have never attended teacher-training institutions; loans are available as incentives, but "strings" require the candidates to teach that subject for a certain number of years in that state in order to get a portion of the loan forgiven; career ladders are enacted which require entry by beginning teachers, but which exempt experienced teachers unless they voluntarily wish to participate; salaries for all teachers are being raised, but not in significant ways; the salary schedule for beginning teachers is a topic for discussion, but to date is the subject of little action.

Meanwhile, experienced teachers have opportunities for attending inservice programs to upgrade skills in areas of need, such as math and science, or to fulfill new requirements for recertification; in at least three states they face competency tests which raise important issues in themselves; in other states, teachers have the opportunity (but are not required) to participate in career-ladder schemes with their accompanying evaluation procedures. Finally, teacher associations themselves have been pressing for more effective teacher evaluation systems, although, interestingly, these efforts to a large extent have met with little response.

Colleges of education are potentially affected in numerous ways, some of which may prove beneficial but all of which may result in overload, given the structural constraints of promising to deliver qualified teachers during a two- or four-year undergraduate program.

Interest groups and elected officials have responded to the crisis in education by proposing reform packages that give the appearance of comprehensive, in-depth reform. When disaggregated, however, their component parts, as they affect the critical aspects of teaching, become too little and even potentially damaging. Because the thrust of the initiatives is to tighten controls over beginning teachers, it is unlikely that they will improve the condition for academic learning for the vast majority of adolescents. The initiatives do not, by and large, address the central problems associated with teaching outlined earlier: the bargain struck to divert attention from concentrated academic instruction; the inclination to manage the social relations of the classroom by sacrificing subject-matter content; the abuse of professional autonomy by entrepreneurial teachers who determine in isolation what knowledge should constitute the content of their classes; and the apparent disengagement of teachers from teaching as their other jobs and responsibilities consume more of their energies. The teaching force nationwide is aging, and relatively few new teachers are being hired, although this will change in the near future. Initiatives that attempt to improve the quality of prospective professionals, rather than the existing force, consequently are unlikely to provide an across-the-board increase in the level of academic learning in high school. To date, the pattern of response common to American education in general seems to be shaping the initiatives directed specifically toward teaching: postponing reform by changing the next generation (Tyack & Hansot, 1981).

PART III
Organizations

9 ⋙ School Organizations

Students and teachers work and learn together in organizations. There are a number of institutional policies and practices, some a century old, that have the unintended consequence of perpetuating the bargain to avoid or minimize academic learning (see Ducharme, 1982). Organizational customs reinforce the effort of some students and teachers to become disengaged from school. The structure and incentives that are most common today mitigate against the academic commitments of everyone involved. Institutional priorities become the enemies of intellectual rigor and can encourage, if not explicitly reward, or even coerce, the flight of students and teachers from sustained academic learning. This chapter will examine several ways that organizations shape and maintain the context within which the arrangement to deemphasize academic content functions, an arrangement that protects the fusion of interests that undergirds the "bargain."

SCHOOL ORGANIZATIONS AND THE BARGAINING PROCESS

America has no national system of education. Rather, responsibility for education is left to the individual states, which allocate various degrees of dependence and autonomy to 16,000 local school districts. Even with such decentralization, however, there is a pattern of organization common to many American secondary schools. The two major common characteristics are universality and comprehensiveness, the former designed to assure an egalitarian goal that the schools serve "everyone," the latter designed, according to Conant, "to provide good elective programs for those who wish to use their acquired skills immediately upon graduation [and] to provide satisfactory programs for those whose vocations depend on their subsequent education in a college or university" (1959, p. 5).

These two basic elements, universality and comprehensiveness, necessitate a third characteristic, bureaucratic structure. The bureaucratic structure is characterized by a division of labor among staff, rules and regulations, reliance on orderly processes, and certain administrative and

155

supervisory practices. More particularly, each secondary school has a principal, one or more assistant principals (depending on size), teachers specialized within subject areas, counselors, and secretaries to keep the paper work flowing and to account for the students. Each has a physical plant, more or less well equipped with corridors and classrooms, specialty areas, lockers, and offices. Each has a variety of courses, fewer for the smaller, more for the larger schools, offered at fixed intervals to batches of students, each of whom has some freedom to choose an appropriate set. Even in small high schools, the courses are quite varied. The students are equally varied, coming from different groups and classes and having differing abilities, interests, and ambitions.

For the most part, those who work and study in schools accept their bureaucratic aspects as necessary, given their size and diversity. Complex tasks require complex organizations. Some scholars, however, maintain that the administrative bureaucracy is more than a facilitator and organizer of people and events. It is the primary socializer in a primarily socializing institution. They argue that while schools may fail to teach all students the content and curriculum, few escape the lessons of obedience to an administrative structure, the importance of rules, regulations, and bureaucratic processes, deference to superiors, or on the other hand, the seeking of ways to find personal satisfaction in informal friendships while giving the minimal compliance to organizational demands. Katz (1975), for example, maintained that the *major purpose* of schools is to teach compliance with bureaucratic procedures. "The purpose [of schools] has been, basically, the inculcation of attitudes that reflect dominant social and industrial values; the structure has been bureaucracy. The result has been school systems that treat children as units to be processed into particular shapes and dropped into slots roughly congruent with the status of their parents" (p. xviii; see also Bowles & Gintis, 1976). Everhart (1983) went even further, arguing that the purpose of schools is not only to teach dominant social and business values but also to ensure that our oppressive cultural and economic system goes unchanged. As he reasoned, the best way to accomplish such goals is to maintain bureaucratic schools that teach obedience and respect for such a system, particularly to working-class students whom society is most intent on oppressing. He accounted for the resistance to school displayed by the working-class junior high students he studied as a form of rebellion against this unfair system. Although almost no school people espouse such views, a number of researchers—including Johnson, N., 1985; Willis, 1977; Everhart, 1983; Cusick, 1973—have described the pervasiveness of rules, regulations, order, and procedures in schools and the rewards given to those who comply, the sanctions reserved for those who rebel. Those who comply succeed in school; it is assumed that they will succeed in life. Those who rebel are routinely sorted to the bottom in school, just as it is assumed they will be sorted to the bottom of society. It is true that students from the lower classes display the most rebelliousness against the schools' socializing efforts and find it most difficult to break from their class origins. Although one should exercise caution in accepting these critical generalizations in their entirety, they are important and deserve strong consideration, as we have suggested earlier, and as will be evident from our conclusion.

To return to this chapter's first objective, it is necessary to describe and discuss a number of institutional policies and practices that perpetuate the bargain. The most important of these is the schools' universality. High schools must admit and attempt to retain all adolescents. They are virtually universal, relatively nonselective, highly inclusive organizations. They testify eloquently to our success in creating a mass secondary educational system. The stigma attached to dropping out, combined with social, economic, and emotional pressures to remain enrolled, make high schools essentially involuntary institutions.

The schools' universality and egalitarianism received a particularly strong boost in the early 1960s when Harrington (1962) suggested that the culture of poverty in America included up to 40 percent of the population and that poverty for many rural whites and urban blacks had become a perennial condition passed from generation to generation. As it was reasoned in political circles, a key to unlocking this cycle of poverty was to make the schools more responsive to poorer children, improve their basic skills, and thereby enhance their job opportunities. As leading economists pointed out, education was to be used as a "transfer of income" to the poor in the hope that upgrading their vocational skills would prove to be an effective answer to the problems of poverty and welfare. The basic mid-1960s perception that schools were insensitive to the poor, particularly the black poor, was given impetus by Kenneth Clark (1965) who reasoned that the schools made *a priori* negative judgments about the ability of black youngsters to the point where teachers did not bother to try to teach them and instead attributed their lack of skills to innate deficiencies. As Clark argued, this blatant racism was built into the school and hidden behind such reasonable sounding educational practices as fixed curricula, tracking, and decision-making based on test data. Clark's argument that the judgments following those practices were inherently biased against blacks was followed by a host of other widely accepted accounts of schools' and teachers' insensitivity to poorer children (by Holt, 1982 [revised]; Kozol, 1967; and Kohl, 1968, for example).

The sum of the pressures brought about by the government's policy of treating education as a transfer of income to the poor, by minorities demanding more responsive schools, and by the sheer increase in the numbers of students attending secondary schools, from 8,869,186 in 1957-1958 to 15,704,000 in 1977-1978, combined to force the schools to "ease off" from making judgments about students and to increase their attempts to accommodate them. Schools increased their efforts to find ways to serve large numbers of students who, even while decently behaved and relatively civil to one another and to teachers, displayed little interest in the subject matter. As this accommodating continued, school authorities found themselves increasingly defensive when making pejorative judgments about these students. As a result, they retreated to a position of institutional passivity and neutrality, that is, easing back from a required curriculum, increasing optional courses and programs, varying the paths to a diploma, allowing students to repeat basic arithmetic again and again and allowing such remedial classes to be counted for the required year of high school math, and not looking too closely at what was actually taught and learned in classrooms.

Organizationally, there were two parts to the response. To serve more diverse numbers of students, the school organization was increasingly differentiated and specialized. But unlike most organizations, wherein increased differentiation and specialization is accompanied by increased scrutiny and supervision, the schools backed off from looking too closely at what was going on in the expanded structure. Such reluctance is understandable, given the dual pressures on the schools to be both responsive and less judgmental.

Whatever value lay in that flexibility, however, must be balanced against the problems of substance and equity that it eventually aggravated. Attempting to devise options for various groups contributed to the problem of adolescents receiving differing "educations" of varying quality and ultimate value. Given that middle-class and professional parents consistently hold high academic aspirations for their children, this tendency to increase freedom of choice has been exploited in a way that has *reinforced* social and economic inequality. If the consequences of unlimited course selection were random, the problem would be one of individual foolishness or an unfortunate blunder. But the consequences are never randomly distributed. The patterns of choice and selection consistently vary by social class, race, strength of affiliation to extended academic schooling based upon projected payoffs, alternatives for investing one's time and effort, the choices of one's closest friends, and other considerations. The choices made consistently aggravate existing problems of equity and access to knowledge. It is ironic, therefore, that mechanisms introduced and continued to enhance equality and individual accomplishment have often been taken advantage of by the privileged classes to reinforce whatever educational advantages they already possessed.

Organizational practices, in other words, have allowed students to elect or negotiate their own accomplishment, or, in many cases, their own educational demise. In the best of circumstances this freedom of choice could be used to build an education probably unequaled in the world. When applied to all high schools, however, where a large percentage of the students lack adequate skills, motivation, alertness, or guidance, such respect for individual choice can circumscribe access to high status or valuable knowledge.

Curricular tracking and ability grouping have been criticized for their availability to economic and social elites to sift and sort students on the basis of nonmeritocratic characteristics, or irrelevant attributes, such as race, social class, gender, and handicapping condition. There is little doubt that these innovations, along with the testing machinery to make them efficient, have been consistently abused, despite their theoretical introduction early in this century, and strengthened into our own time as a noble effort to identify talent that traditional organizational practices would have missed or diverted. As we demonstrated above, misuse and abuse are understandably and deservedly the most common themes in the history and sociology of testing, tracking, and grouping (see Rosenbaum, 1976; Oakes, 1985; Owen, 1985; Goodlad, 1984).

In some respects, however, the recision of organizational practices that constrain student choice provides a comparable opportunity for abuse, although the damage is done under the banner of free choice. Many schools may never escape the circle that leads from imposing discriminating judgments on students to a state of institutional passivity and neutrality, where teachers and administrators appear reluctant to make decisions that will ensure academic learning, ultimately allowing students latitude to create their own educations with discriminatory effects. Institutional neutrality, reflected in the inclination of authorities to back away from their proper responsibility to make decisions about what is best, leaves the decision-making process open to the forces that appear most salient in an adolescent's life. Most students, as a result, will find it difficult to choose wisely as they struggle to reconcile the often countervailing pressures to be popular, or at least to keep the loyalty of some clique, and to be intensely engaged in academic achievement.

Unfortunately, the decision-making vacuum is ordinarily filled in a way that discourages academic achievement. The enormous pressures to do what one's friends are doing, to avoid disparaging one's classmates' lack of ambition, to give the appearance of caring little, to enroll in classes appropriate to one's gender, class, race, or clique: they guide adolescents, especially, in their motivation and thinking about where to invest their energy and effort. A black student who transferred to Highland Park High School on Chicago's suburban north shore reported to Philip Jackson (1981) that "the trouble with the school is that it's too free for the students' own good." Freed from the restrictions common a generation ago, he wasted time and opportunity by skipping class to hang out with his friends. He was angry toward the school for his situation, which he characterized as "scraping the bottom. I just barely graduated" (p. 91). Institutional neutrality allows high school students to make often tragic, irreparable decisions, yet hides the ultimate consequences from them through formal organizational practices such as course election and the refusal to identify the knowledge most worth having, or to discriminate on the relative value of any subject-matter content.

On too few occasions have our schools broken this cycle and determined what is worth knowing and protected the opportunity of all students to learn it, to master it in their own way perhaps, but to master it nonetheless. If it is to ensure equity, the standards-raising movement must confront the related issues of institutional neutrality and invidious grouping and tracking. Teachers and administrators must be able to address the "agonizing issues" that limiting student freedoms will raise and not be intimidated by charges that such action constitutes an "arrogant denial of choice" (Offerman, 1984, p. 51).

In addition to encouraging the fragmentation of knowledge and the development of courses and alternative programs that appeal to adolescents, universal attendance also contributes to the importance of the social relations of the classroom. With a captive audience, teachers must work out mutually satisfying relationships with their students. Universal attendance, combined with a devalued diploma and an extrinsic selection process that assumes the possession of a credential rather than the possession of knowledge, results in high school attendance by a large number of students who must be in high school but who do not really want to be there, or at least have little interest in demanding academic learning.

Teachers must consequently pursue rewarding relationships with many indifferent, if not openly hostile and rebellious, adolescents. High school students who are attempting to build a comfortable life in their unselective host institutions are motivated by their own personal concerns and often care little about acquiring academic knowledge. Such students do not hesitate to challenge the legitimacy of anything that is expected of them. "Why do we have to learn this?" they ask again and again, "What difference does it make if we do this?" Because of an organizational stance that is unwilling and unable to defend the instrinsic value of a high school education or of the knowledge that should constitute secondary schooling, teachers retreat into utilitarianism or vocationalism. They rarely invoke a knowledge standard but instead attempt to engage students with promises (actually implied, thinly veiled threats) about eventual occupational and economic opportunity. But students understand that their compliance is to be given only to acquire the credential, grade-point average, class ranking, or letter of recommendation. Students are aware that they must comply in order to get the extrinsic reward, not the knowledge itself.

Because many teachers find that the intrinsic value of an education, or knowledge, does not motivate most adolescents, they must manage the personal or social relations of their classrooms in such a way that they can avoid humiliation or so that the entire effort does not degenerate into too much of a farce. Many teachers do not prefer it to be this way. But organizational policies (such as mass schooling, institutional passivity and neutrality, the absence of an ethos defending the legitimacy of a coherent body of knowledge), coupled with a devalued diploma, make it hard for them to do anything else. Furthermore, such policies encourage teachers to make bargains that are least likely to erupt into emotional confrontations and to advocate practices such as grouping and passing on the nonlearners, which minimize classroom tension. But such practices are not without costs, a major one being demoralized teachers, such as the one who reported the following to Cusick (1983):

> This girl missed 55 days of class, 55 days and she hadn't handed in an assignment since I checked my book, since October 10, and so I flunked her from the class. But the parent came in and talked to the principal, so I got called in and he said, looking right at me, "Mr._____is it necessary to fail that student?" and I said "yes" and showed him what I'm showing you, and then he looked at me and said again, "Is it really necessary to fail that student?" I said "yes" but the third time he said it, I got the message. (p. 139)

In this instance, that teacher, who himself valued learning, could take no strong moral stance toward the importance of the child learning what he had to teach.

Universalism and egalitarianism have had one additional effect on high school standards, at least according to one segment of the current movement to tighten requirements and raise expectations at the secondary level. In some respects the standards-raising movement can be seen as a critical response to the effects of the equity movement of the past generation. Federal and state legislative and judicial pressure to serve all students, including racial minorities, handicappers, and various classes of disruptive, delinquent, and rebellious students, has been blamed for the willingness of high school teachers and administrators to lower academic and behavioral standards. There is some evidence that teachers have expected less of special classes of students, particularly minorities (Sizer, 1983a; Natriello & Dornbusch, 1984; Oldenquist, 1983).

Governmental attentiveness to the voices of special interest groups concerned with using the schools to solve all sorts of social problems, including inequity, has been derided for its deleterious impact on curricular standards and teacher expectations. In an address to the College Board, for example, Dennis Gray (1980) of the Council for Basic Education held federal and state initiatives to "cure newly emerging social ills" largely responsible for the "curriculum sprawl" that characterizes high school programs today. He commented on the "ruinous overloading of the high school curriculum in the vain expectation that new and socially useful learning would ensue" which has gripped our secondary schools since the mid-1960s. He reasoned that such a diversion of resources "to make our schools the engines of social reform" depleted their capacity to provide basic education (p. 4; see also Cawelti, 1981; Wright, L., 1983). Despite this sort of criticism, however, there is little substantive evidence that the equity movement has had such an impact on standards; indeed, recent gains in standardized test scores by minorities suggest just the opposite.

As a corollary to the universal attendance policy, state reimbursement practices that are designed to get local districts to serve all adolescents are occasionally used to divert some adolescents from the regular classrooms, thereby reducing opportunities for academic learning. State educational funding policies that reimburse districts through a formula based upon average daily enrollment tend to make it attractive to establish programs that keep students officially enrolled, but allow them to complete most of their school assignments off campus, or at least out of the regular classrooms. This funding pattern, increasingly common since the late 1950s, has fueled the expansion and proliferation of work-study, cooperative, alternative education, and evening school programs. Of course, such opportunities are not universally worse than regular classrooms and occasionally can serve to keep some indifferent adolescents at least marginally involved in school. Their potential for abuse is great, however, since there is an irresistable temptation to use the availability of such programs, most of which receive additional state funding, to remove potentially disruptive, bored students who threaten the tranquility of regular academic classrooms, while preserving attendance levels and access to state funds. Furthermore, it is not uncommon for college-bound students to enroll in such programs in order to avoid more demanding academic courses, to spend time off campus and outside, and to earn part-time incomes while earning credit toward graduation.

It has been suggested that a number of structural features essentially universal among secondary schools constrain academic engagement and learning, particularly the development of higher-order reasoning and problem-solving skills. Many thoughtful critics have called attention to the way in which prevailing organizational customs regarding time and knowledge, for example, drastically limit the opportunities of both students and teachers to devote themselves to sustained academic activities. These " 'regularities' and 'axioms' of keeping school—the conventions beyond challenge—make change almost impossible," argues Theodore R. Sizer (1984a; p. 34), drawing partially upon the work of Seymour Sarason (1982). The practice of compartmentalizing subject matter by discipline into courses of one or two semesters and classes of 50 minutes contributes to the fragmentation of knowledge. Coupled with most teacher subject certification practices, this bureaucratic tendency toward specialization and differentiation exacerbates the struggle of defining a body of knowledge that all high school students should master. Adolescents encounter fragments of knowledge randomly over the school day. Fred Newmann, among others, has explored this institutional tendency toward the differentiation rather than the integration of experience and has joined Sizer and Goodlad in calling attention to the "costs" of specialization, including student alienation, disengagement, lack of affiliative ties between teachers and students and among students, unbearable class loads for teachers, and frenetically paced daily schedules for everyone (Newmann, 1980; Sizer, 1984a, 1984b; Goodlad, 1984; Ravitch, 1981; Farrar, Neufeld, & Miles, 1983).

The detrimental effects of the organizational practice of fragmenting knowledge are aggravated by institutional procedures that compromise the ability of students and teachers to use effectively whatever time is available. The premise that "the degree of learning that takes place is a function of the quantity of learning activity" (Sirotnik, 1982, p. 275) is supported by a number of studies showing that increases in student achievement are a function of increased time spent learning (National Institute of Education, 1980). As Harnischfeger and Wiley (1978) pointed out, it is generally agreed that of the four ways to improve learning, three increase the time *allocated* to learning or time actively *engaged* in learning.

Many existing policies governing attendance, movement between classes, withdrawing students for special assignments or tutoring, the scheduling of nonacademic activities during the school day, and intercom interruptions for nonessential announcements distract from everyone's opportunity to concentrate on academic learning. In American high schools, "time on task" is particularly vulnerable because many organizational elements prevent the time allocated from being spent as it is ostensibly planned. Recent reviews of the use and misuse of time in schools, particularly the essential distinction between "allocated" time and "engaged" time, reveal that it is not uncommon for many high schools to "waste" 50 percent of the academic school year (Justiz, 1984, pp. 483-484; Karweit, 1983; Newmann, 1980; Kemmerer, 1983). Karweit (1983) summarized the time-on-task studies and estimated that only "about half to sixty percent of the school day is used for instruction." Here, 60 percent is the time actually spent in school; it does not include time lost from teacher strikes or student absences.

> Assuming that a school day of six hours was held for 180 days a year. The maximum instructional time would be 1080 hours. . . . This figure is reduced by attendance of 170 days (top) and 140 days (bottom), yielding 840 hours and 1020 hours respectively. Next the time is reduced by the non-instructional uses of school time, including scheduling of other events, interruptions, and any other practice which reduces time available, either intended or not. Using estimates of instructional time of 3 and 4 hours of the six, and attendance of 140 and 170 days, produces a range of instructional hours from 420 to 680 per year. Finally, to see the effect of engagement with learning on the number of hours of instruction, we set the engagement rate to be .75 and .90. These engagement rates produce a range of learning time from a low of 310 to a high of 612 hours per year.

Field studies of classrooms indicate large amounts of time consumed by nonacademic endeavors. The first is student accounting. In America, high school students change classrooms every hour and in almost all high schools, they are counted every hour to see if their absences are legitimate. Coleman (1966), Cusick (1983), Sizer (1984b), Everhart (1983), Martin (1977), and Butler (1975) all recorded classrooms in which this child-accounting and the pass system and the resulting interruptions from the "attendance slip collection" took up time that might have been given to academic pursuits. These same researchers noted that some teachers dispatched these maintenance details quickly and with almost no fuss while others spent up to 10 or even 15 minutes of a 50-minute class taking attendance.

Although it is difficult to explain such variation in terms of individual teacher characteristics (Sirotnik, 1982), it is not difficult to understand the elements in the organization that make it necessary for teachers to "count" students every hour. The first is financial. Schools are allocated funds on the basis of per-pupil attendance or average per-pupil enrollment so administrators are obligated to keep accurate records. In addition, there are legal constraints. Principals are generally responsible for the safety of pupils, and they take care to see that they are "not out in the halls running around or riding around town" (Cusick & Peters, 1979). But more important than the financial or legal aspects is the pressure principals feel from parents who might call and want their child or want to know where their child is or saw some students out of school and want to know why they are not in school. Teachers have to count and account for their students every hour, every day.

Similarly, discipline in classes that have many students who are not particularly interested in acquiring abstract knowledge diverts time from instruction. The presence of students, however indifferent, is required by law, and the schools are legally, financially, and politically obligated to keep them, but it does not assure their attention to the material at hand. Teachers have to continually watch and correct students' behavior which is not so bad that they can be asked to leave but still distracts the class and devours time available for instruction.

Administrators pressure teachers to keep control of their classes, even the toughest classes, and are unwilling to tolerate for long a teacher who cannot do that. In fact, Cusick (1983) found that the ability to "handle" their students often was the sole criterion used by administrators to evaluate teachers. Teachers who could not control students were "not welcome in the school," but if they could, then it did not matter what else they did in the way of instruction. A teacher was obligated to "handle his or her own discipline issues" and not send students too often to the office for assistance. That meant that teachers had to deal with student inattentiveness, fooling around, absenteeism, insolence, or lack of preparedness in the classroom and, of course, when those things happen frequently, as they do in schools with larger numbers of low-achieving or disinterested students, they take up a large part of the time allocated to instruction.

In addition, there are a number of nonacademic pastimes that have found their way into the school day. Cusick (1983) found that almost every club and activity in the high school he studied was engaged in some sort of fund-raising endeavor. During the school day students were selling candy, tee shirts, bagels, flowers, and newspaper ads. Teachers encouraged students to raise money for a better yearbook, newspaper, musical activity, trip, or extra equipment. And, of course, fund raising was closely related to the activities side of schools. Peshkin (1978) noted that community members expect more than academics. They expect the school to provide sporting events, plays, holiday programs, and musical events for them as well as their children. Although the activities themselves undoubtedly benefitted the community and the students who participated in them, the fund-raising efforts devoured time and energy that might have been devoted to academic endeavors.

In addition to the child counting, discipline, and the press for activities, there has been a proliferation of specialists who do not teach but who perform some service that depends upon the time of the students (usually individual students) to perform it. Band directors, counselors, yearbook and newspaper sponsors, coaches, school psychologists, special education teachers, remedial teachers, security guards, and assistant principals for discipline or activities, all need the time of individual students to perform their tasks. And few are loath to ask for that time even when it demands that the time be taken from academic classes. This contributes to the coming and going that makes child counting and the attendant pass systems more necessary, complicated, and time-consuming. Teachers complain about interruptions, but few have the power to resist. Someone enters a class and wants a particular student, then he or she goes. Few teachers dare tell the vice principal, counselor, or band director that the child cannot go now. Classrooms in American high schools are not "protected" or sacred environments.

The cumulative effect of child counting, discipline, activities, and requests from without for particular students and the endless announcements about games, activities, warnings, special events, create a place where it can be difficult to provide a serious atmosphere where diligence is the norm. Sizer (1984b) pointed out that during the day he spent with Horace Smith (the composite teacher), in the first class, five of the 22 students were absent (two came in late). In the second class three were absent; the next class was cancelled for an assembly; the next class was interrupted by both the public address system and the attendance girl collecting the slips; in the next class, of 18 students only five were there; the remainder were at the community college for United Nations week. Lightfoot (1983) described a class of seniors, most of whom had gone off to graduation practice. Cusick (1983) described classes released for pep assemblies, teacher inservice programs, special events, and endless announcements. The researchers who record such events do not set out to study the phenomenon of interruptions. But they invariably make note of numerous and trivial events that take time from instruction, after which the teacher has to call the students back to order. There is a message for the students and teachers in all of this. Students learn just how unimportant academic activity really is, and teachers learn that managing the enterprise amid the coming and going is more important than concentrated academic endeavors. Norris Brock Johnson (1985) noted that, as a result, the secondary classroom is not the center of the students' school life. In secondary school "the temporal and spatial context of classroom life is fragmented. Students come and go according to personal schedule. Transience and impermanence are the rule" (p. 244).

Among the popular proposals for reforming secondary schools are those suggesting more time in school and more in-school time devoted to academic subjects. Some proposals such as those in Arkansas, California, and Vermont are phrased in terms similar to Michigan's, which recommends that "the state board of education increase the minimum instructional school year from 900 to 1,000 hours ... and ... establish a minimum of 185 instructional days" (Michigan State Board of Education, 1984, p. 5). Others, such as those in New Jersey, New Mexico, and Texas are phrased in terms of making better use of the time presently allocated by not counting snow days, making sure that special events do not conflict with classes, and/or suggesting better use of classroom time.

When such proposals are discussed, they are sometimes compared with the Japanese schools, where the students spend 240 days each year in school. Not only do Japanese students spend more time in school, but they spend 36 hours each week in class with only four of those hours devoted to nonacademic pursuits. Americans, on the other hand, spend 180 days in school with at most 26 hours weekly devoted to academic pursuits (Rohlen, 1983). Furthermore, in Japanese schools there are no study halls, free periods, independent study time in class, or lunch periods that last more than half an hour. The 1976 figures show that 60 percent of middle-level school children in Japan spend additional study time in "juku" or cram schools to prepare them for the national examinations (Shimahara, 1979).

Given the contrast to America, it is questionable whether increasing the school year to 200 days will help our schools, or whether indeed such proposals could be supported or are even capable of addressing the time issue. In a national survey of the public response to calls for higher academic standards in secondary schools, Freeman, et al. (1985b) found almost no support for increasing the length of the school day or the length of the school year. In addition, those who study the time issue agree that it is not time allocated but time spent on the task that is important. And as we have already shown, in American high schools time on task is particularly vulnerable precisely because there is so much competition for students' time within the organization that it prevents the time allocated to instruction from being spent as it is ostensibly planned. The question is whether proposals to increase time in terms of more days or additional hours are enough to offset the effect of these elements as they accumulate and as they drain available time away from academic endeavors. An extra five days, or one hundred hours, of the same kind of activity is unlikely to make a substantial difference in the time allocated to academic endeavors. If Karweit's estimates are reasonable (field studies indicate that they might even be a little optimistic), then we can assume that the low estimates, that is 310 hours per year allocated to instruction, occur in the more problematic classes with the more difficult and perhaps lower-achieving students, and they are just the students toward whom the proposals are aimed. If those students are presently spending 27 percent of their school time in academic endeavors, an extra five days a year will yield only 27 percent of the 30 hours of instruction in that five days. In effect, the extra five days of instruction will yield only eight more hours of academic activity for those classes. It seems clear that unless the proposals for increased time are accompanied by substantial changes in the way schools allocate time, then any discernable benefit may be negligible.

Administrative priorities can also lead to organizational policies that lessen academic learning. The attention that principals and superintendents must pay to matters of attendance, order, discipline, funding, and public relations reduces their opportunity and inclination to exert responsibility over instruction. Teachers are left with a great deal of autonomy to work out the terms of their employment; to determine the place that teaching will occupy in their lives; to implement curricula derived from their own predilections; and to reconcile in their own way the tension posed by their need to manage the social relations of their classrooms and professional pressure to establish conditions that maximize academic learning. By and large, teachers are rewarded for controlling their classes rather than for ensuring engagement with subject matter. This incentive structure, combined with relatively great classroom autonomy, makes it difficult to resist the temptation to tolerate, if not participate in, the sort of personal interaction that students prefer which undermines concentration and diverts everyone's attention away from the process of acquiring academic knowledge (Cusick, 1983; Cohen, D., 1983, 1984; Sizer, 1984b). With little supervision over instruction, teachers who lack confidence in their mastery of subject matter, or who simply run the risk of being humiliated in confrontations with students over the imposition of rigorous assignments and standards, are encouraged to teach "defensively" in order to minimize the disorder and resistance that could spill out into the halls and arouse the attention of the authorities (McNeil, 1984).

Administrative priorities can encourage student disengagement in other ways. Despite the trade-offs that accompany substantial rates of labor market participation by high school students, administrators concerned with public relations and campus tranquility are pleased that their students work as much as they do. As Linda McNeil (1984) has observed, "many administrators are grateful for the positive, constructive contacts which working students make with the local business community." This sort of public image is far more desirable than "news about students' auto accidents, drinking, shoplifting or general hanging around shopping centers or parks." Jobs reinforce school discipline by clearing upperclassmen "out of the halls and away from school grounds during afternoon classes and after school." McNeil encountered no administrative appreciation of the tensions and compromises that student employment forced on teachers, who felt that without support their only alternative was to lower their expectations for students. In general, many administrators appear to view the bargain warmly, since it preserves educational peace and tranquility, even at the cost of reducing academic engagement and learning. Prevailing priorities pose a significant impediment to any effort that might meaningfully address the cumulative effects of millions of personal decisions to quietly withdraw from intense academic work. They will make it hard to ask adolescents to care about academic learning any more than they do and to adjust their priorities accordingly.

Finally, the posture that administrators adopt toward the importance of academic learning is reflected in their solutions to organizational imperatives and problems. Some administrators, for example, select certain disciplinary practices that could diminish students' interest in acquiring academic knowledge. To some students, suspension symbolizes an absence of organizational commitment to, or respect for, academic instruction. This particular practice could lower the value of classroom learning in the eyes of all students. Furthermore, it does not view discipline as an educational endeavor but principally as an opportunity to display symbolically institutional authority and remove troublemakers from regular classrooms, often at the cost of many students' academic involvement.

American secondary schools have always been faced with public pressure for equalizing access, and in the 1960s that pressure was increased. Schools responded by altering their organizations to allow and encourage access by all adolescents. But as critics have argued and studies have demonstrated, the modes of access adopted by the schools were not sufficient to solve educational problems. In many respects, the ways they opened access paradoxically aggravated the problem of inequality in school learning and achievement. Indeed, the process further exacerbated the (also perennial) problem of quality. For several years now the emphasis has been on quality, and the schools are trying to respond. But they are still under obligation to increase equality and, therefore, are obligated to respond without denying any of the access they allowed in the name of equality.

SCHOOL ORGANIZATIONS AND THE REFORM CAMPAIGN

We have argued that there are three characteristics common to secondary schools in America: *universality* or the egalitarian commitment to everyone, *comprehensiveness* or the effort to educate students of different abilities and interests in the same facility, and a *bureaucratic structure* necessitated by universality and comprehensiveness. We further suggested that there are a number of elements, such as public and per-pupil funding, student accounting, legal obligations, specialization, fragmentation of knowledge, and organizational neutrality that have accompanied the bureaucratization process in schools. As we argued in the first part of this chapter, while the sum of the elements is designed to create smoothly running schools, it also makes it easy for the students and even teachers to ease off from involvement in learning and instead accommodate one another in the bargain. Even when lower-order bargains are struck, if the students are moving along and giving some compliance to the complex organization or as long as school is "being kept," then no one is obligated to look too closely at what is actually taught and learned.

Although this may upset a number of people, it should not surprise students of organizations who understand that schools are complex organizations and the major task for a complex organization is survival. Organizations survive by reducing uncertainty. A complex organization is an open system, "hence indeterminate and faced with uncertainty but at the same time subject to the criteria of rationality and hence needing determinateness and certainty" (Thompson, 1967, p. 10). Theoretically, for schools the task is made more complicated by the fact that the technology of teaching and learning is soft and indeterminate. Unlike a hard technology where a specified action produces a desired outcome, "the technology of education rests on abstract systems of belief about relationships among teachers, teaching materials and pupils; but learning theories assume the presence of these variables and proceed from that point" (Thompson, 1967, p. 19). Schools are not the only organizations obligated to operate with soft technologies. Mental hospitals, many governmental agencies, business consulting firms, and law offices also operate with little certainty about cause/effect relationships at their technical core. Even with a low degree of technical rationality, however, these organizations, like schools, are still obligated to survive, particularly when they are important to a great many people, as are schools. Widespread commitment to our schools' success and survival forces them to develop patterns of instrumental action that, in a sense, cover up or at least minimize the problems of a soft technology. Schools have to behave rationally despite their inherently weak technology.

Our conception of a school organization, then, is of an open system, subject to the criteria of rationality, that is, reducing uncertainty and ensuring its survival but subject to a number of constraints and contingencies beyond its control. Its technology is essentially soft; it cannot choose the number or level of academic inclination of its clients; it is bound to work in a comprehensive facility; it is further bound by year-to-year budgeting practices (most are denied the power to either accumulate capital or to divert working capital into possible experiments); it has legal obligations to all adolescents up to age 16 and all those who desire its services up to age 19. Schools are subject to political control by lay boards and state policies and are further bound by locally generated social and vocational expectations. On the other hand, schools do control a number of their internal variables, such as scheduling, electives, discipline, attendance and promotion policies, testing practices, extracurricular activities, graduation requirements, and curricular and program structure. All of these internal organizational variables are more or less affected by the broad fundamental constraints and contingencies outlined above, but the schools exert some control over them and can alter them to respond to various pressures, such as the current call for higher standards.

In other words, since the schools do not control the larger constraints and contingencies stemming from universalism and comprehensiveness, it is only by manipulating their internal bureaucratic processes that they can respond to the current demands for excellence. In fact that is what has ordinarily happened. Operationally, the effort to reform America's secondary schools has turned into an effort to alter their organizational variables without affecting either the constraints or the contingencies.

The remainder of this chapter will describe those efforts to alter the school organization and examine the effects of those efforts. Campaigns to increase the number of tests and the increasing reliance on testing have already been discussed, as have the efforts to reduce electives, tighten up requirements, make graduation standards more intelligible, and increase the amount and effectiveness of teacher training and teacher supervision. Some of the improvement efforts, however, are more holistic; the best example of the holistic approach is the effective schools movement. The effective schools movement was generally thought to have been fomented by Coleman's (1966) and later Jencks and colleagues' (1972) assertion that differences among student achievement could not be accounted for by differences among schools, but rather by the students' social and class differences. Jensen's (1969) attribution of variations in student achievement to class and race differences reinforced Coleman and Jencks' study by suggesting that schools had failed to reduce achievement differences between poorer minority students and the rest of the population in the wake of vastly increased federal assistance that began with the Elementary and Secondary Education Act of 1965. Assessment of programs for the disadvantaged appeared to show that "compensatory education has been tried and it has failed" (Jensen, 1969).

School people were reluctant to accept these pessimistic conclusions and have focused their attention instead on a set of studies which suggested that school organizations do make a difference in student achievement. One of the most widely heralded was Rutter and colleagues' (1979) study of students in twelve London schools. He found that there were differences in student achievement, discipline, attendance, and student problems outside schools and that the schools which were better on these measures had a different type of organization. The better-achieving schools were characterized by higher and more consistent expectations for both students and teachers, shared norms among teachers about homework, discipline and grading, and joint planning. Although social class surfaced as a variable in some of the schools with better results, the study was generally taken to indicate that organizational elements such as leadership, staff expectations, and teacher behavior could contribute to student achievement. At the same time there was some evidence that private schools were doing better than public schools, even those private schools that were considerably poorer. A study of private schools in British Columbia by Erickson and his colleagues (1979) concluded that schools did better as a result of their *Gemeinshaft* organization wherein people created a community within the school, a community that encouraged better effort on the part of teachers and subsequently higher achievement on the part of students.

These studies supported Brookover et al. (1979) who for years had been conducting studies designed to investigate differences in achievement among poor schools and finding that indeed there were differences, particularly in the "climate" of the school. Edmonds (1981) phrased succinctly three premises from which he conducted the New York City School Improvement Project based in part upon Brookover's research. He maintained that children in the New York public schools were educable, that the educability of the children derived more from the nature of the school which they attended than from the nature of the family from which they came, and that pupil acquisition of basic school skills was not determined by family background (Edmonds, 1981). What happened, according to Purkey and Smith (1982a, 1982b) and MacKenzie (1983), was that selectively chosen studies of classrooms, teachers, and schools were combined with a desire on the part of the school people to affirm the worth of their efforts.

The sum of the effective schools literature is that there are common characteristics of good schools—a stable, good leadership, curricular articulation and organization, school-wide staff development, community involvement, recognition of academic success, maximized learning time, collaborative planning, sense of school as community, clear expectations, and order and discipline (Purkey & Degan, 1985).

There are a large number of reported successes with programs designed to create effective schools from these elements. Eubanks and Levine (1983) reported on Project RISE in Milwaukee where the processes included "the cultivation of the pervasive belief that all students can learn," and included on their list the development of a high level of professional collegiality among staff, the establishment of a strong sense of student identification with the school, grade-level expectations and standards, the use of accelerated learning programs for students performing well below grade level, increases in the amount of time allocated and used for active student learning, and the establishment of a structured environment. Levine and Stark (1982) reported on urban elementary school efforts where the programs concentrated on teaching, planning, outcome-based supervision, monitoring of classrooms, parent involvement, assistance with record-keeping and duplicating for teachers, resource personnel assigned to classrooms, attention to low-achieving students, and attention to teaching higher-order thinking skills. Clark and McCarthy (1983) reported that the New York effort involved community assistance with planning, volunteer compliance, instructional coordination, management information systems, and positive reinforcement for teachers and students.

Although these improvement efforts were reported as successful, some reviewers have been critical. Rowan, Bossert, and Dwyer (1983) reported that the movement's techniques constituted such a "bewildering array" that it is not clear what exactly makes a school more effective. Their studies in California demonstrated that among "effective schools," achievement was still biased according to the social class of students and that the results of the efforts were unstable over time. "Only ten percent of the schools in our sample were effective for three consecutive years" (p. 26). Rowan, Bossert, and Dwyer also objected to the program's lack of clarity about the causal ordering of variables: for example, it is not known if effective principals are effective because they head effective organizations.

Ramsey and his associates (1982) used path analysis to explore causal relations among a number of variables in Seattle's schools. None of the causal modes they tried effectively explained the sources of a school's quality. In addition, they criticized the school improvement literature for being over simplified and noted its lack of clarity about the ways in which the organization affected the teaching and learning that affected the outcomes. Their analysis concluded that current research provides an uncertain basis for the design of school improvement programs.

Most of these criticisms were repeated by Purkey and Smith (1982b) in their discussion of the movement. They asserted that despite the intuitive appeal of the effective schools argument, the research is not only limited but is a "weak reed" (p. 16) on which to base the movement. Further, they raised what is generally a more fundamental question about the movement (particularly when applied to secondary schools): its "top down" nature. This was echoed by Cuban (1984b), who argued that when the rhetoric of effective schools is boiled out, what is left is a focus on test scores as the most visible and important educational goal and that school variables are being manipulated to tighten the school organization to attain high scores. In other words, for all the talk about improving climate, more collegial and democratic decision-making, or creating in Grant's (1981) words "a strong positive ethos," what is actually happening according to Cuban is that school boards articulate policies, develop learning outcomes in the form of test scores, inaugurate school planning processes, review and revise curricula, initiate assessment programs, and link staff evaluation more closely to student outcomes. The effective schools movement is increasing the schools' more bureaucratic aspects. Given the combination of constraints and contingencies, the nonavailability of either new funds or permission to reallocate current revenues, the cry for results coupled with invidious comparisons with schools where the scores are better, or, as Cuban put it, "because time is often short, cries for results are loud, pressures pinch acutely, and routines are already in place, top down implementation is administratively convenient" and "the drift toward organizational tautness is unmistakeable" (p. 139). It is ironic, however, that the effective schools movement, founded in part on Brookover's earlier work, Rutters' work and some of Erickson's work on private schools—all of which stressed a collegial, professional, participative organizational model—should have turned into an effort to strengthen the school bureaucracy. But given the inability of the schools to alter their constraints and contingencies, it is not hard to understand. Schools are responding with what they have to respond with.

Earlier in this chapter, we argued that some of the pressure on schools in the 1960s came from more diverse students. Schools responded with increased organizational specialization and differentiation. But while schools moved in those directions, they did not increase supervision or scrutiny of their processes. In fact, they decreased those elements. The current pressure to increase the schools' academic quality is being met with a slight reduction in specialization and differentiation (such as reducing electives), but the major response of the 1980s is to emphasize the supervision and control of internal processes. Present reform efforts are characterized by a tightening of the organization and an increased supervision and evaluation for both teachers and students. In a sense, those who run the organization are trying to recover a control they feel they gave away in the 1960s.

Cusick and Wheeler observed such a trend in a study (1986) of the effects of standards-raising efforts. For example, in an affluent, suburban school in an eastern metropolitan area, long noted for its academic excellence, the tightening had been going on for several years. In fact it had antedated the current reform movement by at least five years. It included the introduction of elaborate policies and procedures on behavior, district-wide curriculum and some movement toward district-wide content tests, functional tests from the state in mathematics and reading, teacher collaboration on content, an extensive honors program, and an equally extensive special education program accompanied by extensive testing programs. There were more discernible lines between students, tracks, and a resource teacher system whereby supervisory teachers were given real authority relative to their colleagues. Overall this highly respected school had created a more tightly coupled and intelligible organization.

But there were some interesting side effects. One was that the more bureaucratic and regulated organization seemed to reinforce a particular vision about schooling and the ends of education. The teachers and staff said that they were preparing students for a world that is individualized, secularized, materialistic, stratified, competitive, and credentialed. The curriculum supported that vision. At the school's higher levels, students were exhorted to do well on SATs and compile high-grade point averages so they could attend good colleges and assume their rightful places at the top of the envisioned society. The curriculum at the top of the school, while more extensive, was not really different from the curriculum in the special education and vocational classes. At both ends the learning was expressed in terms of skills, competencies, scores, objectives, and tasks. The adult world for which we are actually preparing children, however, may not be limited to individuals making it on their own in a competitive, secular society. This social vision has severe limitations. There are hosts of competing visions and values, many more appealing and perhaps even more realistic, than the simple economic-vocational model presented by and embedded in the school organization.

Administrators, however, rarely have the luxury of addressing complex sets of competing educational visions. Managing the coming and going of 1,750 adolescents, an eight-period day, a teaching staff of 100, and a support staff of 67 is a complicated endeavor. The logistics of running schools support these bureaucratic educational organizations and simple economic vocational world visions to the exclusion of more complex but equally realistic visions. At the least such an arrangement confirms the view of Katz and Everhart, cited earlier, that one of the major functions of schooling is to perpetuate the extant social system, flaws and all.

Coupled with these administrative and bureacratic imperatives and necessities, this limited vision also encourages, if not demands, the adoption of simpler models of learning and achievement. This is one of the most serious unintended consequences of pursuing this limited vision with a tightly coupled school system, such as the one Cusick and Wheeler studied. Although it may appear enviably articulate and efficiently managed, a system with tight connections between its vision, administration, personnel, methods, evaluation, and outcomes is only as good as its vision. Despite its superficial appeal to many school authorities and parents in less advantaged communities, a vision with the limitations of the one reconstructed above is dangerous to embrace enthusiastically.

On the other hand, there are similar dangers in perpetuating loosely coupled systems which primarily protect an equilibrium that sustains and encourages administrators, teachers, and students to bargain away academic standards and learning. Unlike the school discussed above, the vast majority of systems, particularly in our larger cities, are loosely coupled, meaning that they are organizations in which events are purposely left unrelated to one another, supervision is intentionally left weak, and evaluation is purposely left vague. Loose coupling has been essential to the political, legal, and financial survival of schools because it masks low levels of attendance, engagement, and achievement which would be unbearable if revealed to the public that supports schools economically and entrusts them with its children. Public confidence is essential if schools are to survive, and loose coupling avoids the kind of surveillance of instruction and performance that would undermine continued faith and support (Meyer & Rowan, 1978). Organizational theorists have demonstrated how this nonsurveillance of teaching and learning has been functional for many schools, given their fundamental task of "symbolically redefining" graduates as possessing qualities and skills gained through attendance (Kamens, 1977). This process of redefinition occurs independently of whether or not any changes in competency actually occur. Loose coupling, consequently, can also have the unintended consequence of preserving an organization that contributes little to the growth and improvement of its clients, but offers to the public a facade of functional health.

It is essential to appreciate the lesson of how difficult it is in a pluralistic, democratic society to navigate effectively and fairly between educational organizations that are tightly or loosely coupled. Each poses its own special dangers: of a potentially limited and counterproductive vision, or of an unexamined equilibrium that obscures fundamental systemic weakness. In at least one important respect there appears to be an interesting connection between tight and loose coupling. Many efforts to tighten schools organizationally will undoubtedly expose facets of the equilibrium that loose coupling protects. Reforms designed to enhance the articulation and performance of educational organizations, despite their limited vision, may inadvertently reveal the dismal levels of learning that pass for real achievement in many schools.

The schools are under pressure to increase their academic quality, but because the nation continues to support their universalism, or the general comprehensiveness of their programs, they have thus far responded with internal, organizational variables. While there is talk about creating a "strong positive ethos" and "improved learning climate," operationally the schools are pursuing a tighter, scrutinized and evaluated form of organization. It was to be expected. Schools respond with what they have to respond with, and tighter organizations can solve certain problems.

Yet some questions remain unresolved. There is still that soft technical core. Efforts to make schools more organizationally rational do not make the core processes of teaching and learning more rational. Or if they do make them more rational, they do so by substituting a simplified version of education and the world for which students are being prepared. Moreover, it is difficult to ignore the lessons of the 1960s, when teachers, and eventually administrators and school boards, rejected the intuitively appealing "planning, programming, and budget systems," and similar "management by objectives" reforms (Cuban, 1975; Patton & Perrone, 1976; Wolcott, 1977; Clinton, 1977; Bleecher, 1975). Finally, is the organization the proper unit of analysis at all when thinking about educational reform? Despite the brave talk about "effective" schools and communal forms of organization, about a positive ethos and learning climate, it is vital to recall, as Eva Brann has reminded us (1979), that "the effort of a single teacher is the ultimate resort of excellence in education." There remain questions about how organizational reforms affect individual teachers. In fact, there are reasons to believe that many of the proposed reforms may either attempt to defy the nature of our pluralistic school system in a democratic society, or alienate teachers by either diminishing their power relative to administrators or locking them into simple vocational visions of education, visions pursued by equally simple and instrumental versions of pedagogy and curricula.

☶ CONCLUSION: The Pitfalls of Surrogate Learning

Our analysis of bargaining, which prevails in the vast majority of high school classrooms, indicates the depth and scope of the instructional problems endemic to secondary education in the United States. These problems are not immediately apparent. In some ways they are imperceptible because American secondary schools run relatively smoothly. People who work in them are courteous and civil; students are ordinarily well behaved and orderly. Events begin and end on time; procedures are followed. Most administrators and teachers are able to articulate and present a reasonably intelligible account of the relationship between educational goals, the curriculum, and most school events. The problems in our schools are made even more imperceptible because that minority of the public most interested in serious academic endeavors, amibitious parents of aggressive students, can usually find schools or tracks or individual teachers that provide sufficient rigor to enable their children to compete successfully for admission to elite universities. The system's ability to accommodate the aspirations of virtually all constituencies, from the highly to the lowly motivated and engaged, appears both to demonstrate a healthy functional relationship to the larger society and to mask the overall prevalence of low academic standards. This facade of functional health is able to obscure the mutually reinforcing features of entrepreneurial and disengaged teachers, indifferent students, and undemanding academic programs. Most tragically, it is able to mask the inequality that it reinforces and sustains through its open, free, and universal attendance policies, its comprehensive elective curriculum, and its market orientation toward accommodating the "needs of society."

Just as it is essential to acknowledge the extent to which the process of academic learning is embedded in the larger structure of schooling and the relations between educational institutions and their host societies, it is critical to consider the movement to improve high schools in terms of its intended and inadvertent consequences. First of all, the initiatives appear to be based upon a nostalgic view of the origins and nature of problems with academic learning in high schools, which suggests that standards have declined dramatically over the past 20 years and that the diversity of adolescents, in terms of background, ambition, ability, or whatever, is largely responsible for the erosion of academic performance. On the basis of this perspective, the standards-raising movement is attempting to tighten administrative and instructional controls over the students who have been identified as the source of the problem: that minority of adolescents attending primarily urban schools where academic performance standards, as reflected in achievement test scores, are lowest. In contrast to this prevalent viewpoint, we have emphasized that the problem of academic learning is common to the vast majority of high schools, and that the standards-raising efforts should attend to the problematic nature of school learning in perhaps 70 percent of our secondary classrooms.

Despite their misdiagnosis of the problems, the improvement initiatives, nevertheless, will have consequences for many high school students. On the one hand, for the disadvantaged and low-achieving students, many of the reforms will have a detrimental impact. Exit testing, increasing surveillance, monitoring behavior and attendance, and expanding administrative authority over teachers and the curriculum will force many adolescents out of high school. For those who remain, the reforms will make it more legitimate to differentiate them into tracks, with the most able and aggressively academic separated into honors classes, accelerated institutes, and magnet schools, and the less able diverted into classes where they will, at best, be drilled in functional reading, mathematics, social studies, and writing exercises.

Although this differentiation will undoubtedly affect the equitable distribution of instructional resources (since much of the sorting will reflect social class and race as much as ability), it will be attractive to many educational authorities. It appears to offer many advantages. Teachers like it because planning, management, instruction, and evaluation are easier in homogeneous or segregated classes. It will enable schools to retain the appearance of comprehensiveness. Although the realities of scheduling make it likely that tracking will isolate students attending school in the same building, administrators will be able to maintain the image of universality. Segmenting students according to their apparent ability has further advantages. It can appear to satisfy the perennial public outcry for the possession of minimal skills and functional competencies by all students. It does not upset the more academically ambitious students or their aggressive parents. The initiatives that offer essentially supervision, testing, and tighter management controls are relatively inexpensive, limited as they are to the manipulation of organizational variables. By offering what are administrative improvements through altering organizational variables, they give the appearance of solving the problems without disturbing the schools fundamentally or changing their relationship to the larger society and economy.

On the other hand, for able students in academically strong high schools, and for those adolescents with parents who are able to negotiate successfully with bureaucratic educational institutions, and are situated to exploit whatever academic opportunities might be available within the differentiated structure, many of the reforms will magnify their advantages. The initiatives will undoubtedly deliver a greater share of instructional resources to higher-achieving students, in the tradition of providing advantages to talented students tracked in honors classes, for example. Tightening curricular and behavioral standards will differentially reward those students who best understand the nature of school learning and are able to conform to traditional instructional expectations. By making it appear that the high school diploma has more integrity, that the initiatives have made it less accessible and concomitantly more desirable, the reform campaign will seem to increase the value of succeeding at the secondary level, at least initially. In some way, it will be more valuable to endure or to survive successfully an experience that excludes an increasing percentage of the adolescent population, even if the exclusion process is arbitrary and based largely upon irrelevant criteria rooted in differential support for schools, distinctive habits of learning in elementary school, or other social, economic, and cultural realities beyond the control of both schools and the children themselves.

In addition to these direct effects on students, many of the reform initiatives will have other consequences for the way the public thinks about educational purposes and the way the public defines and evaluates the quality of the schooling available in their communities. The sort of managerial tinkering that characterizes many of the proposals and initiatives will inevitably narrow the vision of an acceptable education. Limiting improvements to the manipulation of internal organizational variables, with relatively little appreciation of the larger context of rewards and disincentives within which individuals assess their potential return on schooling, will tend to legitimize one definition of education over all others, one that emphasizes surrogate learning. Such an approach will undoubtedly reinforce the advantages of high achievers, those who appear to flourish under traditional forms of school learning, because it endorses their view of the purpose and nature of education.

As we suggested earlier, it is vital to understand that view and to recognize its implications and limitations. If schooling is defined narrowly, then the quality of education depends upon the validity and consequences of that specific definition. The definition of education that appears to drive many of the reforms has a number of unfortunate, and unappreciated, limitations. It tends to reward proxies for learning rather than learning itself. At its heart is a question that captures the essential qualities of school learning under this definition, a question that is ubiquitous in even the best, most enviably academic schools, "Is this going to be on the test?" This simple question reveals much about the nature of learning in the United States, and in many other nations, including most obviously Japan, as Thomas Rohlen (1983) has reminded us. Whether students ask the question aloud is less important than whether it is on their minds as they move through their lives in classrooms and study halls, as they consider the potential return on employment or social activities or learning. It is a question that begins to be heard in the later elementary grades; it is not particularly prevalent in the lower primary grades in most schools, although ever-younger children are beginning to ask it, as they are inducted into the process of school learning. By the time students are in adolescence, it becomes a question of far more consequences to individual students and their teachers than any question of subject matter or interpretation; indeed, perhaps it becomes *the* subject-matter question for everyone concerned.

This definition of education can sustain an illusion of excellence while allowing students and teachers to bargain away real academic learning. As long as the tests are passed, credits are accumulated, and credentials are awarded, what occurs in most classrooms is allowed to pass as education. By encouraging this vision of education, the current reform campaign risks achieving illusory standards of excellence. Recognizing the implication of this definition should caution against too quickly accepting evidence of improvement in schooling. Implementing a number of the reforms will help some schools "improve" within the terms of this vision of education: scores will rise, attendance rates will increase (as graduation rates fall), evidence of glaring and embarrassing curricular foolishness will diminish, organizations will become more impressively articulated and more tightly coupled. Secondary schooling will appear to improve because the proxies for learning that all students pursue (and that some pursue devotedly) will improve. The real value and meaning of the accomplishments, however, will be eroded by the vision's narrowness and limitations.

Even if the reforms reduce some of the active disengagement of teachers and students, the underlying indifference will remain, for its roots lie largely outside of the simple organizational variables under the jurisdictions claimed by the initiatives. The most prevalent reforms will have relatively little impact on the sort of passive disengagement that characterizes the posture of most adolescents toward academic learning.

The fundamental vision itself encourages and rewards passivity. It asks students to substitute learning how to go to school for learning. It asks them not to learn but to comply. In elementary school, students learn how to comply, how to acquire the proxies for academic learning. That becomes their motivation. While some care about it more and some are more successful in the competition for proxies, most come to care less, and they resist or survive through different degrees of indifference. Should even the successful feel pride in their accomplishments? It seems as though the vision itself undermines the value of their achievements. Savvy adolescents recognize this. They agree or refuse to continue to participate, but their decision is based upon their assessment of a return on investment. Less cunning students become tormented or contented, depending upon their expectations for themselves or the pressure they sense from those about whom they care.

The vision of education underlying the reform campaign is also fundamentally utilitarian and instrumentalist. In our society, education is defended on the basis of its direct utility to individuals. In many respects it is treated as another commodity. Students and their parents offer their commitment and engagement to schooling to the extent that they perceive that their participation will return something to them that they value, perhaps the ability to get ahead, to survive, or to cope. Like virtually all educational reform movements in the past, the current improvement initiatives are marketed politically on the basis of their instrumental value; as with previous efforts as well, the implementation process inevitably narrows the reforms toward ever more utilitarian ends.

Emphasizing such instrumentalist, utilitarian functions for secondary schooling contributes to at least two serious problems. First, as we argued earlier, schools cannot directly control their ultimate utilitarian value. The "worth" of educational credentials is shaped by many relationships and practices external to schools and over which schools rarely have any determining influence. We have suggested, for example, that changes in the labor market, particularly in the supply and demand for specialized skills, and in the admissions practices of colleges and universities dramatically affect the nature of classroom life and academic standards and learning through their impact on adolescents' assessments of the payoff for investing their time and effort in a host of competing alternatives. The larger context of rewards and incentives is shaped by forces far beyond the grasp of either educators or legislators. It is essential to recognize the impact of that context on the pattern and level of engagement of adolescents in academic learning. The utilitarian vision driving schooling sets the level of motivation for each student, thereby affecting the dynamics of classroom interaction.

Second, commitment to schooling is valued differentially in our society because the payoff and rewards vary according to levels of attainment and the reputation of specific educational institutions. In many ways this emphasis upon utilitarianism accentuates social class differences because it reinforces the advantages of children from privileged circumstances who anticipate using advanced credentials to gain access to professional and managerial occupations. The utilitarian value of high school is greater for those competing for admission to institutions of higher education than it is for those seeking employment directly after graduation. Since the motivating power of the credential varies by the nature and level of individual aspirations and opportunities, students who will be able to find some sort of employment with just a secondary diploma (the content of which is rarely examined) understand that it is in their interest to do what is necessary to earn the diploma. They realize also that it is not in their interest to do more than minimally comply with requirements or to resist the temptation to negotiate lower expectations with their teachers. Although the credential is more valuable to students intending to further their schooling, as we have argued above, even they do not have to be deeply engaged in academic learning in order to earn acceptable grades and letters of recommendation. The vast majority of adolescents have accurately assessed the relative utilitarian value or payoff for investing in schooling, with the result that class distinctions will be inevitably exacerbated as the reform movement attempts to artificially manipulate standards and expectations in isolation. This will be an unfortunate, tragic, unintended consequence of the school improvement campaign.

Finally, as we have implied, there is some question as to whether the school or district is the appropriate or legitimate unit within which to examine teaching and learning. It may be that discussing academic learning in isolated organizational language misses the point. Certainly institutions and districts dramatically influence the lives and fortunes of children in school. Yet both teaching and learning are intensely personal. Each teacher and learner approaches the classroom on the basis of a personal assessment of costs and rewards. Bargaining, which lies at the core of the classroom (or any organizational or human relationship) is not an aberration from the norm and cannot be eliminated through more rational administrative processes. As Waller (1932) pointed out more than 50 years ago, and as so much of the observational literature supports, relations between teachers and their students are intensely personal. Their personal nature makes them almost impervious to many apparently reasonable and modest organizational improvement efforts. It is convenient to ignore the personal nature of teaching and learning. It allows reformers to work with administrators who are central to the schools, and administrators are ordinarily optimistic and eager to assist. It makes it relatively easy to develop programs and funding schemes, to speak intelligibly about improvements, and to project an air of hope and confidence that the situation will improve. It is, however, illusory to an important degree. Not only does it ignore the personal nature of the learning and teaching processes and the power of either party to subvert them toward other ends, but it is also condescending because it implies that not only teaching and learning, but also teachers and learners, can always be manipulated toward predictable ends by altering rather superficial organizational variables.

We believe it is critical, even imperative, to improve the quality of education in our nation's secondary schools. However, the present standards-raising movement, although backed by serious and well-intended people, is fundamentally flawed. In an effort to solve the problem of low academic achievement, it has focused on making educational institutions more efficient, prescriptive, and results-oriented without (paradoxically) creating the conditions within the schools for success or recognizing the link between schools and society which fundamentally determines the scope of any real change.

In so doing it is playing out what has become an all-too-familiar scenario in public policy as it has come to affect education in the last twenty years. Reformers have attempted to change public education from the top down with mandates to address a particular problem; with rules, procedures, and standards generated to facilitate goal attainment; and with monitoring and evaluation to assess progress. What has been missing has been an appreciation of how such programs would actually affect the daily lives of students and teachers. Most of the educational reforms of the past twenty years have been initiated in the absence of any understanding of the manner in which the design for change will affect the lives of teachers and students in classrooms and school corridors, the places where learning occurs.

The reforms described and analyzed in this book neatly fit the same pattern of organizational mandates and will likely lead to the same frustrating results. The most prominent reforms in the current movement have been mandated from above, are easy to institute, relatively inexpensive, simple to understand, uniform in their application to all students, and focused on accountability mechanisms. Few have considered their effects on the relationship between teachers and students in the classroom and the trends of the past thirty years both within schools and outside school walls that have exacerbated both student and teacher disengagement from academic learning.

There are good reasons why schools function as they do. There are reasons why teachers are so dependent upon the goodwill of students, why together they are allowed to bargain away standards and academic learning. Bargaining and disengagement are not just surface events. They are bound up with the differential return on academic learning and incentives for teaching in the United States as well as in the way we organize, finance, and administer our schools. They are embedded in our attitudes toward social class, toward what we expect of our children and the children of others, toward equal opportunity, and toward the place of schooling in these vital issues.

By failing to consider such issues, the initiatives mandated thus far have served only to narrow the focus of education to proxies for learning, such as test scores, instead of direct measures (can a child actually read and comprehend or solve a real-world problem?). To do this requires a different way of thinking about education, which is why this study does not conclude with a list of prescribed reforms. Instead it suggests an alternative view of education and learning which could facilitate reform to address the issues we have raised.

In contrast to the forms of gamesmanship which currently characterize school learning in the United States, we endorse a vision of education which leads to genuine empowerment. We have argued that in large part academic learning in high schools is driven by the perceived value and meaning of the high school diploma, a credential that does not represent the acquisition of useful skills and knowledge. Contemporary schooling, in other words, offers a false sense of empowerment. At its core, contemporary schooling is a process of bestowing credentials. Social and economic opportunities are assumed to follow the possession of credentials. Because credentials serve as surrogates or proxies for skills, dispositions, and knowledge, however, their value is established independently of the distribution and prevalence of abilities and skills. Their value is set within the context of a competitive, relatively market-oriented economy that allocates access to scarce resources, including opportunity, income, goods, and power. Because of the necessity to allocate access to scarce resources, the value of credentials is correspondingly manipulated on the basis of the supply of, and demand for, prospective labor in different hierarchically arranged occupations. Credential access and value are shaped or determined by the society's need for differentiated labor as well as the necessity of legitimating the unequal distribution of rewards by offering a semblance of mobility to selected individuals, thereby encouraging a vision of American society as a meritocracy. This is not a conspiratorial process manipulated in isolation by social elites determined to protect their prerogatives and privileges. It is the cumulative product of millions of individual employer and prospective employee decisions about who might be available for certain work and who might feel confident about pursuing certain work. Combined with a relatively stratified, fixed social class structure, the nature of the economy does not encourage—cannot permit—perfect open competition on the basis of the possession of abilities. When an occupation becomes too accessible, or when a level of schooling becomes too universal, its value declines; its value is eroded by its accessibility. When that happens, access is either restricted by pressing for higher standards, thereby restoring some of the occupation's exclusivity, or meaningful competition is shifted to another level within the institution (such as to graduate professional schools) or to a parallel institution (such as to private schools). In a sense, therefore, the value of the credential is established politically and artificially, just as the value of the nation's currency is set politically. Because a credential's worth and a currency's value are set politically, they can be changed, but the change occurs independently of the presumed underlying content of either. Since the credential is simply a proxy, those who wish to discriminate on the basis of its possession and distribution merely have to award it a different value and to use it differently than they had previously. This is what has happened to the high school diploma.

While Americans have pretended that school achievement and attainment—independent of social-class origins—have directly and genuinely determined occupational and economic status, scholarship completed over the past generation has demonstrated that this assumption is unwarranted, at least in the vast proportion of cases. In contrast to the prevailing image of America as a fair, competitive meritocracy, it has been virtually impossible to escape the grasp of social-class origins, regardless of academic performance in school or measured intellectual ability. Because schooling tends to aggravate and reinforce variance in academic ability that is initially rooted in social-class origins, those exceptional individuals who have been able to attain a degree of social and economic mobility have often had to do so in spite of their formal educational experiences rather than because of them. In many respects credentials are symbols of social-class membership rather than accurate reflections of genuine ability or skills. In such a situation, increasing the power of a narrow and limited vision of schooling—where class status is rewarded with credentials and credentials appear to be rewarded with wealth, power, and opportunity—will have ultimately tragic consequences for many families. They will attempt, at enormous cost, to create their own version of the academic vision in which graduation leads to a better life, be it a well paying job or admission to elite institutions of higher education, which are presumed to guarantee affluence and professional status.

But the ability of exclusive elite institutions to contribute so positively to the lives of their clients depends upon the continued existence of so many other nonselective, nonelite institutions willing and able to offer so much less to their clients. Elite institutions cannot absorb everyone because their power rests upon their exclusivity. If everyone could attend an Ivy League university, few would want to because many of the presumed advantages accrue only because everyone cannot attend. In response to the appearance of improved levels of academic attainment on the part of the adolescent population, such institutions would simply set the terms of the competition at a higher level, as they have done consistently over the past century, because they cannot absorb everyone without diluting their ability to make striking contributions to their clients' lives and livelihoods.

For those families which view the high school diploma as a ticket to direct access to jobs and some degree of economic security, the current state of our economy suggests this part of the American dream has died. Getting an education, even a high school education, no longer necessarily means getting a rewarding job. Most expansion in the job market during the rest of this century will be in low-paying, low-skill positions in service occupations. For these jobs, a high school diploma is often unnecessary. Furthermore, one might well suspect that some of the skills learned in high school, those skills of bargaining away requirements, might be dysfunctional to successful performance in many jobs in this sector, where careful adherence to rules and regulations may well be critical.

The current schooling/credentialing/placement system depends upon the appearance of enormous variance in "ability." As more communities and families buy into this vision of the purpose and value of their schools, they will be profoundly disappointed when the relative variance in adult attainment is preserved through the manipulation of the value of the credentials involved. Their children will become more proficient at the gamesmanship that lies at the heart of contemporary schooling, but relative differences in proficiency levels will remain rooted as they are in the cultural capital of different social classes. Of course, this will make it appear as though schools are improving, and working conditions for many teachers and administrators will become more convenient. But those who expect an improvement in achievement test scores to translate into a competitive advantage or eventual economic success for their children will be disappointed. The value of the credential will simply be redefined to recreate the variance, and the variance will be associated with social class, just as it always has been.

Families willing to invest the economic resources and personal pain needed to buy into the prevailing vision of academic schooling deserve more than to have their children become more proficient at playing a tragic game, a game whose rules will be inevitably changed simply because their children were allowed to participate. The rule changes will ensure that their children may never win and may help to convince them that they deserved to lose. Buying into the vision more fully legitimates the process through which inequalities are preserved through the appearance of fair competition.

Such families deserve schools that will empower their children through the learning they offer rather than through the credentials that they award. In order for this goal to be achieved, it is first necessary to sever the connection between bogus credentials and social and economic opportunity. Rejecting the prevailing narrow vision of schooling which rewards proficiency at negotiating rather than learning is worth considering. Empowered learning is foreign to most all of our schools, but it is not a difficult concept to understand. It consists of intellectual and character traits: the ability to act independently and responsibly based upon an accurate assessment of the consequences of one's actions; the possession of values and the ability to exercise sound judgment that encourages the fair treatment of others; personal autonomy and control; problem-solving, critical thinking, and higher-order reasoning skills; and the ability to make informed decisions. Most people would agree with such a definition of what is worth learning.

These skills and knowledge, because they would be genuine, would enable one to function in a competitive market economy if necessary. Our economic system does not preclude individual and collective empowerment. These abilities, however, are not effectively learned in contemporary schools because such skills are not particularly relevant within the terms of a spurious credential system. If they are learned, it is incidental, and for some dysfunctional, to learning the gamemanship and negotiation skills that are more consistently rewarded.

Most of the current reforms and initiatives promote gamesmanship and surrogate learning. They attempt to seduce or induct more children into that way of life. They are based upon the vision of schooling that inevitably promotes surrogate learning instead of empowered learning. To reject this requires reformers who are appreciative of the advantages of empowered learning with the courage to resist the temptations to invest further resources in tidying up after a narrow, limited vision of schooling. The task calls for uncommon courage, since the traditional ranks of reformers owe their positions and advantages to that vision and are particularly well situated to protect their own children's inheritance by investing more in tidying things up even further.

▥ Bibliography

AACTE Task Force on Teacher Certification. "Emergency Teacher Certification: Summary and Recommendations." *Journal of Teacher Education* 35(March-April 1984): 21–26.

Adelman, Clifford. *Devaluation, Diffusion, and the College Connection: A Study of High School Transcripts, 1964–1981.* Report to the National Commission on Excellence in Education, March 1983.

Adelson, Joseph. *Twenty-five Years of American Education: An Interpretation.* Report to the National Commission on Excellence in Education, September 1982.

Adler, Mortimer J. *The Paideia Proposal.* New York: Macmillan, 1982.

Airasian, Peter W., & Madaus, George F. "Linking Testing and Instruction: Policy Issues" *Journal of Educational Measurement* 20(Summer 1983): 103–118.

Amberson, Max. "The Competency-Based Core Curriculum: Innovative and Accountable." *Agricultural Education Magazine* 52(April 1980): 4–5.

Anderson, Beverly L. "What the National Assessment of Educational Progress Has Shown About Education in the 1970's." Paper presented at the Case for Public Education Conference, Wilmington, Del., November 1983.

Anderson, Beverly L., et al. Achievement Standards and Requirements for High School Graduation. Denver, Colo.: Education Commission of the States, August 1983.

Anderson, Lorin W. "Instruction and Time-on-Task: A Review." *Journal of Curriculum Studies* 14(October-December 1981): 289–303.

Anyon, Jean. "Social Class and School Knowledge." *Curriculum Inquiry* 11(Spring 1981): 3–42.

Apple, Michael W. "Teaching and 'Women's Work': A Comparative Historical and Ideological Analysis." *Teachers College Record* 86(Spring 1985): 455–473.

Armstrong, W. Earl. "The Teaching Profession: Retrospect and Prospect." In Lindley J. Stiles, ed., *The Teacher's Role in American Society,* pp. 276–291. New York: Harper & Brothers, 1957.

Arnove, Robert F., & Strout, Toby. Alternative Schools for Disruptive Youth. Paper prepared for the National Institute of Education/Educational Equity Group—School Social Relations under Grants NIE-P-76-0217 and NIE-P-77-0254. September 1978a.

Arnove, Robert, F., & Strout, Toby. "Alternative Schools and Cultural Pluralism: Promise and Reality." *Educational Research Quarterly* 2(Winter 1978b): 74–95.

Arnove, Robert F., & Strout, Toby. The Evolution, Uses and Implications of Alternative Education. Bloomington, Ind.: School of Education, Indiana University, April 1977.

Arnstine, Donald. "The Deterioration of Secondary Education: Media Images, Administrative Nostrums, and College Pressures." *Teachers College Record* 85(Fall 1983): 9–26.

Astin, Alexander W. *The American Freshman, 1966–1981: Some Implications for Educational Policy and Practice*. Report to the National Commission on Excellence in Education, May 1982.

Bailey, Adrienne Y. "Agenda for Action." *Educational Leadership* 41(March 1984): 64–68.

Bailey, Adrienne Y. "The Educational Equality Project: Focus on Results." *Phi Delta Kappan* 65(September 1983): 22–25.

Bailey, Stephen K. *Alternative Paths to the High School Diploma*. Reston, Va.: National Association of Secondary School Principals, 1973.

Bakalis, Michael J. "Power and Purpose in American Education." *Phi Delta Kappan* 65(September 1983): 80–82.

Baratz, Joanne. "Policy Implications of Minimum Competency Testing." In Richard M. Jaeger & Carol H. Tittle, eds., *Minimum Competency Achievement Testing*, pp. 49–68. Berkeley, Calif.: McCutchan Publishing Corporation, 1980.

Barnard, Chester. *The Functions of the Executive*. Cambridge: Harvard University Press, 1938.

Barrett, Wayne. "The Politics of Flunking: Using Tests Against Kids." *The Village Voice* 22(June 1, 1982): 1, 24, 38.

Berryman, Charles, & Schneider, Donald O. "Patterns of Work Experience Among High School Students: Educational Implications." *High School Journal* 66(April/May 1983): 267–75.

Bicknell, John E. *The Prediction of Effectiveness in Secondary School Teaching: A Summary Report*. Albany, N.Y.: New York State Education Department, June 1959.

Birman, Beatrice F., & Natriello, Gary. "Perspectives in Absenteeism in High School." *Journal of Research and Development in Education* 11(Summer 1978): 29–38.

Bleecher, H. The Authoritativeness of Michigan's Educational Accountability Program. Unpublished Dissertation, Michigan State University, 1975.

Bloom, Benjamin. *Human Characteristics and School Learning*. New York: McGraw-Hill, 1976.

"Blowing the Whistle on Johnny." *Time Magazine* (January 30, 1984): 80.

Borden, Christopher, III. "Back to Basics?—Back Is Here." *Educational Horizons* 58(Winter 1979–1980): 85–88.

Borrowman, Merle L. *The Liberal and Technical in Teacher Education: A Historical Survey of American Thought*. New York: Teachers College, Columbia University, 1956.

Bowles, Samuel, & Gintis, Herbert. *Schooling in Capitalist America*. New York:

Basic Books, 1976.

Boyer, Ernest L. *High School: A Report on Secondary Education in America*. New York: Harper & Row, 1983.

Brann, Eva T. H. *Paradoxes of Education in a Republic*. Chicago: University of Chicago Press, 1979.

Breland, Hunter. *Grade Inflation and Declining S.A.T. Scores: A Research Viewpoint*. Princeton, N.J.: Educational Testing Service, September 1976.

Bridgeman, Anne. "States Launching Barrage of Initiatives, Survey Finds." *Education Week* (February 6, 1985): 1–31.

Bridgeman, A., Ranbom, S., & Ward, M. "Legislatures Focus on Salaries, Financing, School Improvement." *Education Week* (March 21, 1984): 5.

Brimm, Jack, et al. "Student Absenteeism: A Survey Report." *National Association of Secondary School Principals Bulletin* 62(February 1978): 65–69.

Brodinsky, Ben. "Back to the Basics: The Movement and Its Meaning." *Phi Delta Kappan* 58(March 1977): 522–27.

Brookover, Wilbur, Beady, Charles, Flood, Patricia, Schweitzer, John, & Weisenbaker, Joe. *School Social Systems and Student Achievement: Schools Can Make a Difference*. New York: Praeger, 1979.

Buchmann, Margret. "Can Traditional Lore Guide Right Choice in Teaching?" *Journal of Curriculum Studies* 13(1981): 339–48.

Buchmann, Margret. "The Flight Away From Content in Teacher Education and Teaching." *Journal of Curriculum Studies* 14(1982): 61–68.

Bullough, Robert V. Jr., Gitlin, Andrew D., & Goldstein, Stanley L. "Ideology, Teacher Role, and Resistance." *Teachers College Record* 86 (Winter 1984): 339–58.

Butler, John H. "An Exploratory Study of Adolescent Interaction in an Innovative Urban High School." Unpublished Dissertation, Michigan State University, 1975.

Cabinet Council on Human Resources. Disorder in Our Public Schools. Memorandum for the Cabinet Council on Human Resources. Washington, D.C.: U.S. Department of Education, January 9, 1984.

California state official [anon.]. Telephone interview with Christopher Wheeler, March 22, 1984.

Campbell, Esther L., Achilles, Charles M., Faires, Charles L., & Martin, Oneida. "School Discipline: Policy Procedures, and Potential Discrimination—A Study of Disproportionate Representation of Minority Pupils in School Suspensions " Paper presented at the Annual Meeting of the Mid-South Educational Research Association, November 1982.

Cawelti, Gordon. "Redesigning General Education in American High Schools." *National Association of Secondary School Principals Bulletin* 65 (March 1981) : 9-15.

"Changing Course." *Education Week* (February 6, 1985): 11-30.

Cheever, Daniel S., & Sayer, Gus A. "How We Defined Our Core Curriculum." *Educational Leadership* 39 (May 1982): 599-601.

Children's Defense Fund. *Children Out of School in America*. Washington, D.C. : Children's Defense Fund, 1974.

Chobot, Richard B., & Garibaldi, Antoine. "In-School Alternatives to Suspension: A Description of Ten School District Programs." *Urban Review* 14(1982) : 317-36.

Christenbury, Leila. "The Elective Curriculum: Origin, Development, and Decline." *English Education* 15(May 1983): 73-91.

Christenbury, Leila. The Origin, Development, and Decline of the Secondary English Elective Curriculum. Unpublished report, prepared at Virginia Polytechnic Institute and State University, 1980.

Christenbury, Leila. "The Secondary English Elective Curriculum." *English Journal* 68(September 1979) : 50-54.

Church, Robert L., & Sedlak, Michael W. *Education in the United States: An Interpretive History*. New York: Free Press, 1976.

Clark, Burton R. "The High School and the University: What Went Wrong in America, Part 1." *Phi Delta Kappan* 66(February 1985a): 391-97.

Clark, Burton R. "The High School and the University: What Went Wrong in America, Part 2." *Phi Delta Kappan* 66(March 1985b): 472-75.

Clark, Kenneth B. *Dark Ghetto*. New York: Harper & Row, 1965.

Clark, Reginald M. *Family Life and School Achievement: Why Poor Black Children Succeed or Fail*. Chicago: University of Chicago Press, 1983.

Clark, Terry, & McCarthy, Dennis. "School Improvement in New York City: The Evolution of a Project." *Educational Researcher* 12(April 1983): 17-24.

Clinton, C. A. *The Politics of Developmental Change*. Final Report to the National Institute of Education, Contract No. OEC-O-72-5245, 1977.

Cohen, David K. "The Conditions of Teachers' Work." *Harvard Educational Review* 54(February 1984): 11-15.

Cohen, David K. "Education and Social Purposes: A Shifting Context." Paper presented at the Case for Public Education Conference, Wilmington, Del., November 1983.

Cohen, David K., & Haney, Walter. "Minimums, Competency Testing and Social Policy." In Richard M. Jaeger & Carol H. Tittle, eds., *Minimum Competency Achievement Testing*, pp. 5-22. Berkeley, Calif. : McCutchan Publishing Corporation, 1980.

Cohen, David K., & Murnane, Richard J. "The Merits of Merit Pay." *Public Interest* 80(Summer 1985): 3-30.

Cohen, David K., & Neufeld, Barbara. "The Failure of High School and the Progress of Education." *Daedalus* 110 (Summer 1981): 62–89.

Coleman, James S. *The Adolescent Society*. New York: Free Press, 1961.

Coleman, James S., et al. *Equality of Educational Opportunity*. Washington, D.C.: Government Printing Office, 1966.

The College Board. *Academic Preparation for College: What Students Need to Know and Be Able to Do*. New York: College Entrance Examination Board, 1983b.

Collins, Randall. *The Credential Society: An Historical Sociology of Education and Stratification*. New York: Academic Press, 1979.

Conant, James B. *The American High School Today.* New York: McGraw-Hill, 1959.

Conant, James B. *The Education of American Teachers.* New York: McGraw-Hill, 1963.

Cooperman, S., Webb, A., & Klagholz, L. F. *An Alternative Route to Teacher Selection and Professional Quality Assurance: An Analysis of Initial Certification.* Report No. PTM 300.80. Trenton, N.J.: New Jersey State Department of Education, 1983.

Crabbe, John K. "Those Infernal Electives." *English Journal* 59 (October 1970): 990-93.

Crain, Robert L. *The Quality of American High School Graduates: What Personnel Officers Say and Do About It.* Baltimore: Johns Hopkins University Center for Social Organization of Schools, Report No. 354, May 1984.

Cromer, Nancy. "Flexibility in the English Curriculum: The Semester Elective Program." *Arizona English Bulletin* 13(October 1970): 15-23.

Crowe, Cameron. *Fast Times at Ridgemont High.* New York: Simon & Schuster, 1981.

Cuban, Larry. "*Hobson* v. *Hanson:* A Study in Organizational Response." *Educational Administration Quarterly* 11(Spring 1975): 15-37.

Cuban, Larry. *How Teachers Taught: Constancy and Change in American Classrooms, 1890-1980.* New York: Longman, 1984a.

Cuban, Larry. "Transforming the Frog into a Prince: Effective Schools Research, Policy and Practice at the District Level." *Harvard Educational Review* 54(May 1984b): 129-151.

Currence, Cindy. "Discipline Codes Must Foster Balance of Order, Autonomy." *Education Week* (January 18, 1984): 8, 18.

Currence, Cindy. "Major Universities Adopt Tougher Teacher-Training Requirements." *Education Week* (June 12, 1985): 5.

Currence, Cindy. "Moratorium on Pay Plan Is Demanded in Florida." *Education Week* (May 22, 1985): 1, 16.

Currence, Cindy. "President's Approach to School Discipline Draws Criticism." *Education Week* (January 25, 1984): 16.

Cusick, Philip A. *The Egalitarian Ideal and the American High School.* New York: Longman, 1983.

Cusick, Philip A. *Inside High School: The Student's World.* New York: Holt, Rinehart & Winston, 1973.

Cusick, Philip A. "A Study of Networks Among the Professional Staffs in Secondary Schools." *Education Administration Quarterly* 17(Summer 1981): 114-38.

Cusick, Philip A., & Peters, W. "The Secondary Principal in the Small Town," *Secondary Education Today* 20(1979): 22-36.

Cusick, Philip A., & Wheeler, Christopher W. "Implementing Reform at the Local Level." Paper presented at the Annual Meeting of the American Educational Research Association, San Francisco, Calif., April, 1986.

Danielson, Louis C. "Educational Goals and Competency Testing for the Handicapped." In Richard M. Jaeger & Carol H. Tittle, eds., *Minimum Competency Achievement Testing,* pp. 201-3. Berkeley, Calif. : McCutchan Publishing Corporation, 1980.

Darling-Hammond, Linda. *Beyond the Commission Reports: The Coming Crisis in Teaching.* Santa Monica, Calif. : Rand Corporation, Report No. R-3177-RC, July 1984.

Darling-Hammond, Linda, & Wise, Arthur. "Teaching Standards or Standardized Teaching." *Educational Leadership* 41(October 1983): 66-69.

Davis, Dick. "One Solution to the Inner-City Attendance Problem." *Phi Delta Kappan* 56(April 1975): 56.

Davis, Janet. "Teachers, Kids, and Conflict: Ethnography of a Junior High School." In James P. Spradley & David McCurdy, eds., *The Cultural Experience,* pp. 103-19. Chicago; Science Research Associates, 1972.

DeLeonibus, Nancy. "Absenteeism: The Perpetual Problem." *The Practitioner* 5(October 1978): 13.

DiPrete, Thomas A., Muller, Chandra, & Shaeffer, Nora. *Discipline and Order in American High Schools.* Chicago: National Opinion Research Center, 1981.

Distefano, Philip. "Can Traditional Grading Survive the Elective Program?" *English Journal* 64(March 1975): 56-58.

Dougherty, Van. State Programs of School Improvement, 1983: A 50-State Survey. Denver, Colo.: Education Commission of the States, 1983.

Doyle, Walter. "Are Students Behaving Worse Than They Used To Behave?" *Journal of Research and Development in Education* 11(Summer 1978): 3-16.

Ducharme, Edward R. "When Dogs Sing: The Prospect for Change in American High Schools." *Journal of Teacher Education* 33(January/February 1982): 25-29.

Ducharme, Edward R., & Agne, R. M. "The Educational Professoriate: A Research-Based Perspective." *Journal of Teacher Education* 33(1982): 30-36.

Duckworth, Kenneth. *Some Ideas About Student Cognition, Motivation, and Work.* Report to the National Commission on Excellence in Education, March 1983.

Duke, Daniel L. *Teaching: The Imperiled Profession.* Albany: State University of New York Press, 1984.

Edmonds, Ronald R. "Making Public Schools Effective." *Social Policy* (September/October 1981): 56-60.

Education Commission of the States. *A Summary of Major Reports on Education.* Denver, Colo.: Education Commission of the States, November 1983a.

Education Commission of the States. *50-State Survey of Initiatives of Science, Mathematics and Computer Education.* Denver, Colo.: Education Commission of the States, September 1983b.

Education Commission of the States, Task Force on Education for Economic Growth. *Action for Excellence.* Denver, Colo.: Education Commission of the States, June 1983.

Educational Testing Service. Bulletin of Information, NTE Programs, 1983-84. Princeton, N.J.: Educational Testing Service, 1984.

Elsbree, Willard S. *The American Teacher: Evolution of a Profession in a Democracy.* New York: American Book, 1939.

English, Fenwick W. "Merit Pay: Reflections on Education's Lemon Tree." *Educational Leadership* 41(December 1983-January 1984): 72-79.

Erickson, Donald A., MacDonald, Lloyd, Manley-Casimir, Michael E., & Busk, Patricia L. Characteristics and Relationships in Public and Independent Schools. San Francisco: Center for Research in Private Education, February 1979.

Erickson, Frederick. "School Literacy, Reasoning, and Civility: An Anthropologist's Perspective." *Review of Educational Research,* 54(Winter 1984): 525-46.

Eubanks, Eugene, & Levine, Daniel. "A First Look at Effective Schools Projects in New York City and Milwaukee." *Phi Delta Kappan* 64(June 1983): 697-702.

Evans, H. Dean. "We Must Begin Educational Reform 'Every Place at Once.'" *Phi Delta Kappan* 65(November 1983): 173-77.

Evenden, Edward S., Gamble, Guy C., & Blue, Harold G. *Teacher Personnel in the United States.* Vol. II of the *National Survey of the Education of Teachers.* U.S. Department of the Interior, Bulletin 1933, No. 10. Washington, D.C.: Government Printing Office, 1935.

Everhart, R. B. *Reading Writing and Resistance—Adolescence and Labor in a Junior High School.* Boston: Routledge & Kegan Paul, 1983.

"Failure in Los Angeles." *Time Magazine* (December 10, 1951).

Fallon, Michael. "Students' Scores on State Tests Up in California." *Education Week* (April 10, 1985): 1, 16.

Farber, Barry A. "Stress and Burnout in Suburban Teachers." *Journal of Educational Research* 77(July/August 1984a): 325-31.

Farber, Barry A. "Teacher Burnout: Assumptions, Myths, and Issues." *Teachers College Record* 86(Winter 1984b): 321-38.

Farrar, Eleanor, Neufeld, Barbara, & Miles, Matthew. *Review of Effective Schools Programs: Implications for Policy, Practice and Research.* Final Report to the National Commission on Excellence in Education, April 1983.

Feiman-Nemser, Sharon, & Floden, Robert E. "The Cultures of Teaching." In Merlin C. Wittrock, ed., *Handbook of Research on Teaching,* pp. 505-26. 2d. ed. New York: Macmillan, 1986

Feistritzer, C. Emily. *The Condition of Teaching: A State by State Analysis.* Princeton, N.J.: Carnegie Foundation for the Advancement of Teaching, 1983.

Fenton, Kathleen S. "Competency Testing and the Handicapped: Some Legal Concerns for School Administrators." In Richard M. Jaeger & Carol H. Tittle, eds., *Minimum Competency Achievement Testing,* pp. 182-88. Berkeley, Calif.: McCutchan Publishing Corporation, 1980.

Ferguson, Richard L. "Issues in the Next Decade of Secondary and Postsecondary Educational Assessment." Paper presented at the Annual Meeting of the American Educational Research Association, New York, March, 1982.

Finn, Chester E., Ravitch, Diane, & Fancher, Robert T., eds., *Against Mediocrity: The Humanities in America's High Schools.* New York: Holmes & Meier, 1984.

Fisher, Thomas H. "Florida's Approach to Competency Testing." *Phi Delta Kappan* 59(May 1978): 599-602.

Fiske, Edward B. "High Schools Stiffen Diploma Requirements." *New York Times,* 1983.

Flakus-Mosqueda, Patricia. Survey of States' Teacher Policies. Working paper no. 2. Denver, Colo.: Education Commission of the States, October 1983.

Freeman, Donald J., Cusick, Philip A., & Houang, Richard T. *Academic Standards in Our Nation's Secondary Schools: The Public's Response.* Final Report to the National Institute of Education, Phase II of Contract No. 400-83-0052, July 26, 1985a.

Freeman, Donald J., Cusick, Philip A., & Houang, Richard T. "Secondary School Reform: What Does the Public Want?" *National Association of Secondary School Principals Bulletin* (October 1985b): 52-62.

Freeman, R. B. *The Overeducated American.* New York: Academic Press, 1976.

French, Russell L. "Dispelling the Myths About Tennessee's Career Ladder Program." *Educational Leadership* (December 1984/January 1985).

Friedenberg, Edgar Z. *Coming of Age in America: Growth and Acquiescence.* New York: Knopf, 1963.

Gallup, Alec. "The Gallup Poll of Teachers' Attitudes Towards the Public Schools." *Phi Delta Kappan* 66(October 1984): 97-107.

Gallup, Alec. "The Gallup Poll of Teachers' Attitudes Toward the Public Schools: Part 2." *Phi Delta Kappan* 66(January 1985): 323-30.

Garibaldi, Antoine. "In-School Alternatives to Suspension: The State of the Art." In Antoine Garibaldi, ed., *In-School Alternatives to Suspension: Conference Report,* pp. 59-70. Washington, D.C.: Government Printing Office, 1978.

Gilman, David Alan. "The Logic of Minimal Competency Testing." *National Association of Secondary School Principals Bulletin* 62(September 1978): 56-63.

Gitlin, Andrew. "School Structure and Teachers' Work." In Michael Apple & Lois Weis, eds., *Ideology and Practice in Schooling,* pp. 193-212. Philadelphia: Temple University Press, 1983.

Glass, Gene V. "Looking at Minimal Competency Testing: Educator Versus Senator." *Education and Urban Society* 12(November 1979): 47-55.

Glass, Gene V. "Minimum Competence and Incompetence in Florida." *Phi Delta Kappan* 59(May 1978): 602-65.

Goodlad, John I. *A Place Called School: Prospects for the Future.* New York: McGraw-Hill, 1984.

Gordon, C. Wayne. *The Social System of the High School: A Study in the Sociology of Adolescence.* Glencoe, Ill.: Free Press, 1957.

Graham, Patricia Albjerg. "Schools: Cacophony About Practice, Silence About Purpose." *Daedalus* (Winter 1984a): 29-57.

Graham, Patricia Albjerg. "Wanting It All." *The Wilson Quarterly* 8(New Year's 1984b): 47-58.

Grant, Gerald. "Character of Education and the Education of Character." *Daedalus* 110(Summer 1981): 135-49.

Grant, Gerald. Education, Character, and American Schools: Are Effective Schools Good Enough? Unpublished paper, Syracuse University, September 1982.

Grant, W. Vance, & Snyder, Thomas D. *Digest of Education Statistics, 1983-1984.* Washington, D.C.: National Center for Education Statistics, 1984.

Gray, Dennis. "The High School: Prospects for Change." Paper presented at the College Board National Forum, October 19, 1980.

Gyves, John J., & Clark, Donald C. "The Interest Centered Curriculum: Is Interest Enough?" *Clearing House* 49(September 1975): 33-37.

Hall, Gene E., Hord, Shirley M., Rutherford, William L., & Huling, Leslie L. "Change in High Schools: Rolling Stones or Asleep at the Wheel?" *Educational Leadership* 41(March 1984): 58-62.

Hampel, Robert L. *The Last Little Citadel: American High Schools Since 1940.* Boston: Houghton Mifflin, 1986.

Handlin, Oscar, et al., *Report of the Harvard University Committee on Teaching.* Cambridge, Mass.: Harvard University Printing Office, May 15, 1957.

Haney, Walter, & Madaus, George. "Making Sense of the Competency Testing Movement." In Peter W. Airasian, George F. Madaus, & Joseph J. Pedulla, eds., *Minimum Competency Testing,* pp. 49-72. Englewood Cliffs, N.J.: Educational Technology Publications, 1978.

Harnischfeger, Annegret, & Wiley, David E. "Conceptual Issues in Models of School Learning." *Curriculum Studies* 10(July-September 1978): 215-31.

Harnischfeger, Annegret, & Wiley, David E. Origins of Active Learning Time. Evanston, Ill. (Northwestern University): ML-GROUP for Policy Studies in Education, October 1981.

Harrington, Michael. *The Other America: Poverty in the United States.* New York: Macmillan, 1962.

Hawkins, Martin. "A New Look at the High School Diploma." *National Association of Secondary School Principals Bulletin* 62(October 1978): 45-50.

Heckman, Paul, Oakes, Jeannie, & Sirotnik, Kenneth. "Expanding the Concepts of School Renewal and Change." *Educational Leadership* 40(April 1983): 26-32.

Heffez, Jack. The Effects of Part-Time Employment on High School Students' Grade Point Averages and Rate of School Attendance. Unpublished report, 1979.

Heffez, Jack. "Employment and the High School Drop Out." *National Association of Secondary School Principals Bulletin* 64(November 1980): 85-90.

Heidelberg, Richard L. "The Cafeteria Concept: Curricular Malnutrition." *Phi Delta Kappan* 53(November 1971): 174-75.

"High School Diplomas." National Education Association, *Research Bulletin* 37(December 1959): 114-15.

"High School Graduation Requirements." National Education Association, *Research Bulletin* 37(December 1959): 122-27.

Hofstadter, Richard. *Anti-Intellectualism in American Life.* New York: Knopf, 1962.

Hollingshead, August B. *Elmtown's Youth.* New York: Wiley, 1949.

Hollingsworth, E., Lufler, H., & Clune, W. *School Discipline: Order and Autonomy.* New York: Praeger, 1984.

Holsinger, Donald B. *Time, Content and Expectations as Predictors of School Achievement in the USA and Other Developed Countries: A Review of IEA Evidence.* Report to the National Commission on Excellence in Education, September 1982.

Holt, John. *How Children Fail.* New York: Belaconte Press, 1982.

Hurn, Christopher J. "The Problems with Comparisons." *Educational Leadership* 41(October 1983): 7-12.

Hurn, Christopher, J., & Burn, Barbara. *An Analytical Comparison of Educational Systems: Overview of Purposes, Policies, Structures, and Outcomes.* Report to the National Commission Excellence in Education, 1983.

Hyman, Irwin A., & D'Alessandro, J. "Oversimplifying the Discipline Problem." *Education Week* (April 11, 1984): 24, 18.

Hyman, R. J. "Testing for Teacher Competence: The Logic, the Law, the Motivation, and the Implications." *Journal of Teacher Education* 35(March-April, 1984): 14-20.

Illinois State Office of Education. Division of Adult Vocational and Technical Education. *Core Curriculum in Agriculture: Phase I Report.* Springfield, Ill., 1980.

Imhoff, Rhoda, & Taylor, Bob L. "The Impact of Declining Enrollment on the High School Curriculum." *North Central Association Quarterly* 55(Winter 1981): 364-68.

Jackson, Philip. *Life in Classrooms.* New York: Holt, Rinehart & Winston, 1968.

Jackson, Philip W. "Comprehending a Well-Run Comprehensive: A Report on a Visit to a Large Suburban High School." *Daedalus* 110 (Fall 1981): 81–95.

James, Thomas, & Tyack, David. "Learning from Past Efforts to Reform the High School." *Phi Delta Kappan* 64(February 1983): 400-406.

Jencks, Christopher, Smith, Marshall, Acland, Henry, Bane, Mary Jo, Cohen, David, Gintes, Herbert, Heyns, Barbara, & Michelson, Stephen. *Inequality: A Reassessment of the Effect of Family and Schooling in America.* New York: Basic Books, 1972.

Jensen, Arthur R. "How Much Can We Boost IQ and Scholastic Achievement?" *Harvard Educational Review* 39(1969): 1-124.

Johnson, James R., Henning, Mary Jo, & Small, Donald D. "A Constellation Model for the Development of a Mini-Course Curriculum." *Educational Technology* 16(September 1976): 25-29.

Johnson, Norris B. *West Haven: Classroom Culture and Society in a Rural Elementary School.* Chapel Hill, N.C.: University of North Carolina Press, 1985.

Johnson, Susan M. "Merit Pay for Teachers: A Poor Prescription for Reform." *Harvard Educational Review* 54(May 1984): 175-85.

Johnston, Don. "Reform in the School: A Student's View." *Baylor Educator* 8(Winter 1983): 9-12.

Justiz, Manuel J. "It's Time to Make Every Minute Count." *Phi Delta Kappan* 65(March 1984): 483-85.

Kamens, David H. "Legitimating Myths and Educational Organization: The Relationship Between Organizational Ideology and Formal Structure." *American Sociological Review* 42(April 1977): 208-19.

Karweit, Nancy. *Time on Task: A Research Review.* Report to the National Commission on Excellence in Education, (Rev. ed.) 1983.

Katz, Michael. *Class, Bureaucracy and Schools.* New York: Praeger, 1975.

Kearns, J. M. State Competency Testing for Teacher Certification. Unpublished paper, 1983.

Keith, Timothy. "Time Spent on Homework and High School Grades: A Large-Sample Path Analysis." *Journal of Educational Psychology* 74(1982): 248-53.

Kemmerer, Frances. National Reports: Research and Recommendations. Albany, N.Y.: Center for Educational Research and Policy Studies, State University of New York at Albany, August 1983.

Kerr, Donna H. "Teaching Competence and Teacher Education in the United States." In Lee S. Shulman & Gary Sykes, eds., *Handbook of Teaching and Policy,* pp. 126-49. New York: Longman, 1983.

Kingston, Albert J., & Gentry, Harold. "Discipline Problems in Georgia Secondary Schools, 1961 and 1974." *National Association of Secondary School Principals Bulletin* 61(February 1977): 94-99.

Kirk, Letitia A. The Relationship Between Ability Grouping and Academic Achievement. Unpublished paper, 1982.

Kirschenbaum, Howard. The Free Choice English Curriculum. Unpublished report, 1969.

Kirst, Michael. "The Impact of Postsecondary Admissions Policies on Secondary Education." *Educational Leadership* 41(October 1983): 16.

Klausmeier, Herbert. Highlights in the Development and Validation of the Wisconsin Program for the Renewal and Improvement of Secondary Education. Madison, Wis.: Wisconsin Center for Education Research, 1983.

Klausmeier, Herbert, Serlin, R., & Zindler, M. Improvement of Secondary Education Through Research: Five Longitudinal Case Studies. Madison, Wis.: Wisconsin Center for Education Research, April 1983.

Klausmeier, Herbert J., & Weber, Laurence J. "Improving Secondary Education in Wisconsin." *Educational Leadership* 41(March 1984): 80-84.

Klein, Karen. "Minimum Competency Testing: Shaping and Reflecting Curricula" *Phi Delta Kappan* 65(April 1984): 565-67.

Koerner, James D. *The Miseducation of American Teachers.* Boston: Houghton Mifflin, 1963.

Kohl, Herbert R. *36 Children.* New York: New American Library 1968.

Kozol, Jonathon. *Death at an Early Age.* Boston: Houghton Mifflin, 1967.

Krathwohl, David R. "The NTE and Professional Standards." *Educational Leadership* 41(October 1983): 74-7.

Kulik, Chen-Lin C. "Effects of Ability Grouping on Secondary School Students." Paper presented at the Annual Meeting of the American Educational Research Association, April 13-17, 1981.

Labaree, David F. "Academic Excellence in an Early American High School: Lessons for the 1980s." *Social Problems* 31(June 1984b): 558-67.

Labaree, David F. "Curriculum, Credentials, and the Middle Class: A Case Study of a Nineteenth Century High School." *Sociology of Education* 59(January 1986): 42-57.

Labaree, David F. "Setting the Standard: Alternative Policies for Student Promotion." *Harvard Educational Review* 54(February 1984a): 67-87.

Labaree, David F. *Setting the Standard: The Characteristics and Consequences of Alternative Student Promotional Policies.* Philadelphia: Citizens Committee on Public Education, 1983.

Lanier, Judith E. "Research on Teacher Education." In Merlin C. Wittrock, ed., *Handbook of Research on Teaching,* pp. 527-69. New York: Macmillan, 1986.

Larkin, Ralph W. *Suburban Youth in Cultural Crisis.* New York: Oxford University Press, 1979.

Lasley, Thomas J., & Wayson, William W. "Characteristics of Schools with Good Discipline." *Educational Leadership* 40(December 1982): 28-31.

Latimer, John Francis. *What's Happened to Our High Schools?* Washington, D.C.: Public Affairs Press, 1958.

"Lawmakers Continue Action on Education Reform." *Education Week* (May 2, 1984): 15.

Learned, William S., & Wood, Ben D. *The Student and His Knowledge: A Report to the Carnegie Foundation on the Results of High School and College Examinations of 1928, 1930, and 1932.* Bulletin No. 29. New York: Carnegie Foundation for the Advancement of Teaching, 1938.

Leonard, George. "Car Pool: A Story of Public Education in the Eighties." *Esquire* 99(May 1983): 58-66, 70, 72-73.

Lerner, Barbara. "American Education: How Are We Doing?" *The Public Interest* 69(Fall 1982): 59-82.

Levanto, Joseph. "High School Absenteeism." *National Association of Secondary School Principals Bulletin* 59(October 1975a): 100-104.

Levanto, Joseph. "The Problems of Attendance: Research Findings and Solutions." Paper presented at the National Association of Secondary School Principals Annual Convention, February 1975b.

Levin, Henry M. "A Cost-Effective Analysis of Teacher Selection." *Journal of Human Resources* 5(1970): 25-33.

Levin, Henry M. "Educational Performance Standards: Image or Substance." *Journal of Educational Measurement* 15(Winter 1978): 309-19.

Levine, David U., & Stark, Joyce. "Instructional and Organizational Arrangements that Improve Achievement in Inner-City Schools." *Educational Leadership* 40(December 1982): 41-46.

Levine, Marsha. School Reform: A Role for the American Business Community. A background paper prepared for the Committee for Economic Development, 1983.

Lewin-Epstein, Noah. *Youth Employment During High School-An Analysis of High School and Beyond: A National Longitudinal Study for the 80's.* Chicago, Ill.: National Longitudinal Center for National Center for Educational Statistics, May 1981.

Lightfoot, Sara Lawrence. *The Good High School: Portraits of Character and Culture.* New York: Basic Books, 1983.

London, Howard B. "Academic Standards and the American Community College: Trends and Controversies." Report to the National Commission on Excellence in Education, July 1982.

Lortie, Dan. *Schoolteacher: A Sociological Study.* Chicago: University of Chicago Press, 1975.

Lucas, Paul. "The Curriculum Ended with a Whimper." *English Journal* 64(April 1976): 54-57.

Lufler, Henry S., Jr. "Discipline: A New Look at an Old Problem." *Phi Delta Kappan* 59(February 1978): 424-26.

Lynd, Albert. *Quackery in the Public Schools.* Boston: Little, Brown, 1953.

Lynd, Robert S., & Lynd, Helen Merrell. *Middletown: A Study in Modern American Culture.* New York: Harcourt, Brace & World, 1929.

Lynd, Robert S., & Lynd, Helen Merrell. *Middletown in Transition: A Study in Cultural Conflicts.* New York: Harcourt, Brace & World, 1937.

MacKenzie, Donald E. "Research for School Improvement: An Appraisal of Some Recent Trends." *Educational Researcher* 12(April 1983): 5-16.

Madaus, George. "Making Sense of the Competency Testing Movement." *Harvard Educational Review* 48 (November 1978): 462-84.

Madaus, George. "NIE Clarification Hearing: The Negative Team's Case." *Phi Delta Kappan* 63(October 1981): 92-94.

Madaus, George F., & McDonagh, John T. "Minimum Competency Testing: Unexamined Assumptions and Unexplored Negative Outcomes." *New Directions for Testing and Measurement* 3(1979): 1-14.

Martin, William H. A Participant Observation Study of an Outdoor Education Experiential Curriculum Experiment Operating in a Public Secondary School. Unpublished dissertation, Michigan State University, 1977.

Marvin, Paul. "Should We Adopt a Statewide Curriculum?" *Agricultural Education Magazine* 52(April 1980): 11-12.

Maul, Ray C. "The 1956 Teacher Supply and Demand Report." *Journal of Teacher Education* 7(March 1956): 52-53.

McClung, Merle S. "Competency Testing Programs: Legal and Educational Issues." *Fordham Law Review* 47 (1979): 698-701.

McClung, Merle S., & Pullin, Diana. "Competency Testing and Handicapped Students." *Clearinghouse Review* (March 1978).

McCurdy, Jack. "Sending the Message: New Admissions Standards for a New Decade." *Phi Delta Kappan* 63(April 1982): 547-50.

McDermott, R. P. "Achieving School Failure: An Anthropological Approach to Illiteracy and Social Stratification." In G. D. Spindler, ed., *Education and Culture Process.* New York: Holt, Rinehart & Winston, 1974.

McNeil, Linda M. "Contradictions of Control: The Organizational Context of School Knowledge." Final Report to the National Institute of Education, Wisconsin Center for Public Policy, June 1982.

McNeil, Linda M. Lowering Expectations: The Impact of Student Employment in Classroom Knowledge. Madision, Wis.: Wisconsin Center for Education Research, February 1984.

McNeil, Linda M. "Negotiating Classroom Knowledge: Beyond Achievement and Socialization." *Journal of Curriculum Studies* 13(October-December 1981): 313-28.

Meyer, J., Chase-Dunn, C., & Inverarity, J. *The Expansion of the Autonomy of Youth: Responses of the Secondary School to the Problems of Order in the 1960's.* Stanford, Calif.: The Laboratory for Social Research, Stanford University, 1971.

Meyer, John W. "Levels of the Educational System and Schooling Effects." In Charles E. Bidwell & Douglas M. Windham, eds., *The Analysis of Educational Productivity,* Vol. 2, pp. 15-63. Cambridge, Mass.: Ballinger, 1980.

Meyer, John W., & Rowan, Brian. "The Structure of Educational Organizations." In M. Meyer, et al., eds., *Environment and Organizations,* pp. 78-109. San Francisco: Jossey Bass, 1978.

Michigan State Board of Education. *Better Education for Michigan Citizens: A Blueprint for Action.* Lansing, Mich.: Michigan State Board of Education, 1984.

Miles, Matthew B., Farrar, Eleanor, & Neufeld, Barbara. *Review of Effective School Programs: II: The Extent of Adoption of Effective Schools Programs.* Report to the National Commission on Excellence in Education, January 1983.

Mitchell, Douglas. "Metaphors of Management or How Far From Outcomes Can You Get?" Paper presented at the Annual Meeting of the American Educational Research Association, March 1982.

Mitchell, Douglas, & Encarnation, Dennis. *Alternative State Policy Mechanisms for Influencing School Performance.* Stanford University: Institute for Research in Educational Finance and Governance Program Report No. 83-132, 1983.

Mitchell, Richard. *The Graves of Academe.* Boston: Little, Brown, 1981.

Mizell, M. Hayes. "Designing and Implementing Effective In-School Alternatives to Suspension." In Antoine Garibaldi, ed., *In-School Alternatives to Suspension: Conference Report,* pp. 133-50. Washington, D.C.: Government Printing Office, 1978.

Moles, Oliver. "In-School Alternatives to Suspension: Stability and Effects." Paper presented at the Annual Meeting of the American Educational Research Association, April, 1984.

Monk, David H., & Jacobson, Stephen L. "Reforming Teacher Education." *Education and Urban Society* 17(2) (February 1985): 223-36.

Montgomery County Public Schools Department of Education Accountability. "A Preliminary Evaluation of the Pilot In-School Suspension Program." Montgomery County, Maryland, Public Schools, August 1981.

Nathan, Joe. "Graduation Requirements and Alternative Schools." *Eccentric* 37(February/March 1976): 15-18.

Nathan, Joe, & Jennings, Wayne. "Educational Bait and Switch." *Phi Delta Kappan* 59(May 1978): 621-39.

National Association of School Boards. "Diplomas Are Good for Nothing—True or False?" *Updating School Board Policies* 7(January 1976): 1-4.

National Association of Secondary School Principals Special Task Force Report. *Graduation Requirements.* Reston, Va. National Association of Secondary School Principals, 1975.

National Association of State Directors of Special Education. "Competency Testing, Special Education and the Awarding of Diplomas," February 1979.

National Commission on Excellence in Education. *A Nation at Risk.* Washington, D.C.: Government Printing Office, 1983.

National Education Association. *Status of the American Public School Teacher, 1980-81.* Washington, D.C.: National Education Association, 1982.

National Education Association. *Teacher Supply and Demand in the Public Schools, 1980-81.* Washington, D.C.: National Education Association, 1981.

National Education Association. *Teachers' Views about High School.* Washington, D.C.: National Education Association, 1983a.

National Education Association. *The Teaching Profession.* Washington, D.C.: National Education Association, December 1983b.

National Institute of Education. *Time to Learn.* Washington, D.C.: Government Printing Office, 1980, pp. 695-717.

National Institute of Education. *Violent Schools—Safe Schools: The Safe School Study Report to the Congress.* Vol. I. Washington D.C.: Government Printing Office, 1977.

Natriello, Gary, & Dornbusch, Sanford. *Teacher Evaluative Standards and Student Effort.* New York: Longman, 1984.

Neill, Shirley. "The Competency Movement: Problems and Solutions." *AASA Critical Issues Report,* 1978.

Nelson, F. Howard. "New Perspectives on the Teacher Quality Debate: Empirical Evidence From the National Longitudinal Survey." *Journal of Educational Research* 78(January/February 1985): 133-40.

Neufeld, Barbara. Working in High Schools: Inside Views of the Organization. Cambridge, Mass. Huron Institute, March 1980.

"The New Basics for Everyone?" *Educational Leadership* 41(October 1983): 28-33.

New Jersey school official [anon.]. Telephone interview with Christopher Wheeler, March 2, 1984.

New York State Education Department. Student Affairs Task Force. What Should We Do With Our Senior Year? Albany, N.Y.: New York State Education Department, 1975.

New York Times, February 26, 1984, p. 15.

New York Times, March 11, 1984, p. 14.

Newmann, Fred M. *Organizational Factors and Student Alienation in High Schools: Implications of Theory for School Improvement.* Madison, Wis.: University of Wisconsin. Final Report to the National Institute of Education, Grant No. NIE-G-79-0150, September 1980.

Newmann, Fred M., & Behar, Steven L. The Study and Improvement of American High Schools: A Portrait of Work in Progress. Madison, Wis.: Wisconsin Center for Education Research, October 1982.

Oakes, Jeannie. *Keeping Track: How Schools Structure Inequality.* New Haven: Yale University Press, 1985.

Oakeshott, M. "Education: The Engagement and Its Frustration." In R. F. Dearden, P. H. Hirst, & R. S. Peters, eds., *Education and the Development of Reason,* pp. 19-49. London: Routledge & Kegan Paul, 1972.

Odden, Allan. "Financing Educational Excellence." *Phi Delta Kappan* 65(January 1984): 311-18.

Offerman, Donald A. "Designing a General Education Curriculum for Today's High School Student." *Educational Leadership* 41(March 1984): 50-54.

Official of a Florida teachers union [anon.]. Telephone interview with Christopher Wheeler, March, 1984.

Official of a Tennessee teachers union [anon.]. Telephone interview with Christopher Wheeler, March, 1984.

Oldenquist, Andrew. "The Decline of American Education in the '60's and '70's." *American Education* 19(May 1983): 12-18.

Ornstein, Allan C. "Curriculum Contrast: A Historical Overview." *Phi Delta Kappan* 63(February 1982): 404-8.

Owen, David. *High School: Undercover with the Class of '80.* New York: Viking Press, 1981.

Owen, David. *None of the Above: Behind the Myth of Scholastic Aptitude.* Boston: Houghton Mifflin, 1985.

Panwitt, Barbara. "A Changing More Challenging Twelfth Grade . . . Antidotes for Senioritis." *National Association of Secondary School Principals Curriculum Report* 9(September 1979): 13.

Parnell, Dale. "The Oregon Walkabout." *Phi Delta Kappan* 56(November 1974): 205-206.

Patton, M. Q., & Perrone, V. Does Accountability Count without Teacher Support? Kalamazoo, Mich.: Unpublished report, 1976.

Pedulla, Joseph, & Reidy, Edward. "The Rise of the Minimal Competency Testing Movement." In P. Airasian, G. Madaus, & J. Pedulla, eds., *Minimal Competency Testing.* Englewood Cliffs, N. J.: Educational Technology Publications, 1979.

Peng, Samuel S., Fetters, William B., & Kolstad, Andrew J. *High School and Beyond: A National Longitudinal Study for the 1980's. A Capsule Description of High School Students.* Washington, D.C.: National Center for Educational Statistics, April 1981.

Pepe, Thomas J., Tufts, Alice L., & Gluckman, Ivan B. "Academic Penalties for Attendance Reasons: A Legal Memorandum." Reston, Va.: National Association of Secondary School Principals, 1985.

Peshkin, Alan. *Growing Up American: Schooling and the Survival of Community.* Chicago: University of Chicago Press, 1978.

Peterson, Paul E. *Making the Grade: Report of the Twentieth Century Fund Task Force in Federal Elementary and Secondary Education Policy: Background Paper.* New York: Twentieth Century Fund, 1983.

Pipho, Chris, & Flakus-Mosqueda, Patricia. "States Raise Requirements for High School Grads." *State Education Leader* (Winter 1984): 5.

Platt, John. "Social Traps." *American Psychologist* 28(August 1973): 641-51.

Plisko, V. W. Staffing Trends and the Status of Teachers. *The Condition of Education,* 1980 education. Statistical report of the National Center for Education Statistics. Washington, D.C.: U.S. Department of Education, 1980.

Popkewitz, Thomas S., Tabachnick, B. Robert, & Wehlage, Gary. *The Myth of Educational Reform.* Madison, Wis.: University of Wisconsin Press, 1978.

Powell, Arthur G., Farrar, Eleanor, & Cohen, David K. *The Shopping Mall High School: Winners and Losers in the Educational Marketplace.* Boston: Houghton Mifflin, 1985.

Prichard, K. W., Fen, S. N., & Buxton, T. H. "Social Class Origins of College Teachers of Education." *Journal of Teacher Education* 22(1971): 219-28.

Pugach, M. C., & Roths, J. E. "Testing Teachers: Analysis and Recommendations." *Journal of Teacher Education* 34(1983): 37–43.

Pullin, Diana. "*Debra P. V. Turlington:* Judicial Standards for Assessing the Validity of Minimum Competency Tests." In George F. Madaus, ed., *The Courts, Validity, and Minimum Competency Testing.* Boston: Kluwer-Nijhoff Publishing, 1983.

Pullin, Diana. "Mandated Minimum Competency Testing: Its Impact on Handicapped Adolescents." *Exceptional Education Quarterly* 1(August 1980): 107–15.

Pullin, Diana. "Minimum Competency Testing and the Demand for Accountability." *Phi Delta Kappan* 63(September 1981): 20–22.

Pullin, Diana. Minimum Competency Testing, the Denied Diploma, and the Pursuit of Educational Opportunity and Educational Adequacy. Los Angeles: Center for the Study of Evaluation, U.C.L.A., 1982.

Purkey, Stewart, & Degan, Susan. "Beyond Effective Schools to Good Schools: Some First Steps." *Perspectives.* Center for Educational Policy and Management, Eugene, Oreg., Spring 1985.

Purkey, Stewart C., & Smith, Marshall S. Effective Schools: A Review. Madison, Wis.: Wisconsin Center for Education Research, June 1982a.

Purkey, Stewart C., & Smith, Marshall S. "Too Soon to Cheer? Synthesis of Research on Effective Schools." *Educational Leadership* 40(December 1982b): 64–69.

Ramsey, M., Hillman, L., & Matthews, T. "School Characteristics Associated with Instructional Effectiveness." Paper presented at the Annual Meeting of the American Educational Research Association, 1982.

Ravitch, Diane. "Excellence in Humanities Teaching." *Educational Leadership* 41(October 1983a): 14–15.

Ravitch, Diane. "The Schools We Deserve." *The New Republic* (April 18, 1981): 329–40.

Ravitch, Diane. *The Troubled Crusade: American Education, 1945–1980.* New York: Basic Books, 1983b.

Remmers, H. H., & Radler, D. H. *The American Teenager.* Indianapolis: Bobbs-Merrill, 1957.

Resnick, Daniel P., & Resnick, Lauren B. "Improving Educational Standards in American Schools." *Phi Delta Kappan* 65(November 1983): 178–80.

Resnick, Lauren B., & Resnick, Daniel P. *Standards, Curriculum and Performance: A Historical and Comparative Perspective.* Revised Report to the National Commission on Excellence in Education, September 28, 1982.

Richardson, Richard C., Jr., Fisk, Elizabeth C., & Okun, Morris A. *Literacy in the Open-Access College.* San Francisco: Jossey-Bass, 1983.

Riesman, David. *On Higher Education: The Academic Enterprise in an Era of Rising Student Consumerism.* San Francisco: Jossey Bass, 1980.

Rodman, Blake. "Unions Turn to Courts to Block Florida's 'Uniform' Merit-Pay Program." *Education Week* (February 20, 1985): 6.

Rogers, Richard. "Restructuring the Curriculum for Vocational Agriculture in California." *Agricultural Education Magazine* 52(April 1980): 16–17.

Rohlen, Thomas P. *Japan's High Schools.* Berkeley, Calif.: University of California Press, 1983.

Rosenbaum, James. *Making Inequality: The Hidden Curriculum of High School Tracking.* New York: Wiley, 1976.

Rosenbaum, James E. "Social Implications of Educational Grouping." In David C. Berliner, ed., *Review of Research in Education,* Vol. 8, pp. 361–401. Washington, D.C.: American Educational Research Association, 1980.

Rosewater, Ann. Minimum Competency Testing Programs and Handicapped Students: Perspectives on Policy and Practice, Washington, D.C.: Institute for Educational Leadership, June, 1979.

Ross, John W., & Weintraub, Frederick J. "Policy Approaches Regarding the Impact of Graduation Requirements on Handicapped Students." *Exceptional Children* 47(November 1980): 200–203.

Rowan, Brian, Bossert, Steven T., & Dwyer, David C. "Research on Effective Schools: A Cautionary Note." *Educational Researcher* 12(April 1983): 24–31.

Rudolph, Frederick. *Educational Excellence: The Secondary School—College Connection and Other Matters: An Historical Assessment.* Report to the National Commission on Excellence in Education, August 1982.

Rutter, M., Maughan, B., Mortimer, P., Ouston, J., with Smith, A. *Fifteen Thousand Hours: Secondary Schools and Their Effects on Children.* Cambridge, Mass.: Harvard University Press, 1979.

Sandefur, J. T. Competency Assessment of Teachers: 1980-1983. ERIC Clearinghouse No. SP 023 584, 1983.

Sarason, Seymour B. *The Culture of the School and the Problem of Change.* 2d. ed. Boston: Allyn & Bacon, 1982.

Schlechty, Philip, & Vance, Victor. "Do Academically Able Teachers Leave Education? The North Carolina Case." *Phi Delta Kappan* 63(February 1981): 106-12.

Schlechty, Philip C., & Vance, Victor S. "Recruitment, Selection, and Retention: The Shape of the Teaching Force." *Elementary School Journal* 83(March 1983): 469-87.

Seeley, David S. "Educational Partnership and the Dilemmas of School Reform." *Phi Delta Kappan* 65(February 1984): 383-88.

Seidman, Robert H. "Toward a General Model of the Shifting Benefits and Liabilities of Educational Attainment." Paper presented at the Annual Meeting of the American Educational Research Association, April 1980.

Sentelle, Sam P. "A Helping Hand for the Chronic Truant." *Educational Leadership* 37(March 1980): 471-72.

Serow, Robert C., & Davies, James J. "Resources and Outcomes of Minimum Competency Testing as Measures of Equality of Educational Opportunity." *American Educational Research Journal* 19(Winter 1982): 529-39

Shanker, Albert. "The First Real Crisis." In Lee S. Shulman & Gary Sykes, eds., *Handbook on Teaching and Policy,* pp. 471-83. New York: Longman, 1983.

Shaw, Robert, & Walker, Wayne. "High School Graduation Requirements. From Whence Did They Come?" *National Association of Secondary School Principals Bulletin* 65(October 1981): 96-102.

Shimahara, Nobuo K. *Adaptation and Education in Japan.* New York: Praeger, 1979.

Sirotnik, Kenneth. "What You See Is What You Get—Consistency, Persistency, and Mediocrity in Classrooms." *Harvard Educational Review* 55(February 1983): 16-31.

Sirotnik, Kenneth A. "The Contextual Correlates of the Relative Expenditures of Classroom Time on Instruction and Behavior: An Exploratory Study of Secondary Schools and Classes." *American Educational Research Journal* 19(Summer 1982): 275-92.

Sizer, Theodore R. "Compromises." *Educational Leadership* 41(March 1984a): 34-37.

Sizer, Theodore R. *Horace's Compromise: The Dilemma of the American High School.* Boston: Houghton Mifflin, 1984b.

Sizer, Theodore R. *A Review and Comment on the National Reports.* Reston, Va.: National Association of Secondary School Principals. 1983a.

Sjogren, Cliff. *College Admissions and the Transition to Postsecondary Education: Standards and Practices.* Report to the National Commission on Excellence in Education, June 1982.

Smith, G. Pritchy. "The Critical Issue of Excellence and Equity in Competency Testing." *Journal of Teacher Education* 35(March-April 1984): 6–9.

Smith, Timothy L. "Native Blacks and Foreign Whites: Varying Responses to Educational Opportunity in America, 1880–1950." *Perspectives in American History* 6(1972): 309–35.

Southern Regional Education Board. The Need for Quality: A Report to the Southern Regional Education Board by its Task Force on Higher Education and the Schools. Southern Regional Education Board, June 1981.

Spady, William. "The Illusion of Reform." *Educational Leadership* 41(October 1983): 31–32.

Spady, William G., & Mitchell, Douglas E. "Competency Based Education: Organizational Issues and Implications." *Education Research* February 1977.

"The Status of the American Public-School Teacher." National Education Association, *Research Bulletin* 35(February 1957): 5–63.

Smith, Paul. Telephone interview with Christopher Wheeler, April 9, 1984.

Stedman, Laurence C., & Smith, Marshall. "Recent Reform Proposals for American Education." *Contemporary Education Review* 2(Fall 1983): 85–104.

Stiles, Lindley J., ed., *The Teacher's Role in American Society.* New York: Harper & Brothers, 1957.

Stinnett, T. M. A Manual of Standards Affecting School Personnel in the United States, 1974. ERIC Document Reproduction Series No. ED 097 335, 1974.

Stock, Richard, & Hansen, Lee. *Proposals for High School Improvement.* Ann Arbor, Mich.: Ann Arbor Public Schools, September 1983.

Sweeney-Rader, Jane, Snyder, Gayle L., Goldstein, Harriet, & Rosenwald, Priscilla. "School Suspensions: An In-House Prevention Model." *Children Today* 9(March-April 1980): 19–21.

Sykes, Gary. "The Deal." *Wilson Quarterly* 8(1984): 59–77.

Sykes, Gary. "Public Policy and the Problem of Teacher Quality: The Need for Screens and Magnets." In Lee S. Shulman & Gary Sykes, eds., *Handbook of Teaching and Policy,* pp. 97–125. New York: Longman, 1983.

Tanner, Daniel. "The American High School at the Crossroads." *Educational Leadership* 41(March 1984): 4–13.

Task Force on Educational Assessment Programs. "Competency Testing in Florida: Report to the Florida Cabinet, Part I." Tallahassee, Fla.: Task Force in Educational Assessment, 1979.

"Teachers in the Public Schools." National Education Association, *Research Bulletin* 27(December 1949): 132.

"Teachers Revise Teacher-Pay Scheme." *Education Week* (August 22, 1984): 20.

Teachman, Gerard W. "In School Truancy in Urban Schools." *Phi Delta Kappan* 61(November 1979): 203–5.

Tennessee State Department of Education official [anon.]. Telephone interview with Christopher Wheeler, March 16, 1984.

Thompson, James. *Organizations in Action.* New York: McGraw-Hill, 1967.

Thompson, Scott, & Stanard, David. "Student Attendance and Absenteeism." *The Practitioner* 1(March 1975): 1–12.

Timpane, Michael, et al. *Youth Policy in Transition.* Washington, D.C.: Government Printing Office, 1976.

Toch, Thomas. "Teacher Response Linked to Evaluation System." *Education Week* (March 21, 1984): 1, 14–15.

Toth, Susan Ellen. *Blooming: A Small Town Girlhood.* Boston: Little, Brown, 1978.

Tractenberg, Paul. "Legal Implications of Minimum Competency Testing: Debra P. and Beyond." Paper presented to the Education Commission of the State, Denver, Colo. (October 15, 1979).

Tregend, Alina. "Florida to Pay $20 Million to 'Merit' Schools in 1985–86." *Education Week* (August 22, 1984a): 20, 27.

Tregend Alina. "Half of Florida Districts, Citing Bias, Shun 'Merit-School' Program." *Education Week* (October 3, 1984b): 5.

Tyack, David B., & Hansot, Elizabeth. "Conflict and Consensus in American Public Education." *Daedalus* 110(Summer 1981): 1–25.

U.S. Department of Education. *Meeting the Challenge: Recent Efforts to Improve Education Across the Nation.* Washington, D.C.: U.S. Department of Education, November 15, 1983a.

U.S. Department of Education. *Supplement to Meeting the Challenge.* Washington, D.C.: U.S. Department of Education, 1983b.

U.S. Department of Education. *The Nation Responds: Recent Efforts to Improve Education.* Washington, D.C.: U.S. Department of Education, May 1984.

U.S. General Accounting Office. What Assurance Does Office of Education's Eligibility Process Provide? GAO Publication No. HRD 78–120. Washington, D.C.: U.S. General Accounting Office, 1979.

U.S. State Department official [anon.]. Telephone interview with Christopher Wheeler, June, 1984.

University administrator [anon.]. Personal interview with Christopher Wheeler, March 24, 1984.

Unruh, Adolph. "Teachers and Classroom Discipline." *National Association of Secondary School Principals Bulletin,* 61(February 1977): 84–87.

Van Til, William, ed., *Issues in Secondary Education: 75th Yearbook of the National Society for the Study of Education Part II.* Chicago: University of Chicago Press, 1976.

Vance, Victor S., & Schlecty, Philip C. "The Distributions of Academic Ability in the Teaching Force: Policy Implications." *Phi Delta Kappan* 64(September 1982): 22–27.

Vars, Gordon F., & Applegate, Jane H. "It's Time to Rediscover the Needs of Youth." *High School Journal* 67(October-November 1983): 42–45.

Walberg, Herbert J. "We Can Raise Standards." *Educational Leadership* 41(October 1983): 4–6.

Waller, Willard. *The Sociology of Teaching*. New York: Wiley, 1932.

Walsh, John. "Does High School Grade Inflation Mask a More Alarming Trend?" *Science* 203(March 1979): 982.

Wangberg, Elaine G., Metzger, Devon J., & Levitov, Justin E. "Working Conditions and Career Options Lead to Female Elementary Teacher Job Dissatisfaction." *Journal of Teacher Education* 33(September-October 1982): 37–40.

Weaver, W. Timothy. *America's Teacher Quality Problem: Alternatives for Reform*. New York: Praeger, 1983.

Weaver, W. T. "Educators in Supply and Demand: Effects on Quality." *School Review* 86(1978): 522–93.

Weaver, W. T. "In Search of Quality: The Need for Talent in Teaching." *Phi Delta Kappan* 61(1979): 29–46

Weaver, W. Timothy. "Solving the Problem of Teacher Quality, Part 1." *Phi Delta Kappan* 66(October 1984a): 108–15.

Weaver, W. Timothy. "Solving the Problem of Teacher Quality, Part 2." *Phi Delta Kappan* 66(November 1984b): 185–88.

Wechsler, Harold S. *The Qualified Student: A History of Selective College Admission in America*. New York: Wiley, 1977.

Wegmann, Robert G. "Homework and Grades: Where Is the College Student Coming From?" *College Student Journal* 8(February-March 1974): 13–22.

Weick, K. "Educational Organizations as Loosely Coupled Systems." *Administrative Science Quarterly* 21(3) (1976): 1–19.

Wheeler, C. W. NCATE: Does It Matter? IRT Research Series No. 92. East Lansing, Mich.: Michigan State University College of Education, 1980.

Williams, Junious. "In-School Alternatives to Suspension: Why Bother?" In Antoine Garibaldi, ed., *In-School Alternatives to Suspension: Conference Report*, pp. 1–23. Washington, D.C.: Government Printing Office, 1978.

Willis, Paul. *Learning to Labor*. Hampshire, England: Gower Publishing House, Ltd., 1977.

Wilson, Alfred P., & Singer, Jerry D. "High School Attendance Policies in the State of Kansas." Paper presented at the Annual Rural and Small School Conference, November 15, 1982.

Wimpelberg, R., & Ginsberg, R. "Are School Districts Responding to *A Nation at Risk?*" *Education and Urban Society* 17(February, 1985) 2: 186–203.

Wise, Arthur E. "A Critique of Minimal Competency Testing." Paper presented at the Educational Adequacy Program, Basic Skills Group, National Institute of Education, 1977.

Wise, Arthur E. *Legislated Learning: The Bureaucratization of the American Classroom*. Berkley: University of California Press, 1979.

Wise, Arthur E. "Minimum Competency Testing: Another Case of Hyper-Rationalization." *Phi Delta Kappan* 59(May 1978): 596–608.

Wise, Arthur E., & Darling-Hammond, Linda. "Teacher Evaluation and Teacher Professionalism." *Educational Leadership* 42(December 1984/January 1985): 28–33.

Wise, Arthur E., & Darling-Hammond, Linda, McLaughlin, Milbury W., & Bernstein, Harriet I. *Teacher Evaluation: A Study of Effective Practices.* Santa Monica, Calif.: Rand, 1984.

Wolcott, H. Teacher *vs.* Technocrat. Eugene, Oreg.: University of Oregon Center for Educational Policy and Management, 1977.

Wolf, Richard M. "Controversy: American Education: The Record Is Mixed." *Public Interest* 72(Summer 1983): 124–32

Wolfle, Dael L. *America's Resources of Specialized Talent.* The Report of the Commission on Human Resources and Advanced Training. New York: Harper's, 1954.

Wright, Douglas. *School District Survey of Academic Requirements and Achievement.* Washington, D.C.: U.S. Department of Education, National Center for Education Statistics, April 1983.

Wright, Linus. "Making Secondary Education First Rate." *Baylor Educator* 8(Winter 1983): 4–8.

Wu, Shi-Chang. *The Foundations of Student Suspension.* Report to the National Institute of Education, December 1980a.

Wu, Shi-Chang, et al. *Student Suspension: A Critical Reappraisal.* Report to the National Institute of Education, 1980b.

⋒ Index

ꕤ About the Authors

Michael W. Sedlak is an historian of education who earned his bachelor's degree from the University of Washington and his master's and doctoral degrees from Northwestern University. He has published widely in the history of education, professional schooling, and youth policy. He is currently Associate Professor in the College of Education and a senior researcher with the Institute for Research on Teaching at Michigan State University.

Christopher Wheeler is a political scientist who received his bachelor's degree from Oberlin College and his M.A. and Ph.D. degrees from Columbia University. His research interest is educational policy and its effects on school districts and classroom teachers. His studies include the federal administration of compensatory education, classroom implementation of Title IX and gender equity, accreditation standards and their implementation by the National Council for the Accreditation of Teacher Education, and interest group politics in Sweden. Dr. Wheeler is currently Professor in the College of Education and a senior researcher in the Institute for Research on Teaching at Michigan State University.

Diana Pullin holds both a Ph.D. in Education and a law degree from the University of Iowa. For the past ten years she has been actively involved as both a practicing attorney and as an education researcher. She has represented educators, teachers' associations, school districts, and students, in lawsuits involving schools. While associated with the Harvard Center for Law and Education, she litigated several major cases concerning educational accountability and educational equity for minority and special needs children. She is most known for her representation of the students and parents who brought the landmark federal court challenge to Florida's minimum competency testing program. Presently, Dr. Pullin is Associate Dean of the College of Education at Michigan State University.

Philip A. Cusick is Professor and Chairman in the Department of Educational Administration at Michigan State University. He is the author of *Inside High School: The Students' World,* and *The Egalitarian Ideal And The American High School.* For several years, he taught English and reading in secondary schools and now teaches in the areas of organizational theory and research.